ARCHITECTURAL REVOLUTION ON THE OTTOMAN FRONTIER

ARCHITECTURAL REVOLUTION ON THE OTTOMAN FRONTIER

Greece and Albania in the Age of Ali Pasha

 Emily Neumeier

THE PENNSYLVANIA STATE UNIVERSITY PRESS
UNIVERSITY PARK, PENNSYLVANIA

Publication of this book has been supported by a grant from the New Foundation for Art History.

Publication of this book has been supported by a grant from the Barakat Trust.

Library of Congress Cataloging-in-Publication Data

Names: Neumeier, Emily, author.
Title: Architectural revolution on the Ottoman frontier : Greece and Albania in the age of Ali Pasha / Emily Neumeier.
Other titles: Buildings, landscapes, and societies.
Description: University Park, Pennsylvania : The Pennsylvania State University Press, [2025] | Series: Buildings, landscapes, and societies series | Includes bibliographical references and index.
Summary: "Reinterprets the history of Ottoman architecture under the patronage of Ali Pasha of Ioannina, a provincial governor who came to rule a vast domain that spanned most of modern-day Greece and Albania"—Provided by publisher.
Identifiers: LCCN 2024028791 | ISBN 9780271097749 (hardback)
Subjects: LCSH: Ali Paşa, Tepedelenli, 1744?–1822. | Architecture, Ottoman—Greece—History—19th century. | Architecture, Ottoman—Albania—History—19th century.
Classification: LCC NA1097 .N48 2025 | DDC 720.949509/034—dc23/eng/20240722
LC record available at https://lccn.loc.gov/2024028791

Copyright © 2025 Emily Neumeier
All rights reserved
Printed in China
Published by The Pennsylvania State University Press, University Park, PA 16802–1003

The Pennsylvania State University Press is a member of the Association of University Presses.

It is the policy of The Pennsylvania State University Press to use acid-free paper. Publications on uncoated stock satisfy the minimum requirements of American National Standard for Information Sciences—Permanence of Paper for Printed Library Material, ANSI Z39.48–1992.

Frontispiece: William Haygarth, *View of Jannina* (fig. 18), detail.

for Sotiris

CONTENTS

LIST OF ILLUSTRATIONS	ix
ACKNOWLEDGMENTS	xiii
NOTE ON TRANSLATIONS AND TRANSLITERATIONS	xvii
Introduction	1
CHAPTER 1 .... "Amidst No Common Pomp": Redefining the Governor's Palace	25
CHAPTER 2 .... Revising the Rules of Engagement: Fortifications on a Liquid Frontier	67
CHAPTER 3 .... Building Local Support: Patronage for Multiconfessional Communities	101
CHAPTER 4 .... Poetic Justice: Experiments in Architectural Epigraphy	141
Conclusion	175
NOTES	179
BIBLIOGRAPHY	195
INDEX	207

ILLUSTRATIONS

FIGURE 1	The Ottoman Empire circa 1812, with the territory governed by Ali Pasha and his sons highlighted	2
FIGURE 2	Louis Dupré, *The Palace and Fortress of Ioannina, View from the Lake*	3
FIGURE 3	Spiridon Ventouras, *Portrait of Ali Pasha*	4
FIGURE 4	The territory governed by Ali Pasha and his sons circa 1812	5
FIGURE 5	Edward Lear, *View of Tepelena from the North*	6
FIGURE 6	Dominique Papety, *Litharitsa, Fortress of Ali Pasha*	7
FIGURE 7	The Çapanoğlu Mosque in Yozgat	11
FIGURE 8	View of the mosque and mausoleum within the İshak Pasha palace at Doğubayazıt	13
FIGURE 9	The *sabil-kuttab* of Mehmed Ali Pasha in Cairo	14
FIGURE 10	The Rumi Darwaza, the gate to the first forecourt of the Great Imambara complex in Lucknow	17
FIGURE 11	View of Ali Pasha's fortress on the Vrino channel in Butrint	21
FIGURE 12	William Purser and Edward Francis Finden, *Tepaleen, the Palace of Ali Pacha*	27
FIGURE 13	Jean-Denis Barbié du Bocage, map of the city of Ioannina	32
FIGURE 14	Ali Pasha's palace complex in the southeastern citadel of Ioannina	34
FIGURE 15	The main entrance to Ali Pasha's palace complex in the southeastern citadel of Ioannina	35
FIGURE 16	Henry Edmund Allen, *The Serai and Tomb of Ali Pasha, Ioannina*	36
FIGURE 17	Ernest Hébrard, photograph of the main gate to the walled quarter of Preveza	36
FIGURE 18	William Haygarth, *View of Jannina*	37
FIGURE 19	The southern entrance to the Tepelena citadel	38
FIGURE 20	Jean-Guillaume Barbié du Bocage, detail of a map showing the town of Preveza and its surrounding area	40
FIGURE 21	Vincenzo Coronelli, map of Preveza	40
FIGURE 22	Frédéric Boissonnas, photograph showing the location of Ali Pasha's "Bouka" palace in Preveza	41
FIGURE 23	Matrakçı Nasuh, *View of Istanbul*	42
FIGURE 24	The fortified way station at Pente Pigadia	47

FIGURE 25	The *hans* and residences in the *çiftlik* of Ali Pasha and his sons in the provincial districts of Yanya and Delvine 48
FIGURE 26	William Haygarth, *Presentation to Ali Pacha at Joannina* 51
FIGURE 27	Interior of the Zekate House in Gjirokaster 51
FIGURE 28	Louis Dupré, *Ali Pasha of Ioannina Hunting on the Lake at Butrint in March 1819* 55
FIGURE 29	Charles Cockerell, *View of the Interior of the Kiosk in Ali Pasha's Garden Palace in Ioannina* 56
FIGURE 30	Eugène Delacroix, *The Death of Sardanapalus* 59
FIGURE 31	The first page and front cover of an Ottoman register listing Ali Pasha's property seized by the sultan's troops from the palace in the Ioannina citadel 61
FIGURE 32	Details of a rifle of British manufacture that was gifted to Ali Pasha and then decorated with gold and silver by local craftsmen 64
FIGURE 33	Giorgio Vasari, *The Battle of Lepanto (The Fleets Approaching Each Other)* 68
FIGURE 34	The eastern coast of the Ionian Sea, with the major cities and sites where Ali Pasha commissioned coastal fortifications indicated 70
FIGURE 35	Ottoman ground plan of the fortress at Porto Palermo 73
FIGURE 36	Fortifications in the areas of Saranda and Butrint 75
FIGURE 37	Southeastern tower at the Likurs fortress, Saranda 75
FIGURE 38	Ali Pasha's fortress in the Vrino Channel at Butrint 76
FIGURE 39	The fortress constructed at Agia-Anthousa, northwest of Parga 76
FIGURE 40	Preveza and the surrounding region, with major towns and other important sites indicated 77
FIGURE 41	Map of the city of Preveza, with the major fortifications that were constructed or renovated in the early nineteenth century indicated 78
FIGURE 42	The Fortress of Agios Georgios in Preveza 79
FIGURE 43	View from one of the battlements at the Plagia fortress looking north to the town of Lefkada across the strait 80
FIGURE 44	View of the Fortress of Antirrio looking southeast toward the strait at the entrance to the Gulf of Corinth 80
FIGURE 45	French plan of the Fortress of Agios Andreas in Preveza 82
FIGURE 46	The southeast bastion at the Fortress of Agios Andreas, Preveza 83
FIGURE 47	Main entrance to the Tekes Fort 84
FIGURE 48	The south bastion at the Fortress of Agios Georgios, Preveza 86
FIGURE 49	Map showing the location of the Aktion Fortress in relation to the territory of the Septinsular Republic and Confederation of Continental Cities in 1801 93
FIGURE 50	An ethnographic map of Epirus organized according to language and religion 102

FIGURE 51	Postcard showing the Mosque of Mehmed Ali Pasha on the Cairo Citadel	105
FIGURE 52	The Fethiye Mosque in the southeastern citadel of Ioannina	107
FIGURE 53	Plaque with an inscription recording the late eighteenth-century renovation of the Fethiye Mosque in Ioannina	109
FIGURE 54	Mausoleum at the Arslan Pasha Mosque in Ioannina	110
FIGURE 55	Edward Lear, *View of the Citadel of Tepelena*	111
FIGURE 56	Early twentieth-century photograph of the Ali Pasha Mosque in Preveza	112
FIGURE 57	The Fethiye Mosque in Ioannina	113
FIGURE 58	The Arslan Pasha Mosque in Ioannina	113
FIGURE 59	Mihrab of the İzzet Pasha Mosque in Safranbolu, Turkey	114
FIGURE 60	Mihrab of the Beylerbeyi Mosque in Istanbul	114
FIGURE 61	The Osman Shah Mosque in Trikala	114
FIGURE 62	The Veli Pasha Mosque in Ioannina	115
FIGURE 63	Edward Lear, detail of *View of Ioannina*	116
FIGURE 64	A section of an Ottoman panoramic view of Ioannina looking south	120
FIGURE 65	Photograph of the *semahane*, mausoleum, and living quarters of the Kurt Ahmet Pasha Tekke in Berat	122
FIGURE 66	Muntaz Dhrami, *Ali Pashe Tepelena, 1740–1822*	124
FIGURE 67	The Monastery of Kosmas Aitolos	127
FIGURE 68	A printed icon showing events from the life of Kosmas Aitolos	128
FIGURE 69	The ruined apse of the Church of the Theotokos, located within the Monastery of Kosmas Aitolos	130
FIGURE 70	Detail of the foundation inscription embedded in the exterior wall of the apse at the Church of Kosmas Aitolos	131
FIGURE 71	The northern entrance to the Church of Kosmas Aitolos	132
FIGURE 72	Foundation inscription of the Church of Agios Nikolaos in Vasiliki, a village north of Trikala	134
FIGURE 73	Interior of the Fethiye Mosque in Ioannina	137
FIGURE 74	The Church of Shen Meri in the village of Labova e Kryqit	138
FIGURE 75	Detail of wall decorations in the southeast arcade in the interior of the Church of Shen Meri in Labova e Kryqit	138
FIGURE 76	Detail of the decorations painted on the central dome of the Fethiye Mosque in Ioannina	139
FIGURE 77	Bilingual inscription in Greek and Ottoman Turkish once located above the eastern entrance of the Tepelena citadel	142
FIGURE 78	Remains of the Temple of Augustus and Rome in Ankara	144

FIGURE 79	Foundation inscription of the Selimiye Mosque in the Üsküdar neighborhood of Istanbul	145
FIGURE 80	Foundation inscription of the Çapanoğlu Mosque in Yozgat	146
FIGURE 81	Greek inscription commemorating Ali Pasha's renovation of the city walls in Ioannina	147
FIGURE 82	Entrance to the Ioannina citadel on the southeastern side of the city walls	148
FIGURE 83	The main entrance portals to the city walls and southeastern citadel of Ioannina	149
FIGURE 84	Arabic inscription commemorating the renovation of Ioannina's city walls	154
FIGURE 85	Zoomorphic plaque above one of the gates to the walled district of Ioannina	155
FIGURE 86	Zoomorphic plaque above one of the entrances to the southeastern citadel of Ioannina	156
FIGURE 87	Zoomorphic plaque on the southwestern bastion of the Fortress of Agios Andreas in Preveza	157
FIGURE 88	Zoomorphic plaque located on the left above the main entrance of the Aktion Fortress, Preveza	158
FIGURE 89	Zoomorphic plaque located on the right above the main entrance of the Aktion Fortress, Preveza	158
FIGURE 90	Relief sculpture of the lion of Saint Mark above the main entrance to the Venetian "New Fortress" in Corfu Town	159
FIGURE 91	Plaque on the exterior of the Santa Maura Fortress in Lefkada	160
FIGURE 92	Greek inscription above the main entrance to the fortification at Porto Palermo	161
FIGURE 93	Map showing the location of the village of Gardiki and the Valiares Han	163
FIGURE 94	W. Davenport and George Hunt, *The Vizier Ali Pacha, Giving the Fatal Signal, for the Slaughter of the Gardikiotes Shut up in the Khan of Valiare*	164
FIGURE 95	The early nineteenth-century ruins of Gardiki, with the modern village of Prongji in the distance	166
FIGURE 96	William Haygarth, *Khan at the Foot of the Pindus at Malacasi*	167
FIGURE 97	George Zongolopoulos, *Monument of Zalongo*	170
FIGURE 98	Edward Lear, *View of Ioannina from the South*	171
FIGURE 99	The main entrance gate to the walled city of Ioannina	172

ACKNOWLEDGMENTS

THIS BOOK COULD NOT have been realized without the unwavering support of countless colleagues and friends. First and foremost, my heartfelt thanks to my mentors Renata Holod, Bob Ousterhout (in memoriam), André Dombrowski, and Christine Philliou, who deftly guided this project from its inception. Other individuals who played a key role during its formative stages include Tülay Artan, Filiz Yenişehirlioğlu, Lucienne Thys-Şenocak, and Heghnar Watenpaugh. Finally, Machiel Kiel, Stefan Weber, Kostis Kourelis, Günsel Renda, Çiğdem Kafescioğlu, Gülru Necipoğlu, İnci Kuyulu, András Riedlmayer, and Maximilian Hartmuth were all very generous with their time and offered crucial feedback and suggestions.

While conducting the research for this book, I benefited greatly from the tireless assistance of individuals at a wide variety of library and research institutions, including the Presidential State Ottoman Archives in Istanbul, the Directorate General of Pious Foundations in Ankara, the Service historique de la Défense at Vincennes in Paris, the British Library, and the National Archives in London. I am particularly indebted to Dimitris Dimitropoulos at the National Hellenic Research Foundation; Maria Georgopoulou, Irini Solomonidi, and Maria Smali at the Gennadius Library; Xenia Politou and Anna Ballian at the Benaki Museum; Varvara Papadopoulou and Virginia Mavrika at the Ephorate of Antiquities in Greece; Mirela Koçollari at the Institute of Cultural Monuments in Tirana; and Sokol Çunga at the Central State Archive of Albania, who all ensured that I had access to all of the relevant archives and objects. I would not have been able to interpret much of this material without the several instructors who broadened my linguistic horizons: Yorgos Dedes, Abdullah Uğur, Hakan Karateke, Mika Tsekoura, and Maria Andrikogiannopoulou. Throughout the course of fieldwork, Dritan Egro, Artan Shabani, Nevila Molla, Smirald Kola, Jonathan Eaton, Rupert Smith, Alexandros Alexakis, Gregory Manopoulos, Christos Stavrakos, Georgios Liakopoulos, Nikolaos Magouliotis, and Kostas Chalkias were all instrumental in opening doors—both literal and metaphorical—and pointing me in new directions of inquiry. I owe particular gratitude to Nikos Karabelas and Auron Tare for so generously sharing their expertise and resources, and to my travel companions Benjamin Anderson, Jordan Pickett, Yael Rice, and Nir Shafir for serving as an invaluable team of interlocutors during numerous site visits. My research travels and language training were made possible through funding provided by the American Research Institute in Turkey, a Fulbright-Hays grant from the US Department of Education, the University of Pennsylvania, and the Institute of Turkish Studies.

Several ideas and arguments put forth in this book were first developed in public fora. Many thanks to those who created these opportunities for me to preview my findings, including Mina Moraitu, George Manginis, Lita Tzortzopoulou-Gregory, Maria Georgopoulou, Elias Kolovos, Paschalis Androudis, Dimitris Loupis, Paris Papamichos Chronakis, Ömür Harmanşah, Antony Greenwood, Christine Philliou, Katerina Lagos, Vasilis Panagiotopoulos, Dimitris Dimitropoulos, Alexia Petsalis-Diomidis, Edhem Eldem, Elizabeth Key Fowden, Jeremy Walton, Benjamin Anderson, Felipe Rojas, Anthony Kaldellis, Stéphane Pradines, Stephennie Mulder, Eva-Maria Troelenberg, and Nikos Karabelas. I would never have managed to write this book without the thoughtful comments and close reading of my writing partners Devin Byker, Rachel Schneider-Vlachos, Zoe Griffith, Michael Polczynski, Coleman Connelly, Corey Katz, Jonathan Mullins, Erika Weiberg, Monica Hahn, Kartik Nair, Rebeca Hey-Colón, and Jess Marie Newman. I also profited from testing some of the broader theoretical claims of this book in the context of Architecture as Performance: Space, Society, and Spectacle in the Ottoman Empire, a graduate seminar I led in the spring of 2023. I thank the participants—Ryan Mitchell, Miray Eroglu, Emma Holter, Juhyung Park, Julia Pearse, Amira Pualwan, Dominique Samarco, Rachel Vorsanger, Becca Huang, and Ari Lipkis—for joining me in thinking about the performative aspects of the built environment. Financial support for writing and revising this book was provided with generous grants from the Getty Foundation, the American Council of Learned Societies, and Temple University. I am grateful to the staff of the American School of Classical Studies in Athens, and especially those at the Gennadius Library, for offering their space, expert assistance, and friendship as the manuscript took shape.

This book would not have been possible without the assistance of the attentive staff at Penn State University Press. I would like to thank Ellie Goodman and Maddie Caso for their consistent encouragement and support, the Buildings, Landscapes, and Societies series editor Jesús Escobar for championing this project from the outset, and Alex Ramos, Suzanne Wolk, Regina Starace, and Brian Beer for shepherding all the materials through the last stages of production. I also would like to acknowledge the series board and anonymous reviewers for offering thoughtful responses, which proved to be essential as this book took its final form. Additional thanks to Matthew Jacobson and Lisa Backhouse for creating the maps and plans, and to Tyler Rockey for his assistance in tracking down image permissions. Funding for the publication of this volume was provided by the New Foundation for Art History, the Barakat Trust, and the Tyler School of Art and Architecture at Temple University.

Finally, there are many people whose friendship and support made this long journey an enjoyable experience. Special thanks to Zoe Griffith, Benjamin Anderson, Jordan Pickett, Elvan Cobb, Nikolaos Vryzidis, Katerina Stathi, Tasos Tanoulas, Eva-Maria Troelenberg, Ali Boyd, Megan Boomer, Jamie Sanecki, Elisabeth Fraser, Jane Hathaway, Melis Taner, Hilal Uğurlu, Nilay Özlü, Ünver Rüstem, and Deniz Türker for opening their homes, offering insights on what is often a mysterious process, and always being there with words of encouragement. To Yavuz Sezer, who passed while this book was under way, I know that we will find each other again for a scalding cup of çay at the Karaköy iskele. As for my family, all my love to little Nikoletta, who came into the world as I was preparing the manuscript, and whose winning smile has sustained me in even the most trying moments. I am extremely grateful to my parents, Mary and Burton Neumeier, and my incredible in-laws, Niki Simou and Dimitris Dimitriadis, who were instrumental in making sure that I had ample space and time to write. And to my dearest Sotiris, who has been with me through every step of this process, who has met every doubt and fear with a kind word, this book is for you. Onward to our next adventure!

NOTE ON TRANSLATIONS AND TRANSLITERATIONS

UNLESS OTHERWISE INDICATED, all translations and transliterations of Ottoman Turkish, Greek, and French sources and terms are my own.

For Ottoman Turkish terms, I provide the complete diacritical markings of frequently repeated words the first time they appear and use the modern Turkish spelling in subsequent instances. When transliterating Greek sources and terms, I follow a modified version of the transcription system established by the Hellenic Organization for Standardization.

In historical travel accounts and archival records, authors writing in English often used spelling conventions that are no longer standard. I have opted to preserve the spellings that appear in the original texts when quoting such sources.

Introduction

By the summer of 1820, the situation was looking rather grim for Ali Pasha. Thousands of soldiers, representing the full might of the Ottoman sultan, were descending upon his territory to force the surrender of all his titles and properties. Ali Pasha was a longtime governor on the western edge of the Ottoman Empire, controlling a large swath of land that today comprises most of northern Greece and southern Albania (fig. 1). During a tenure that spanned more than thirty years, he had ushered the region into relative prosperity, evidenced by several large-scale urban construction projects that the governor himself had sponsored. Ali Pasha's administrative capital in Ioannina thrived as an intellectual center and as a cosmopolitan hub for merchants hailing from Venice to Vienna. Foreign consuls from Britain, France, and Austria encountered a diverse, multiconfessional court that included Sufi shaykhs, Orthodox clergy, polyglot translators and scribes from the Ionian Islands, luminaries of the Greek Enlightenment movement, and those who would go on to play a prominent role in the Greek War of Independence. The governor's numerous architectural interventions shaped Ioannina as it stands today—the city's striking profile of a citadel jutting out onto the surrounding lake being the result of several building campaigns launched by Ali Pasha in the first years of the nineteenth century (fig. 2).

How did it all go wrong? The governor's considerable military strength and vast personal wealth, not to mention his frequent practice of meeting independently with European diplomats, eventually made him a liability in the eyes of the Ottoman authorities in Istanbul. Sultan Mahmud II accused the governor of treason and issued orders for his deposition.[1] Ali Pasha refused to resign and, hoping to negotiate some kind of resolution, sought refuge in his fortified palace complex within the Ioannina citadel. The British consul William Meyer was on hand to observe the final days of the beleaguered governor. As troops made their way to the city's bastions, Meyer reported in a dispatch to London that Ali Pasha, despite his family's desperate appeals to flee, "expressed the determination to meet his fate in the capital of that country, which has been the theatre of his fortunes and his triumphs."[2] After a protracted siege, news reached the Ottoman Porte in Istanbul in early 1822 that the sultan's agents had finally managed to capture and behead the self-styled Lion of Ioannina.[3]

The saga of Ali Pasha's destruction unfolded in tandem with the outbreak of the Greek War of Independence, which was spreading like wildfire throughout the region. For both of these events, Ottoman troops were mobilized to shut down bold experiments in local

FIGURE 1
The Ottoman Empire circa 1812, with the territory governed by Ali Pasha and his sons highlighted. Map by Matthew J. Jacobson.

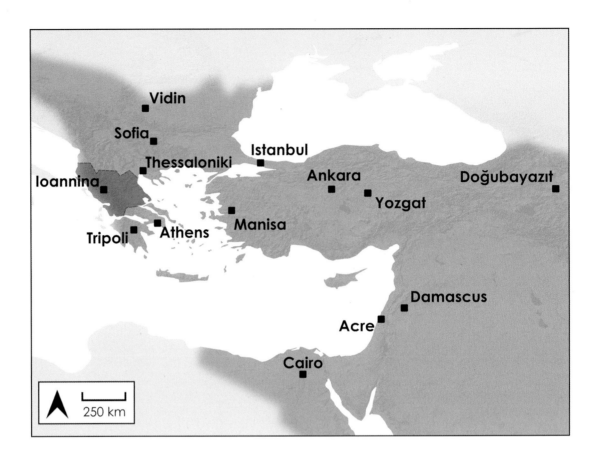

This book is a spatial history of an Ottoman frontier zone. In the early nineteenth century, some of the most consequential innovations in Ottoman architecture were taking place not in the capital of Istanbul but in the farthest reaches of imperial territory. A number of provincial power brokers, rising to prominence during an unstable period of political crises, sparked an explosion of building activity throughout the Eastern Mediterranean. I investigate this wider phenomenon through the case study of Ali Pasha (fig. 3), who epitomized the trend by emerging as one of the most prolific patrons of architecture in the history of the empire. Born in what is now Albania to a family of local notables, Ali Pasha embarked on a precipitous climb to authority in his youth.

self-definition. While one of these experiments famously succeeded, with the Hellenic Republic of Greece recognized as a sovereign state in 1830, the other was quashed in a decisive manner by the imperial center. In this study, I examine how the architecture that Ali Pasha commissioned was a key element in the governor's own improvisations in regional identity formation: an ambitious building program that was so revolutionary, it ultimately got him killed. Although Ali Pasha's aspirations to a semi-independent dynastic state ended with his death, during his lifetime as an Ottoman administrator he spent several decades using the built environment to leave his mark on the world around him—constructing a "theatre of his fortunes and his triumphs."

FIGURE 2
Louis Dupré, *The Palace and Fortress of Ioannina, View from the Lake*. From Dupré, *Voyage à Athenes et à Constantinople* (Paris: Dondey-Dupré, 1825), plate 9. American School of Classical Studies at Athens, Gennadius Library.

His path eventually crossed with those of contemporaries like Napoleon and Lord Byron, who took great interest in this individual situated at the geographic intersection between Western Europe and the Ottoman realms. Ali Pasha came to rule a vast domain (fig. 4), which he and his family transformed with infrastructure projects and architectural complexes, including palaces, fortifications, mosques, dervish lodges, and even Orthodox churches. Such commissions were not a mere reflection of but a catalyst for a shift in the sociopolitical order, part of an ongoing process of challenging the standards of patronage established by the imperial court and relocating administrative authority from center to province. The present volume represents the first in-depth study of Ottoman architecture during what has often been described as the age of revolution, the pivotal moment at the turn of the eighteenth century when there was no obvious blueprint for power, written from the perspective of one of the most notorious figures of the time.[4]

THE BUILT ENVIRONMENT AS THEATER

By taking up an examination of a single patron's architectural program, I adopt what the art historian Ellen Kenney describes as a "prosopographical" approach, recognizing that a "patron's biography and building activity are intricately interwoven."[5] Yet this book is not a biography of Ali Pasha per se, or even a series of in-depth character studies of individual monuments, but rather an account of how an entire

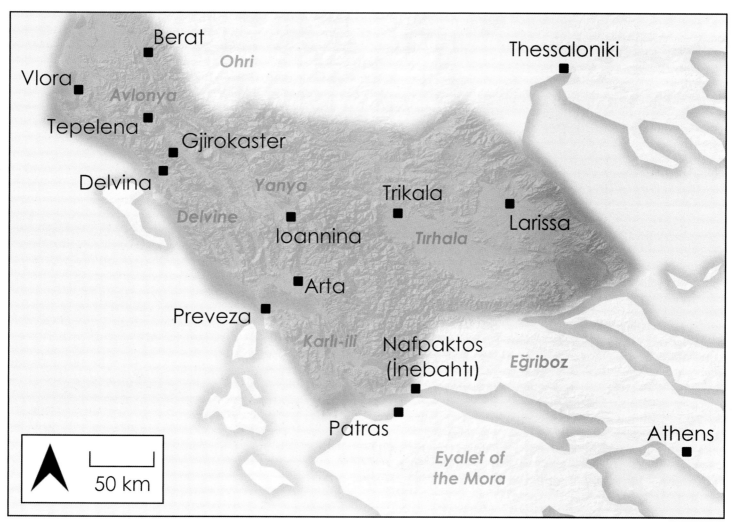

FIGURE 3 (opposite)
Spiridon Ventouras, *Portrait of Ali Pasha*, 1818. Oil on canvas, 71 × 58 cm. The Thanassis and Marina Martinos Collection.

FIGURE 4
The territory governed by Ali Pasha and his sons circa 1812, with the major cities and Ottoman provincial districts indicated. Map by Matthew J. Jacobson.

FIGURE 5
Edward Lear, *View of Tepelena from the North*, 1848. Ink, pencil, and watercolor on paper, 32.2 × 51 cm. MS Typ 55.26, Houghton Library, Harvard University.

built environment was shaped during the tenure of one provincial official's administration. Ali Pasha's buildings are notable not for their singularity but for their ubiquity. The governor ordered the construction of massive city walls and fortified palace complexes not only in his capital in Ioannina but in all the big towns that came under his rule, from the shores of Preveza to the heights of Tepelena (fig. 5). In these cities, spanning a distance of more than 150 kilometers, the governor commissioned major projects like congregational mosques in a coherent style and design—creating a recognizable "brand" for Ali Pasha's era. This homogenizing effect was partly due to the teams of building specialists who were constantly moving throughout the region from one construction site to another. Ali Pasha also invested heavily in infrastructure networks, including roads, way stations, bridges, aqueducts, and customs houses—what I term interstitial architecture—that knitted together the vast topography falling under his jurisdiction. This volume therefore aims to deal with monuments not as stand-alone set pieces but within their broader geographic context, thinking through how the governor's spatial strategies comprised the full manipulation of a territory.

There are many reasons why this story of patronage on the periphery has been left largely unwritten. First and foremost, quite a few of the buildings commissioned by Ali Pasha have almost entirely disappeared. In the immediate aftermath of the governor's execution, several of his constructions were either destroyed or damaged. For example, the Istanbul officials who were appointed to take over the administration of this region opted to leave the charred husk of Ali Pasha's fortified palace at Litharitsa in Ioannina to sit and molder, the remains

FIGURE 6
Dominique Papety, *Litharitsa, Fortress of Ali Pasha* (in ruins), ca. 1846–47. Watercolor, gouache, and pencil on paper, 17.3 × 28.5 cm. Bequest of François Sabatier. Louvre Museum, RF 1773.67. Photo: Michel Urtado. © RMN-Grand Palais / Art Resource, New York.

visible for decades after his execution (fig. 6). Such pointed acts of ruination on the part of the Ottoman central authorities reveal how the buildings themselves—tectonic mementos of one local ruler's ambition—were perceived as an ongoing threat to the imperial order. Evidently, it was not sufficient to eliminate the person; his constructions had to be neutralized as well. My attempt here to reconstruct the built environment in its fullest scope avoids the common pitfall in architectural history that favors the study of surviving monuments. This approach reverses the subsequent campaigns of erasure that were designed to obliterate Ali Pasha's unique political project. While this book is about the governor's rise to power, the narrative of Ali Pasha's architecture is also by necessity linked with his equally dramatic fall.

Ali Pasha's architectural legacy has also been complicated by the emergence of the modern states of Greece and Albania, whose government agencies in the twentieth century tended to overlook and, in some cases, neglect outright the monuments from the preceding Ottoman era. The relative lack of interest in preserving and studying Ottoman material in the twentieth century stood in stark contrast to the wealth of academic literature and restoration efforts devoted to ancient sites, which proved to be more effective vehicles for the construction of national identity.[6] The story of Ali Pasha, a controversial figure who was born in Albania and died in Greece, tends to fall through the disciplinary cracks of Balkan studies, a field that is often framed according to contemporary national geographies.[7] By examining this provincial power holder through the lens of architecture and, more broadly, a built environment that transcends modern political borders, this volume offers a view of a zone that was remarkably syncretic during a time when nationalist discourses were only beginning to form. In this way, the case study of Ali Pasha also contributes to broader initiatives to examine the Ottoman heritage of this region, which have begun to emerge in recent decades with the fall of communism in Albania and the growing interest in Greece's multicultural past.[8]

The fact that Ali Pasha's buildings were deemed unserviceable or even downright threatening to the ruling authorities in Ottoman Istanbul and subsequently in the modern nations of Greece and Albania raises the question of architecture as a stage for the performance of political power. Through his architectural patronage, Ali Pasha built up the surrounding region as a series of "theaters" in which he himself enacted his authority and tested what was possible in realizing his own political aspirations.[9] William Meyer's assessment of the governor's last stand as taking place within the "theatre of his fortunes and his triumphs" explicitly ties a physical geographic space to Ali Pasha's personal achievements and status. The consul's description captures succinctly how the built environment in Ottoman lands had at that point become less a symbol of empire than a locus for innovative self-representation.

The concept of architecture as theater offers a productive framework for interpreting Ali Pasha's corpus of monuments in several respects. First, scholars of performance studies have observed theater's potential to upend the status quo.[10] In a similar fashion, Ali Pasha's buildings are situated in the liminal space of an Ottoman frontier zone, where the customs of architectural patronage were being questioned and redefined. The metaphor of theater is also useful in that stage performance provides a space where one can envision new or alternative realities.[11] Theater is typically less about the scientific representation of the world than it is engaged with creating a realm of illusion in which the importance of actors and their actions is magnified by being placed within an extraordinary setting.[12] Ali Pasha's buildings, such as the splendid reception halls of his numerous palaces, likewise work to convince multiple audiences—from the heads of local villages to foreign diplomats—of the governor's grandeur and influence. This conspicuous fashioning of Ali Pasha's public persona through architecture points to a moment of social mobility and upheaval in the established order of Ottoman ruling hierarchies, when someone who began his career as a small-time mountain brigand could become one of the wealthiest and most powerful people in the empire. In Ali Pasha's theater of fortune and triumph, the spectator is asked to imagine not how the world is but how it *could* be.

The political drama of Ali Pasha's final conflict with the Ottoman sultan was so compelling that the story of the siege of Ioannina was being translated to the stages of London and Paris mere months after the wayward governor's death.[13] In these performances, the buildings that Ali Pasha commissioned were transformed into scenography, a literal realization of the governor's territory as a theater. Meanwhile, within the Ottoman context, Ali Pasha's own cultural productions also mine the theme of the land itself as a backdrop for the performance of political ascendancy. After more than a decade of rule, the governor commissioned a folk song in Greek verse to celebrate his achievements as a capable and just leader. This ballad—composed by Haji Sehreti, a Muslim secretary in Ali Pasha's court—is commonly known as the *Alipasiad*, a naming convention recalling the heroic songs of ancient Greek literature such as the *Iliad*.[14] It is also on the scale of epic poetry, being composed of around 6,500 lines of rhyming couplets (the *Iliad* is approximately 15,500 lines, for comparison). The existence of multiple manuscript copies with a good deal of variation in the text suggests that this poem was transmitted orally, with different performers embellishing the song with their own verses over time.[15] The final lines of the poem reflect on the nature of Ali Pasha's rule:

> From the four corners he gave them order.
> And his law was heard throughout the land,
> In the West and in the East they converse about it.
> In the West and in the East, they speak about this [man],
> When they recognize his name all over they tremble.
> He bestowed just rule to the corrupt Albania,
> Thereafter he ventured from Tepelena,
> And, in his own post settled in Ioannina.
> Ten provinces are now found under his command.[16]

In this concluding summa, Haji Sehreti describes the scope of Ali Pasha's fame in spatial terms, stressing how his renown has seemingly permeated every nook and cranny of the landscape, from the winding mountain defiles of Epirus in the west to the plains of Thessaly in the east. The final word in this passage—"command" (ορισμόν, *orismon*)—is particularly notable, because the term in Greek originates from the verb *orizo*, which means to determine, define, set down, or inscribe. It is the same verb that gives English the word "horizon," in the sense that the horizon is the line between earth and sky that determines the farthest boundary of space perceivable by the human eye. Ali Pasha's command thus depends on the concept of a geographic expanse defined in terms of both imperial administrative boundaries (the "ten provinces" within the governor's jurisdiction) and the farthest limits (the "four corners") of what the poem's audience could perceive as their commonly shared homeland.

While a cultural monument like the *Alipasiad* remains unique (I know of no other Ottoman governor who commissioned epic verse in the style of Homer), it is indicative of a much wider transformation in power relations throughout the imperial borderlands. For it was during the long eighteenth century that the Ottoman Empire experienced profound changes in provincial administration and became a series of defined theaters in which regional identity was being staged on the ground.

LOCAL RULERS IN THE AGE OF REVOLUTION

Ali Pasha can be counted among a group of provincial notables who held sway over large territories of the Ottoman Empire at the end of the eighteenth century—typically referred to by historians as the *â'yân*.[17] Tellingly, it proves something of a challenge to establish an all-encompassing definition for this class of local rulers, mostly owing to an inherent diversity of backgrounds, leadership and organizational styles, the specific type of administrative positions held, and their relationships with the imperial center. Yet it can be generally observed that, in the eighteenth century, the choicest offices and revenues in provincial administration, which had traditionally been awarded to those who had trained and risen through the ranks at the sultan's court in Istanbul, became available to local notables already based out in the provinces. In this way, individuals beyond the Istanbul elite were incorporated into the upper echelons of the Ottoman administrative apparatus.

The rise of a new group of provincial administrators and the decentralization of government appointments went hand in hand with two factors: the establishment in 1695 of tax-farming grants (*mâlikâne*) that could be awarded for life rather than for just a few years, and the growth of local economies based on the management of increasingly frequent military incursions.[18] Thus, as wars against foreign powers drained the Ottoman central treasury, the government granted more autonomy to local notables who proved effective at quickly marshalling soldiers and supplies and moving them from one region to another. The emergence of the *ayan* class of provincial power holders was a gradual process, and it was only in the last decades of the eighteenth century that a clear hierarchy formed, distinguishing larger and smaller ruling families. At the turn of the century, precisely when Ali Pasha was coming into his own in today's Greece and Albania, he and half a dozen other families spread throughout the empire were managing networks of lesser notables from their regional bases of power.

By spotlighting the architectural production of one local ruler against the background of broader developments in Ottoman political and economic history, this book bridges multiple disciplines. I am particularly engaged with the rich scholarship on provincial notables that has shifted the focus in Ottoman studies from imperial center to periphery. In the 1960s, Albert Hourani proposed a new examination of what he described as the "politics of notables."[19] In subsequent decades, historians have analyzed the socioeconomic bases for the influence of the *ayan*, especially the extent to which access to foreign trade, tax-farming rights, and ability to acquire and form a large number of *çiftlik* (farming villages) contributed to the appearance and endurance of this group in the eighteenth century.[20] As a result, these provincial power holders have become the key to understand the workings of—and potential challenges to—the Ottoman state at the regional level.[21] In her volume *Empire of Difference*, Karen Barkey gives pride of place to this class of local notables by tracking how Ottoman administration in the eighteenth century came to function as a system of constant brokerage and negotiation between imperial authorities and peripheries.[22] In another recent monograph, Ali Yaycıoğlu also characterizes the state at this time as a "horizontal and participatory empire, in which central and provincial actors combined to rule the empire together," yet he emphasizes that the new "social and political order . . . did not bring long-term stability."[23] In the field of history, the "age of revolution" has typically been defined by the French Revolution, which resulted in the overthrow of the reigning monarchy and a complete restructuring of the country's government.[24] The age of revolution in the Ottoman sphere was more a matter of the imperial court's attempts to navigate constant political uncertainty. This uncertainty not only took the form of riots and rebellions but also involved the slow and steady chiseling away of the sultan's ruling authority in the provinces—and the *ayan* played an important role in both respects.

These endeavors in the field of Ottoman history to characterize the *ayan* and their place in state administration call for an investigation of the material presence of these figures. How was empire negotiated and produced through new approaches to the organization of space

FIGURE 7
The Çapanoğlu Mosque in Yozgat, the initial construction of which was completed in 1779. Photo by author.

and the built environment? Recognizing architecture as a type of historical document in and of itself is a methodology that offers a nuanced view of this class of notables on the rise in the Ottoman provinces.

ARCHITECTURAL PATRONAGE AT THE EDGE OF EMPIRE

While the present volume on Ali Pasha's architecture focuses on monuments constructed in Greece and Albania, in many ways this project began in Turkey, in a town called Yozgat. Situated in the central plains of Anatolia, Yozgat is relatively remote, a far cry from Turkey's mega-urban sprawls of Istanbul and Ankara. It is for this reason that I was particularly struck during my first visit by the large Ottoman-era mosque situated in the heart of the municipal center (fig. 7). Elegant and weighty in its design, this building would not have been out of place in the imperial capital, and thus seemed rather outsized for the town. The time that I spent in Yozgat would ultimately lead to the central research questions raised in this book about the shifting dynamics of architectural patronage on the edge of empire. How can we explain the appearance of this massive foundation in what had presumably been one of the more distant corners of the Ottoman provinces?

The central congregational mosque in Yozgat was built by the Çapanoğlu family, an *ayan* household of local rulers who were contemporaries of Ali Pasha. The first phase of construction, which comprised the central domed prayer space, was initiated by Çapanoğlu Mustafa Bey in 1779.[25] More than a decade later, in 1794, his brother and successor as provincial governor, Süleyman Bey, expanded the mosque with a new façade and covered porch that almost doubled the holding capacity of the building. This foundation served as the focal point of a wider effort on the part of the Çapanoğlu family to transform what had been a small village into the district capital of the Anatolian plateau in a matter of years. The two phases of the mosque's construction, clearly distinguished by different-colored stones, could be considered a visual metaphor for how these patrons steadily accrued power and sought to establish themselves as a dynasty of local notables.[26] There is a saying in modern Turkish: "Bu işin altında bir Çapanoğlu var," which can be loosely translated as "[Be careful, because] there is [probably] a Çapanoğlu behind this." It is most often used to caution someone when dealing with a sticky situation lest they provoke the ire of an influential figure who could be implicated in the matter. This popular expression preserves the memory of how, in a relatively short amount of time, the Çapanoğlu family came to have their hands in seemingly every affair. When I first asked myself how such a large congregational mosque came to be built in Yozgat, the answer was ultimately straightforward—there was a Çapanoğlu behind it.

Throughout the long duration of the Ottoman Empire, there were always government officials and local notables who were active in urban life and commissioning buildings in the provinces. In the sixteenth and seventeenth centuries, however, high-ranking administrators would be sent from Istanbul to a particular district, perhaps set up a public foundation (*vakıf*) in the course of their service, and then in a few years' time move on to their next position in another location. Local families also commissioned buildings, but they typically possessed the means to fund only one or two foundations.[27] By the eighteenth century, the financial and political capital concentrated in the hands of some *ayan* families enabled them to oversee the construction of numerous architectural projects and public works over a much longer period, in a few cases across several decades. This book contributes to a budding area of scholarship that recognizes the significance of these developments in provincial building projects and examines what could be described as "*ayan* architecture."[28] Ayda Arel has observed how building activity in the eighteenth-century Ottoman provinces could flourish during this period of political unrest and within a new system of accruing financial capital, all through a case study of the fortified "feudal" estates of the Cihanoğlu, a family of landowners active in what is today southwest Turkey.[29] Filiz Yenişehirlioğlu expanded this line of inquiry with an introductory survey of the architectural production of a handful of *ayan* groups throughout Anatolia, including the Çapanoğlu and Cihanoğlu families.[30] Her comparative approach and reading of the buildings themselves as historical documents—especially because this material can be much more difficult to trace in Ottoman government archives than sultanic foundations—has deeply informed the present study.

The precise nature of Ali Pasha's architectural patronage comes into sharper focus when considered alongside the building efforts of his fellow *ayan* rulers. In this way, the governor, who is often treated in secondary literature as an isolated figure who is only vaguely connected to the Ottoman context, can be more squarely situated within the political and cultural environment in which he operated. In other words, to understand the architecture of Ioannina, one must also go to

Yozgat. In addition to the Çapanoğlu family, we can find other regional governors based in Anatolia who were undertaking impressive building projects. In 1784, İshak Pasha, who was a member of the influential Çıldıroğlu clan, constructed a large combination palace and mosque complex in Doğubayazıt, located today on the border between Turkey, Iran, and Armenia (fig. 8).³¹ His successors continued to add to and maintain the site, constructed in a distinctively regional style that is characterized by elaborate stone carving in high relief reminiscent of local Seljuk and Armenian religious architecture. The entire structure is dramatically perched on a cliff overlooking abundant plains and an important trade route along the Silk Road, a site that conveys the Çıldıroğlu family's command over these economic resources. Moving south to the Arab provinces, several members of the ʿAzm family initiated a building boom in Damascus that endured for the better part of the eighteenth century, investing in large real estate clusters that brought together marketplaces, schools, and bathhouses.³² One prominent member of this family, Asʿad Pasha, placed a large palace complex immediately adjacent to a massive domed *khan* (caravanserai) that he also built. The mansion stands as an extravagant example of residential architecture in the region, with a number of reception areas surrounding a large paved courtyard that are decorated with *ablaq* masonry of alternating courses of white and black stone.³³ Meanwhile, in Egypt, Mehmed Ali Pasha claimed the Cairo Citadel in the 1820s and '30s with a sprawling palace built in a neoclassical style and a Friday mosque complex that looks to be straight out of Istanbul.³⁴ The governor also established a large garden palace and industrial complexes on the outskirts of his capital and in the Nile Delta beyond.³⁵ In the heart of old Cairo, Mehmed Ali Pasha inserted himself along one of the main thoroughfares by contributing a *sabil-kuttab*, a type of public foundation unique to the city that combines a fountain with a religious school. While the governor's fountain from 1820 thus participates in a specific local building tradition, the façade and interior have been executed in an Ottoman

FIGURE 8
View of the mosque and mausoleum within the İshak Pasha palace at Doğubayazıt. Photo by author.

FIGURE 9
The *sabil-kuttab* of Mehmed Ali Pasha in Cairo. Photo by author.

baroque fashion with sinuous vegetal designs and classicizing capitals (fig. 9). Finally, turning to one of Ali Pasha's neighbors in the Balkans, the rebellious local ruler Pasvantoğlu Osman Pasha constructed a tekke (dervish lodge) along with a mosque and library complex in Vidin, on today's border between Bulgaria and Romania.[36] The foundation inscription in Ottoman Turkish above the library's door records the foundation as 1802–3 (1217 H), a few years after Pasvantoğlu's capital had been unsuccessfully besieged by imperial authorities.[37] Revealingly, this text makes no mention of the sultan and instead dedicates the complex to the memory of Pasvantoğlu's father, who had been executed by the Ottoman state for conspiracy to revolt.[38]

Even this cursory review of the architecture of this new class of provincial notables reveals that the late eighteenth and early nineteenth centuries witnessed a dramatic transformation of imperial space. It may seem counterintuitive that there was a proliferation of architectural patronage in the Ottoman Empire during an age of revolution, as times of instability do not usually lend themselves to the mass mobilization of funds, labor, and materials necessary to construct buildings. Yet the fact that Ali Pasha and his fellow *ayan* managed to do just that calls into question the paradigm of the Ottoman lands as the "sick man of Europe"—money may not have been flowing into the coffers of the imperial capital, but that does not mean it was not being put to use elsewhere. Decentralization does not necessarily equal decline.

The field of Ottoman architecture has traditionally been defined by Istanbul, particularly the large sultanic mosque complexes dotting the Golden Horn, whose slender minarets and tall domes lend the city its celebrated silhouette. Yet, while in many ways the capital served as a microcosm of empire, the narrative of one city's urban development cannot adequately account for a geopolitical arena that touched three continents. Several scholars have investigated how architecture in the provinces served as a tool for expanding and managing the empire. This is especially the case in the sixteenth and seventeenth centuries, when architectural forms developed by the corps of royal architects (haṣṣa miʻmârları) in Istanbul were disseminated and replicated throughout the provinces, a process of "Ottomanization" that announced the supremacy of the sultan's suzerainty.[39] There has also been a recent movement to trace modernization efforts throughout the Ottoman provinces beginning in the second half of the nineteenth century, in which historians have situated industrial and urban development projects, especially in the port cities around the Eastern Mediterranean, within emerging global economies.[40]

By examining *ayan* architecture, this volume bridges the chronological gap between the eras of Ottomanization and modernization and, in doing so, also moves beyond a state-centric view.[41] As Tülay Artan suggests, an account of architectural patronage outside the context of the imperial court can bring to light the hybrid identities across regional spaces "that both coexisted with, and were counterposed to" a dominant sense of cultural Ottoman-ness.[42] A rich literature on borderlands undergirds this study, which considers the edges of empire not as regions that passively receive center-driven initiatives but rather as interconnected zones of flux and ambivalence where a pluralistic consciousness is formed.[43] Precisely because the *ayan* were not part of the elite classes in Istanbul, their buildings were distinguished by the aspirations common to any arriviste group looking to secure its legitimacy, and this process did not always involve forging ties with the imperial center. Borrowing, and expanding upon, a term from Catherine Asher's study of governor palaces in the Mughal Empire, I refer to the architecture of Ottoman provincial notables as "subimperial" in that these buildings operate within the context of an imperial order but cannot necessarily be considered as participating in a state-driven discourse of sovereignty.[44]

Ayan architecture is defined by its eclecticism. All the provincial notables mentioned above preferred to employ local building specialists working in distinctive regional styles rather than to requisition architects from the sultan's *hassa mimarları* in Istanbul.[45] The patronage of this new ruling class thus emphasized geographic rootedness and the lavish expenditure of newfound financial capital, all to develop and secure patron-client relationships among the local communities that proved to be essential for the endurance of this reconfigured system of political power. In some instances, especially in the case of Ali Pasha, one of the more incendiary members of the *ayan* class, architecture could serve as a potential site of transgression against the imperial order.[46] In the sixteenth century, under the tenure of the chief royal architect Sinan, there emerged certain expectations of propriety in the construction of buildings relative to the sociopolitical status of their patrons, which has been described as a system of "decorum" in architecture.[47] While this system was from the outset a "fragile form of social contract open to negotiation" and adaptation, the point stands that Ottoman architecture should be understood within a cultural context in which people were highly attuned to interpreting the rank of a patron according to the formal typology and siting of monuments.[48] In the seventeenth and eighteenth centuries, architectural decorum arguably remained intact in the sense that certain stylistic features continued to be reserved for royal use. Yet this period also witnessed an expansion of who was included in the ruling class of Istanbul, whose members served as the arbiters of taste and pursued self-expression through the commissioning of architecture.[49] At the end of the eighteenth century, the *ayan* were thus part of what had already been an ongoing process of testing the limits of decorum, but their approach to patronage is distinctive in that the challenges they posed to this system were exceptionally widespread and characterized by a very high degree of self-assurance. In the territory under his control, Ali Pasha constructed numerous sumptuous palaces, established coastal fortifications that were in direct violation of international treaties, commissioned a church in his own name, and ordered a program of epigraphic inscriptions in Greek verse that make no reference to the sultan and instead celebrate the governor's descent from ancient Greek deities and local Hellenistic kings. For Ali Pasha, architectural decorum was hardly a matter of "negotiation," and the fact that he was able to carry on in such a manner for years points to the strength of the *ayan* in this period.

This class of provincial rulers played the most decisive role in shaping the built environment of the Ottoman lands during the long eighteenth century, a period that for the purposes of this study is bracketed by the emergence of the *malikane* system in 1695 and the 1839 Edict of Gülhane that launched the Tanzimat modernization reforms.[50] Given that these subimperial actors were interested in building their own spheres of influence, often beyond the tastes and trends of Istanbul, it is not surprising that several of these figures—most prominently Ali Pasha, Pasvantoğlu Osman Pasha, and Mehmed Ali Pasha—also found themselves embroiled in clashes with the sultan's troops. While architectural historians typically approach patronage as a benign or even benevolent act, this book raises the question of the revolutionary potential of architecture. The burned ruins of Ali Pasha's palace in Ioannina serve as a testament to the significance—and risk—of building beyond one's station (see fig. 6).

Ali Pasha must be recognized not only as a product of the Ottoman context but also as part of an even wider phenomenon of regional power holders carving out their own territories in the face of destabilizing empire. Several oceans away but at precisely the same time, a number of local notables emerged on the Indian subcontinent at the edges of the Mughal Empire. One such clan was the Nawabs of Awadh in Uttar Pradesh, who asserted their authority in several commissions, including numerous palaces, gardens, and city gates.[51] While the members of this family shared in the imperial architectural traditions established by the Mughals, such as building large tomb complexes capped by prominent central domes, they also distinguished themselves as Shi'i patrons, constructing in their capital of Lucknow shrines such as the Great Imambara, founded by the Nawab Asaf al-Dawla in 1786–91 (fig. 10).[52] All of these monuments feature an exuberant local style characterized by scalloped arches and elaborate plaster ornamentation. When brought into conversation with one another, these case studies from the Ottoman lands and South Asia suggest that the turn of the eighteenth century witnessed a global moment in which the long reach of different

FIGURE 10
The Rumi Darwaza, the gate to the first forecourt of the Great Imambara complex in Lucknow. Photo by author.

empires was giving way to a series of more local, circumscribed theaters of influence.

Throughout this book, I thus employ comparisons to other examples of "frontier" architecture, to provide a broader frame of reference for Ali Pasha's architectural interventions. The horizontal nature of the Ottoman Empire, especially at the end of the eighteenth century, meant that provincial power holders, operating with immense amounts of newfound wealth and political authority, were looking askance at their contemporaries and were engaged in a competition to carve out their own territories.[53] Among the *ayan* class, Ali Pasha stands out as a patron of architecture in multiple respects. He was certainly one of the most prolific, in terms of the breadth of the geographic area he covered and the sheer volume of projects he oversaw. Through his own funding and organization efforts, the governor built everything from military fortifications and palace complexes to Friday mosques and roadside dervish lodges. He was able to undertake such an extensive building program because he was so effective at amassing resources and remained in power for a very long time, more than three decades. Such a comprehensive approach to architecture in many ways anticipated the modernization reforms that would sweep through the Ottoman Empire in the middle of the nineteenth century. Ali Pasha was able to maintain a very fine balance of keeping the Porte's wrath at bay with regular contributions of funds and soldiers, while at the same time taking advantage of his position on the border of the empire to set up an expansive infrastructure that could support his ambitions of semiautonomous rule, seemingly leaving no corner of his realm untouched.

INTRODUCTION 17

ALI PASHA AND HIS REALM

Ali Pasha was born around 1750 in a village just outside the city of Tepelena, in what is today Albania.[54] Both his father and his grandfather had served as the administrators of the local *ṣancaḳ* (provincial district), but Ali's father died when he was still a young man.[55] Nevertheless, he managed to forge a path for himself in the military service of Kurt Ahmed Pasha, the governor of the neighboring district of Berat. Ali ultimately butted heads with his patron but during this time built his own network of contacts and raised sufficient funds to start recruiting mercenaries himself. In 1784, he successfully lobbied the Porte to award him the titles of both *mîr-i mîrân* (governor-general, a military distinction) and *mutaṣarrıf* (administrative governor) of the Delvine district, following in the path of his forebears with the latter position.[56] Meanwhile, in correspondence from his own chancery and in local inscriptions, Ali Pasha is typically styled as the "vizier," an Ottoman title indicating high political rank that is conferred on some provincial governors.

In short order, Ali Pasha expanded his zone of influence by acquiring the titles to several other adjacent administrative districts, including the governorship of Trikala (Ott. Tırhala, 1786) and Ioannina (Ott. Yanya, 1788), as well as the position of "Commander of the Mountain Passes" (*derbendler başbuğu*) in 1788.[57] This last title was of particular importance, as it allowed Ali Pasha's own men to monitor all the key mountain passes throughout the wider province (*eyâlet*) of Rumelia, i.e., most of the southern Balkans.[58] Besides managing the collection of taxes throughout an extensive geographic area and ensuring that these revenues were sent on time to the sultan's treasury, Ali Pasha also proved himself to be indispensable to the Porte by maintaining troops that could be summoned and sent forth at a moment's notice.[59] Based in his capital of Ioannina, Ali Pasha not only gained positions for himself but was also constantly shuffling his family members around to adjacent territories, including the districts of Eğriboz and Karlı-ili for his son Muhtar Pasha in 1799; the province of the Morea (Ott. Mora, 1807) and then the Trikala district (1812) for his eldest son, Veli Pasha; and the district of Berat for Muhtar and his other younger son Salih Pasha in 1811 (see fig. 4).[60] Thus, as the traveler Henry Holland surmised, Ali Pasha's "dominion has been derived, not from any transient effort of revolution, but from a slow and persevering system of aggrandizement, and a policy compounded of caution and enterprise, which has given pretense to usurpation and permanence to conquest."[61] To put it another way, the "four corners" of Ali Pasha's realm celebrated in the *Alipasiad* did not take shape overnight but were years in the making.

This book examines the extent to which Ali Pasha's architectural efforts functioned to establish his own prestige within the landscape by reifying a local identity shared by the communities under his rule. But how did this local identity manifest in the provinces that were under the vizier's governorship? The most logical starting point in defining the geographic contours of the "local" would be the various administrative districts to which Ali Pasha and his sons laid claim. Determining the exact boundaries of any given territory in the Ottoman Empire before the mid-nineteenth century, however, remains a surprisingly difficult task.[62] At the time, the state's concept of administrative space did not entail drawing lines on a map.[63] Rather than rely on a cartographic system, Ottoman officials defined empire through textual inventory. The Ottoman government archives in Istanbul are overflowing with list upon list: registers that identify a particular provincial district by its central capital city and name the numerous surrounding villages (*karye*) that could determine the extent of the geographic unit. When these villages are plotted on a map, the resulting cloud of place markers often shows a degree of overlap between administrative districts, making it difficult to delineate clear boundaries and revealing a system of provincial geography that was relatively fluid and flexible. For this reason I have opted to omit firm border lines in the maps that represent the administrative districts that fell within Ali Pasha's territory in figures 1 and 4.

What we can say is that Ali Pasha and his sons eventually governed an area that comprised what had once been the ancient regions of Epirus, Acarnania, and Thessaly, with the Ottoman districts falling along similar topographic boundaries: the Ionian Sea to the west, the Tomorr and Morava mountains to the north, the Vermio and Olympus mountains to the east, and the Gulf of Corinth to the south. This area (and, really, the Balkans in general) can be characterized as a system of plains and mountain ranges. Access from one region to the next was restricted to a handful of choke points through the mountains, hence the significance of Ali Pasha's winning the title of commander of the passes.

Divided from the rest of the mainland by the Pindus Mountains, Ali Pasha's core homeland of Epirus (what is now northwestern Greece and southern Albania) maintained a long tradition of regionalism and even insularity well before the early nineteenth century.[64] Ali Pasha was distinctive, however, in that he consolidated several microregions and tribes of diverse languages, ethnicities, and creeds under a coherent political order. He was the archetype of the Balkan strongman, savvy in clan politics and commanding both the fear and the respect of the local populace by administrating with a firm hand.[65] Although this general characterization of authoritarian rule has been legitimately critiqued by scholars as an Orientalist stereotype, the fact remains that Ali Pasha himself trafficked in this kind of language and considered his unification of Epirus one of his great achievements as governor.[66] During an audience with the traveler Thomas Hughes, Ali Pasha boasted that he had fearlessly traversed this region "when a thousand muskets were aimed against his life; but that now we should find perfect security and tranquility diffused over the whole district."[67] The *Alipasiad* picks up on this theme of the governor and his sons as the heralds of a Pax Epirotica. The poet Haji Sehreti writes:

> I tell of the wondrous deeds of all the noted warriors,
> Who performed these [acts] brilliantly [in the service] of these viziers.
> With my pen I tell of the things they have done,
> Giving the Albanians and Rumelians order.[68]

The *Alipasiad* itself—an epic folk song composed in the Epirote Greek dialect by a Muslim in Ali Pasha's court—already demonstrates the complex layers of local identity in the region. Meanwhile, this specific passage highlights how the vizier framed his claim to legitimacy by co-opting the wider concept of "order" (νιζάμι, *nizami*), a familiar construct used by the Ottoman sultans to make their own claims to power, perhaps most notably in the contemporaneous Nizam-i Cedid (New Order) reforms instituted by Sultan Selim III beginning in the late eighteenth century.[69] In this poem, however, the sultan is bypassed completely in favor of extolling the deeds of Ali Pasha.

Bringing the people of Epirus together under a single banner was a long and frequently violent process. Ali Pasha's most significant coup in this respect was the conquest in 1802 of Souli, an impregnable mountain community that had refused to recognize his authority as governor. Another significant move toward territorial expansion was Ali Pasha's victory in a long internecine dispute with İbrahim Pasha, the neighboring governor of Berat, resulting in the Porte's removal of İbrahim from his position in 1812 and the ceding of the district to Ali Pasha. The *Alipasiad* notes the ability of the governor "To usher in the age of Ali Pasha in all the towns, / Where they desire to make conflict with this [man]."[70]

In the face of all these challenges, how did the vizier consolidate power throughout the region, ushering in "the age of Ali Pasha," and what was the role of architecture in this process? While the first three chapters of this book detail Ali Pasha's innovations in the building typologies that tend to form the core of Ottoman architectural patronage (i.e., the palatial, the military, and the religious), the final chapter addresses the theme of public texts as sites of political tension and even violence. Chapter 1 begins with an examination of the vizier's palaces, which were the very heart of Ali Pasha's peripatetic court. A series of urban residential complexes served as stages for the performance of the governor's political power before local, state, and foreign audiences through elaborate ceremonies and by offering a commanding view of the wider landscape (see fig. 2). These residences were also built to impress as repositories for Ali Pasha's personal wealth, with treasuries of gifts and luxury items on display. In addition to the palaces themselves, the vizier also invested in a system of roads and way stations to support his retinue's movements from one residence to another. Such mobility had not been possible for earlier administrators, who were typically assigned to one province—and only one official residence—at a time. Ali Pasha thus redefined the governor's palace, transforming it from a single, stand-alone set piece into a node within a wider spatial network that was continuously being activated to legitimate his claims to authority.

This survey of the governor's urban interventions is followed, in chapter 2, with an investigation of a line of military installations along the Ionian Sea, raising the question "Who has the right to build a fortress?" In this region, the macropolitics of the Napoleonic Wars were telescoped into microlevel tussles among international actors over key disputed zones that were often a matter of only a few square kilometers. In the course of a decade, from 1805 to 1815, Ali Pasha commissioned the construction or extensive renovation of eleven coastal fortifications, which involved a tremendous investment of both finances and labor (fig. 11). These building projects—and the governor's frequent clashes with both Istanbul and European neighbors over their construction—counter the assumption that the Ottoman capital was spearheading such projects in order to maintain the border. Rather, Ali Pasha's maritime fortifications can be understood as a strategy meant to intimidate neighboring populations who proved resistant to his own ambitions of territorial expansion. I thus reassess the criteria that scholars typically use to evaluate military architecture, considering how the governor's fortifications were primarily designed as long-range antagonistic spectacles—the look

FIGURE 11
View of Ali Pasha's fortress on the Vrino channel in Butrint, looking west, with the island of Corfu in the background. Photo by author.

and placement of an installation within a wider terrain being just as important as its short-range defensive capabilities.

Turning from matters of international diplomacy to internal affairs, chapter 3 considers how Ali Pasha took a pragmatic approach in addressing the multiconfessional communities living under his rule by establishing an astonishingly wide array of religious complexes. First, he paired his official residences with Islamic pious foundations, especially Friday mosques, whose minarets mark each of the major urban centers in his domain (see fig. 5). Ali Pasha and his sons also sponsored Sufi dervish lodges on the outskirts of these towns and in the surrounding hinterlands, a once pervasive typology of roadside architecture that has now almost completely disappeared in Greece and Albania. But the governor did not build only for his own faith tradition. Archival documentation and fieldwork reveal that Ali Pasha and his Christian wife, Vasiliki, were directly responsible for commissioning multiple church foundations. Even though these structures were in relatively remote locations, the significance of these gestures should not be understated, as the construction of a Christian monument by a Muslim official is unprecedented in the history of Ottoman architecture.

The fourth and final chapter concerns the vizier's efforts to inscribe his personal brand of politics into the local topography through the medium of architectural epigraphy. By the early nineteenth century, firm standards governed the creation of public texts in the Ottoman Empire, and Ali Pasha defied these norms at every turn. Most significantly, I document how the governor commissioned multiple epigraphic inscriptions in Greek verse, a format echoing local folk song, that all emphasize both Ali Pasha's local roots and his commitment to being just (even if at times ruthless) in his administration. These inscriptions were accompanied by heraldic insignia that are engaged with a regional visual tradition of the Venetian lion. In one example from the city walls of Ioannina, the heterodox epigraphic program was removed by the central Ottoman authorities shortly after Ali Pasha's death, a clear act of *damnatio memoriae*. This competition over public texts and thus collective memory reveals how the drama between imperial center and periphery could be played out within the built environments of the Ottoman provinces.

To recover the world that Ali Pasha built, this volume brings together a wide range of sources that have thus far received only scant attention. This includes the material record itself, which I examined during numerous site visits in both Greece and Albania. While I make use of technical ground plans to analyze the construction techniques of the architects and engineers in the governor's service, I also frequently deploy historical traveler views and photographs from my own movements through these spaces during fieldwork in order to capture how this architecture was staged in the environment, often against dramatic natural backdrops and with clear attention to the long-distance visibility of these sites. As noted above, the survival rate of Ali Pasha's buildings is variable, and in order to reconstruct these sites, I triangulate my fieldwork with an abundance of archival material, whose far-flung nature—from Istanbul to London—reflects the impressively wide scope of Ali Pasha's audiences and influence. It is my hope that this book will prove relevant to modernists dealing with case studies where there is a paucity of extant architecture. This is an issue that many assume to be consigned to the fields of ancient art and archaeology, yet there are many examples of built environments from the more recent past that have been lost to natural disasters or political upheaval.

Because the governor was a significant figure in the Ottoman Empire, I delve into the State Ottoman Archives in Istanbul as well as the archives of the Directorate General of Pious Foundations in Ankara to capture the view from the imperial center.[71] In addition to housing the collection of orders tracking Ali Pasha's actions and movements (*haṭṭ-i hümâyûn*), these archives contain a score of valuable registers that record the movable and immovable property of the governor, along with his pious endowments (*vakıf*). By examining such registers, I have been able to identify and glean socioeconomic information about a number of Ali Pasha's public foundations, this data sometimes being the sole remaining trace of a particular monument in the material or archival record.

In addition to employing documentation generated by the Ottoman state, this book makes use of an extraordinary local resource for Ali Pasha's governance in Epirus, which is the vizier's own chancery. This collection of more than fifteen hundred documents resides today at the Gennadius Library in Athens.[72] Most of these memoranda, registers, and petitions that reflect the day-to-day life of the court are written in Greek, albeit with an abundance of Ottoman Turkish, Albanian, and Arabic vocabulary, a reflection of the eclecticism of the local dialect before the standardization of Greek after the revolution. Happily, a digital humanities project has been launched at Stanford University to map information found in this archive using a variety of data visualization tools.[73] The preliminary findings of this project complement my own arguments about the importance of the *ayan* class securing the support of local communities by revealing a complex and dynamic network of patron-client relationships maintained by Ali Pasha and his sons across Epirus. In addition to this archival collection, which provides a more ground-level view of the vizier's architectural patronage, I present epigraphic inscriptions, Greek folk songs, and contemporary literary works to round out the local reception of Ali Pasha's building endeavors.[74]

As a complement to these state and local sources, this book makes use of the diplomatic reports and travel accounts of both French and British agents who were stationed in Ali Pasha's court.[75] While travel narratives were composed after the fact, sometimes several years after a particular journey, consuls fired off missives monthly or even weekly as events unfolded in Epirus. The diplomatic record also offers a great deal of information about military constructions and infrastructure projects, as this intelligence was considered highly sensitive at the time and would not have been included in travel accounts, which were intended for a general reading public. The preponderance of European accounts of this region is a reflection of Ali Pasha's relatively relaxed policy on allowing foreign visitors to travel throughout his territory. It is largely for this reason that Epirus attracted an increased flow of Western European travelers, especially after the Napoleonic Wars had effectively closed the Italian peninsula to those hoping to go on their "grand tour." The details offered in the accounts of these visitors—such as the geographic location of a mosque or a description of a palace's decoration—enable us to reconstruct these architectural and urban spaces as they stood at the beginning of the nineteenth century.

By bringing together a multiplicity of sources, this study draws one of the most detailed portraits of an Ottoman borderland to date. These documents make it abundantly clear that Ali Pasha was, after all, just one person, and that the buildings constructed during his rule are the result of a multitude of architects, masons, craftspeople, day laborers, financiers, and common taxpayers who all played a part in making this world a reality. Throughout this book, we will meet this cast of characters: from Master Petros, a Christian from Albania who was Ali Pasha's chief architect, to Guillaume de Vaudoncourt, a French colonel dragooned into overseeing the construction of one of the governor's coastal fortifications. Nevertheless, Ali Pasha takes center stage throughout this study, primarily because his approach to architecture was so evidently an opportunistic endeavor of self-aggrandizement, which in many instances was out of step, if not in outright conflict, with the conventions of patronage established by those who had come up through the Ottoman court. In examining this one provincial governor's building activity, the land itself emerges as a symbolic space in which the dynamics between center and periphery were played out. This was political upheaval through architecture—and it was by and large improvised. With the significant financial and material investment involved in the construction of buildings, it is usually taken for granted that architectural patronage is programmatic, the result of a grand vision or plan. Yet Ali Pasha never composed any kind of manifesto on architecture—indeed, that is the point. In an iterative fashion, building by building, the governor kept pushing the limits of what was possible, experimenting within the inherited system of empire, yet all the while laying the literal groundwork for a quasi-autonomous or even potentially independent state that was extinguished in its nascent stages.[76] Situated as he is on the eve of the Greek War of Independence and Ottoman government reform, Ali Pasha plays a crucial role in our understanding of the modern era. Multiple aspects of the vizier's patronage, including his dedication to infrastructure, openness to foreign visitors and building specialists, accommodation of non-Muslim communities, and interest in cultivating a sense of local identity in Epirus, foreshadow the modernization and nationalization movements that would emerge throughout the rest of the nineteenth century and in many ways carry on into the present. While Ali Pasha's legacy was actively silenced by various stakeholders in the aftermath of his death in 1822, the stubborn material fact of his architectural projects can still be traced in the physical and archival record. These ghostlike fragments haunt the land of Epirus—a persistent presence that speaks to the enduring impact of a local actor like Ali Pasha during a time of revolution.

"Amidst No Common Pomp"
REDEFINING THE GOVERNOR'S PALACE

CHAPTER 1

Within the architectural landscape of the Ottoman Empire, it was the palace above all other building types that served as the preeminent emblem of the sultan's ruling authority. For subjects and foreigners alike, the "Porte," a reference to a monumental gateway at the Topkapı Palace in Istanbul, became shorthand for the entire imperial administrative apparatus.[1] Beginning in the sixteenth century, the height of Ottoman geographic expansion, the sultan would go on military campaigns with a tent complex designed to be a portable replica of the Topkapı, complete with collapsible towers and crenellated "walls" made of fabric.[2] In effect, the sultan never left the confines of his official residence even when he was on the move, forging an unbreakable link between the built environment and the sovereign himself.

In his role as provincial governor on the borderlands of the Ottoman Empire, Ali Pasha fully comprehended the metonymic power of the palace as an architectural type. The concept of the official residence, which had been carefully cultivated over the centuries as a symbol of the sultan's sovereignty, was co-opted in the eighteenth century by members of the new *ayan* class of local rulers, who sought to experiment with representing their own political agency, and Ali Pasha was a standout among his peers. If the vizier's capital in Ioannina was the "theatre of his fortunes and his triumphs," Ali Pasha's palaces could be understood as the stages on which he performed the rituals of statecraft. In these buildings, the governor was both star and director, and his audiences often traveled great distances in the hope of seeing him.

The palace was the heart of Ali Pasha's administration and a crucial site for securing the legitimacy of his rule. However, unlike the Ottoman sultan, who at that point was inextricably bound to a single monumental residence at the opening of the Golden Horn in Istanbul, Ali Pasha strove to map out his jurisdiction by commissioning multiple palace complexes, prominent coordinates within an expanding territory. As a result, his court became increasingly mobile. By the end of his more than thirty-year reign, the governor's entourage was routinely circulating among these residences along a well-developed system of roads and way stations. These palaces thus served not only as the settings for court ritual but also as signposts of Ali Pasha's omnipresent authority within the wider geopolitical landscape.

The governor's numerous residences embodied a new style of political order in the region. In previous centuries, it was standard for an Ottoman administrator to maintain a residence in the urban center of the district that he managed. Perhaps the most important aspect of Ali Pasha's palace architecture is the sheer volume of sites, which sets it apart from this established pattern. In earlier periods, a governor serving in the Ottoman provinces would typically hold only one appointment at a time.[3] Yet, by the early nineteenth century, Ali Pasha and his sons were administrators of what was effectively a contiguous territory comprising multiple provincial districts (see fig. 4). This ruling family of Epirus exercised their prerogative of constructing an unparalleled number of residences within a geographic area reaching from the Adriatic to the Aegean. While many of Ali Pasha's contemporaries in other parts of the empire were also building lavish palaces—the massive complex of İshak Pasha, commanding the plains of Doğubayazıt, and Mehmed Ali Pasha's baroque reception halls in the suburbs of Cairo stand out as examples—the vizier and his sons distinguished themselves by maintaining official residences in every major city under their command and throughout the surrounding hinterlands.[4] These dwellings could be considered multivocal in that their structures and the rituals performed within them anticipated a variety of different audiences. Local elites, neighbors from the Ionian Islands, messengers from the Porte, and Western European travelers all collided with and observed one another in these spaces. Ali Pasha's intense focus on palace architecture, which sets him apart from his predecessors and his peers, provides a view of the polycentric and versatile nature of his ruling strategy.

As discussed in the introduction, because so few of the governor's residential buildings survive intact, these spaces can be reconstructed only through a careful survey and synthesis of the archival record. In what follows, papers from the governor's own chancery provide a view of the day-to-day affairs of Ali Pasha's court.[5] This massive cache of documents gives us a sense of the endless bustle and itinerant nature of palace life. The archive shows that the governor's scribes, writing from whichever city Ali Pasha happened to be in at the time, were constantly dispatching missives to agents in Istanbul or to the leaders of nearby villages to requisition troops or summon workers for one of the governor's latest building projects. Meanwhile, property registers drawn up by Ottoman state officials after Ali Pasha's death offer a wholesale account of both the real estate and movable objects that the governor had amassed throughout his long career. Finally, European travel narratives prove useful for understanding the appearance of these residences and the activities within. Because Western travelers were typically barred admission to other structures, such as mosques or dervish lodges, Ali Pasha's palaces were the monuments to which these individuals had the most immediate access, playing a formative role in European impressions of this individual and his domains.

A case in point is a vivid description of one of Ali Pasha's residences from Lord Byron. His narrative poem *Childe Harold's Pilgrimage* concerns the journey of a disillusioned young man searching for insight in foreign lands. Much of the text is considered to be autobiographical, based on Byron's own journeys through Italy and the Ottoman Empire, including Ali Pasha's realm.[6] The governor and his architecture are given pride of place in the work. Byron describes the hero Childe Harold's approach to Ali Pasha's palace in the town of Tepelena:

The Sun had sunk behind vast Tomerit,
And Laos wide and fierce came roaring by;
The shades of wonted night were gathering yet,

FIGURE 12
Drawn by William Purser and engraved by Edward Francis Finden, *Tepaleen, the Palace of Ali Pacha*. From Lord George Gordon Byron, *The Works of Lord Byron: With His Letters and Journals, and His Life*, by Thomas Moore, Esq., 17 vols. (London: John Murray, 1832–33), vol. 2, frontispiece. American School of Classical Studies at Athens, Gennadius Library.

When, down the steep banks winding warily,
Childe Harold saw, like meteors in the sky,
The glittering minarets of Tepalen,
Whose walls o'erlook the stream; and drawing nigh,
He heard the busy hum of warrior-men
Swelling the breeze that sigh'd along the lengthening glen.

He pass'd the sacred Haram's silent tower,
And underneath the wide o'erarching gate
Survey'd the dwelling of this chief of power,
Where all around proclaim'd his high estate.
Amidst no common pomp the despot sate,
While busy preparation shook the court,
Slaves, eunuchs, soldiers, guests, and santons wait;
Within, a palace, and without, a fort;
Here men of every clime appear to make resort.[7]

That Byron's own visit to Tepelena in 1809 served as the basis for this fantastical scene attests to the inherently theatrical quality of Ali Pasha's residences (fig. 12). As a spectator, Byron was evidently captivated and inspired by what he saw at the governor's court.

This passage from *Childe Harold's Pilgrimage* touches on some of the most salient characteristics of Ali Pasha's households, especially in terms of the use of space and the diverse profile of visitors. These urban residences tended to command a view of the wider area and were in visual dialogue with the surrounding environment, especially with the main routes of entry to the city in question. Upon his approach to Tepelena, Childe Harold saw the minarets glittering "like meteors in the sky," an impression also evoked by a breathtaking view of the palace's fortification walls drawn four decades later by Edward Lear (see fig. 5). Additionally, Ali Pasha's residences stood in locations slightly removed from the town proper, taking on a distinctive military character by being protected with fortification walls and guarded gateways—as Byron remarks, "within, a palace, and without, a fort." The text also introduces the wide range of people who circulated within the court, from Italian engineers to the local archbishop: "Here men of every clime appear to make resort." Byron's traveling companion, John Hobhouse, recalled in his own memoir the cosmopolitan nature of Ali Pasha's retinue in Tepelena; upon entering the palace courtyard, the pair made the acquaintance of two physicians, one French and the other a local Christian "who spoke the German, French, Italian, Turkish, and Albanian languages" in addition to his mother tongue of Greek.[8] The archival record of the governor's chancery—written predominantly in Greek, Italian, and Ottoman Turkish by both Muslim and Christian scribes—verifies that multiculturalism was the rule rather than the exception in Ali Pasha's milieu.

Yet the most revealing line from Byron's ekphrasis of the palace at Tepelena describes how the ruler sat "amidst no common pomp." The phrase emphasizes the ostentatious spectacle on display in Ali Pasha's court, its "pomp" impressing a wide range of visitors, and Byron was no exception. What is more, this passage suggests that the governor transcended the standard ceremony that had been expected of functionaries at his level. I focus here on this concept of excess in Ali Pasha's buildings because these architectural experiments redefined the provincial palace in almost every respect. As a patron and political figure, the governor worked continuously to normalize the extraordinary.

Ali Pasha's spatial rendition of previously unseen levels of wealth and influence among the provincial notable class should be understood within the wider context of an Ottoman society that was highly conscious of rank. A "mirror for princes" literary genre arose in Istanbul in the sixteenth and seventeenth centuries, advising the sultan and his courtiers to build according to their position in the political hierarchy. For example, in his well-known *Counsel for Sultans* (*Nuṣḥatü's-Selâṭîn*) from 1581, the bureaucrat Mustafa Ali, who himself served in various positions in the provinces, excoriates the lavish expenditures of Ottoman administrators, calling their largesse unjust and inappropriate. He warns against an overattachment to fine houses, "in particular the possession of vaulted arches and gold-ornamented porches."[9] As a member of the educated elite, Mustafa Ali was distressed by what he perceived as the potential breakdown of imperial order:

> It is undoubtedly a requirement of Faith and state, the base of the firm structure of kingdom and nation that man strives for cleanliness, for elegance and neatness in wear and furnishings, and for a show of décor in the harness of his charger of power. But in this, too, moderation must be observed, excess must be avoided, and warning should be taken from the display of its free indulgence. In particular, each person must conduct himself in conformity with his situation and in harmony with his rank; he must not overstep his degree relying upon his money and must not engage

in extravagant acts, having in mind to excel over his peers and equals.[10]

Mustafa Ali was writing long before the *ayan* class came to power in the provinces, yet this passage shows that by then there was a notable shift away from the customary protocol of state ceremony that discouraged officials from acting beyond their station. Ali Pasha, an Ottoman governor perched in his residences "amidst no common pomp," was precisely the kind of person whom Mustafa Ali had feared the most.

PALACES AND OTTOMAN ADMINISTRATION

In the field of Ottoman architecture, the term for palace (*sarây*) in its most restricted sense refers to the official residence of the head of state, i.e., the sultan, and his dynastic household.[11] Studies of architecture in the Ottoman Empire have revolved around the royal palaces in Istanbul—the most famous being the Topkapı Palace—and the earlier sultanic residences in Edirne.[12] Yet, in the Ottoman lands, the term *saray* described not only the dwellings of the sultan but also any large residence of an individual of high political rank. In Istanbul, these palaces were located both in the city center and in the suburbs along the shores of the Bosphorus. Unfortunately, mostly owing to a lack of textual and material evidence, our understanding of elite palaces in Istanbul is still quite sparse, especially when compared to the volume of literature for other early modern cities such as Florence or Paris. One exception is the *Tuhfetü'l-Mi'marin* (*Choice Gift of the Architects*), an autobiography by the famed sixteenth-century Ottoman architect Mimar Sinan, which names the various palaces constructed by the corps of royal architects. This list includes not only the main imperial palaces but also residences for the *vâlide* (mother of the sultan), grand viziers, and a grand admiral, Kapudan Sinan Pasha, on the hippodrome.[13] The palaces of the Ottoman court society also served as sites of political ceremony and reception, especially in the seventeenth and eighteenth centuries, when greater authority was assumed by individuals such as the grand vizier and the *valide*.[14]

Looking beyond Istanbul, Ali Pasha's palaces invite a wider investigation of another type of residential architecture found throughout the Ottoman lands: the *saray* of the provincial governor. Every district and province maintained an official residence for its respective administrator. During the fifteenth and sixteenth centuries, this class of building also served as a princely palace, as it was standard practice to send the young heirs to the throne (*şehzâde*) to various districts—most notably Manisa and Amasya—to hone their skills in statecraft.[15] In later centuries, the princes became increasingly restricted to the confines of the harem in the Topkapı Palace, and the business of administering the provinces was left to officials who had worked their way up within the palace system.

As a location in which many day-to-day affairs were handled, the governor's *saray* played a fundamental role in the operation of empire. All these palaces were semipublic urban spaces, where the local administrator of the given district would receive guests and hold court, hearing petitions and meeting with town officials and notables. This system changed with the modernization reforms of the mid-nineteenth century, when provincial administration began to be based within the *hükümet konağı*, usually translated as "government office," a type of civic architecture separate from the governor's residence that housed offices and meeting chambers. In the pre-Tanzimat period, therefore, the governor's palace functioned as the primary site where subjects of the sultan could experience meaningful contact with the administrative apparatus of the government. A sustained look at Ali Pasha's residences in Epirus offers a rare opportunity to consider what administrative buildings in the Ottoman provinces looked like and how they may have changed over time. Ali Pasha's emphasis on residential architecture stands in contrast to the building patterns of Ottoman provincial administrators from previous centuries, who tended to focus most of their investments on pious endowments, which would in turn support large, urban mosque complexes. Although Ali Pasha and his sons did construct mosques and, as will be discussed further in chapter 3, also garnered local support through the patronage of dervish lodges and churches, their palace complexes emerged as the most substantial and visibly impressive contribution to the urban environment of the cities in their territory.

Despite the role of provincial palaces as sites of ceremony and encounter between a variety of government administrators and the general public, the systematic study of these structures as a building type has been largely neglected in the field of Ottoman architecture. One reason for this lacuna could be the dearth of surviving physical evidence, a situation that belies the prevalence and importance that these buildings once had in the Ottoman Empire. Many residences built in the early modern era for the use of provincial governors were eventually destroyed by fire or lost their relevance after the modernization reforms and were left in ruin or demolished to make way for new types of civic architecture in the second half of the nineteenth century. In 1834, for example, the traveler Richard Burgess met with the new administrator of Ioannina, the man who arrived after Ali Pasha's execution, and found him residing in the governor's old palace on the citadel.[16] By the 1870s, just a few decades later, that structure had burned down and been replaced with another administrative building constructed in an updated neoclassical style, which in turn was serving as a public hospital by the first half of the twentieth century.[17]

While the majority of these governor palaces in the Ottoman provinces no longer survive, several examples can be examined using archival documents and literary sources. One essential resource for understanding how the wider Ottoman administration represented itself in the provinces is the *Seyâhatnâme* (*Book of Travels*), the seventeenth-century account of the famous Ottoman globe-trotter Evliya Çelebi. The *Seyahatname* offers a wealth of information about urbanism and architecture throughout the empire, and this account has already been used to great effect by art historians.[18] Evliya's descriptions of cities are fairly formulaic. For every district capital, he first includes information about the power hierarchy in the area, identifying who occupied all the administrative positions at the local level. Notably, the political capacity of the governor is intimately tied to architecture: Evliya usually accompanies this roll call with a short commentary on the governor's palace and its location in the urban fabric, as well as any other larger residences worth mentioning. The implication is that the governor's residence was one of the most important sites in an Ottoman provincial town, the place where affairs of state were orchestrated.

Evliya sometimes refers to the provincial governor's palace as belonging to a specific individual. In an example from Albania, he calls the *saray* in Delvina (Ott. Delvine) the "palace of

Memo Pasha."[19] This tendency raises the question of who technically owned these residences and thus who was responsible for their upkeep. Ottoman archival documents suggest that, at least in the early nineteenth century, governors' palaces were tied to political positions, not persons, and were therefore under the stewardship of the state.[20] For instance, in 1815 the central government saw to it that sufficient funds were collected to construct a new governor's *saray* in the port town of Silistra, today on the modern border between Bulgaria and Romania.[21] That it was the Porte's responsibility to build and maintain these structures is a fact of crucial importance, because it appears that Ali Pasha directed and funded the construction of his numerous palace complexes without much oversight from Istanbul.

In one revealing episode, Ali Pasha thwarted the state's authority to remove and install governors from their posts, which was signaled by the physical occupation of the provincial palace. This incident took place in Manastir (modern Bitola), which was the capital city of the Ottoman *eyalet* of Rumeli. All of the districts governed by Ali Pasha and his sons fell under the jurisdiction of this wider province. A document dated 1815 in the State Ottoman Archives in Istanbul explains that Ali Pasha intentionally destroyed the palace at Manastir amid turbulence over the governorship of the Rumeli *eyalet*.[22] For a short period in 1801–2, Ali Pasha was appointed to the position but was then removed.[23] What followed was a power struggle between Ali Pasha and a rival named Behram Pasha, who also occupied Manastir for some time. By 1815, it seems that Ali Pasha was able to summon his old supporters among the notables of the city and was again in command, only to be removed once more in 1817.[24] It was then that Ali Pasha moved his troops to Sofia to establish a temporary alternative capital there, and, "so that future governors would not be able to hold a residence in Manastir, by some ruse [Ali Pasha] had the palace there burned to the ground." He was nothing if not thorough. Local reports confirmed that "everything besides the kitchen is completely incinerated and is beyond repair."[25] Ali Pasha understood the symbolic potential of the governor's palace, and in order to prevent any political rival from usurping his position by occupying the residence built by Istanbul, he saw to it that the site was, in a word, eliminated. He was evidently the type of figure who could not bear to share the limelight. In his own residences, Ali Pasha found subtler but no less important strategies for redefining the role of the governor's palace in the provinces.

THE URBAN PALACE COMPLEXES OF EPIRUS

Among the variety of domestic architecture constructed by Ali Pasha, including large palace complexes, fortified way stations, and suburban recreational pavilions, the most important examples are the residences found in the three cities key to his administration: the capital of Ioannina, Ali Pasha's hometown of Tepelena, and the Mediterranean port city of Preveza.[26] One of the most notable characteristics of these three palaces is their location—all three are found within the heart of the city but behind the walls of the citadel—a feature that departs from the practices of earlier Ottoman administrators in the region.

The highest concentration of palatial architecture under the patronage of Ali Pasha and his sons was in Ioannina, the seat of the Yanya district and the cultural and economic powerhouse of the wider region. The approximate location of these residences can be observed

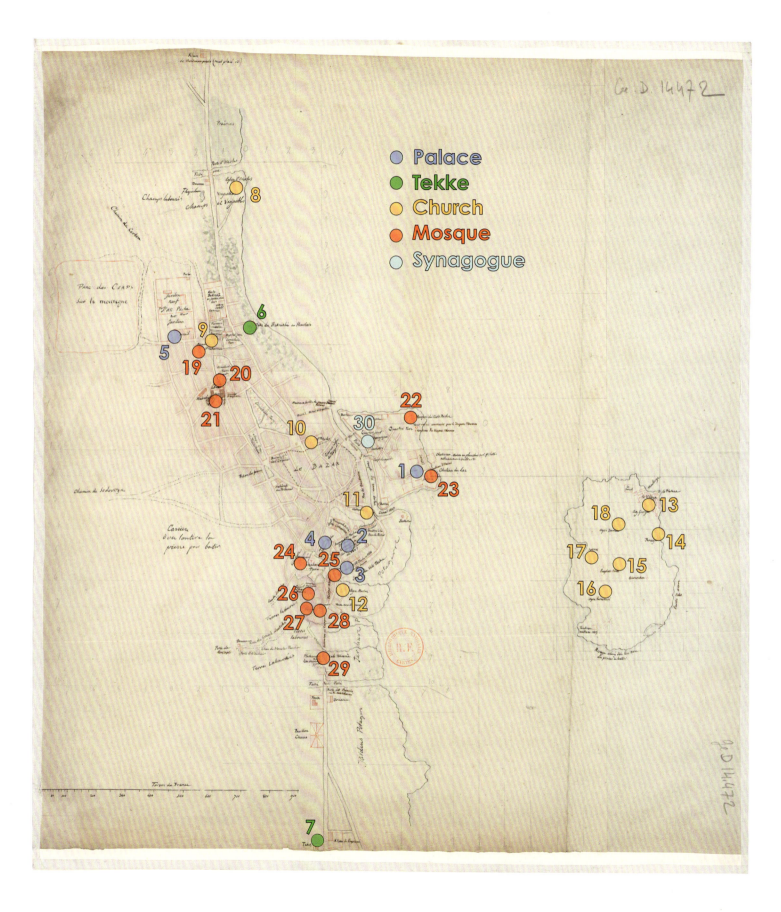

in an 1820 map of Ioannina now at the Bibliothèque nationale de France, drawn by the cartographer Jean-Denis Barbié du Bocage (fig. 13).²⁷ Looking at this map, produced in the last year that Ali Pasha was officially in power, one can see the main governor's palace in the Ioannina citadel (no. 1), a newer palace constructed by Ali Pasha *extra muros* on the Litharitsa hill in the southern part of the city (no. 2), the residences of his sons Veli Pasha (no. 3) and Muhtar Pasha (no. 4) at the foot of this hill, and the "old" and "new" garden palace complexes in the northern suburbs of the city (no. 5). Through the construction of no less than five palace complexes in Ioannina, Ali Pasha and his sons transformed the texture of the city fabric during a lightning-quick building campaign that took place over about a decade's time.

Ali Pasha's illustrious career began and ended in the palace complex in the southeastern citadel of the walled city of Ioannina (no. 1), referred to in Ottoman and Greek sources as the *iç ḳale* (ιτς καλέ), or inner fortress. Although it is not clear exactly when construction began on this site, the majority of these structures had to have been erected between 1785, when Ali Pasha was appointed governor of the province, and June 1805, when the traveler William Martin Leake referred to this area as the "new serai."²⁸ Leake also named Petros, an Albanian Christian from the city of Korçë and Ali Pasha's chief engineer, as the head architect for the project.²⁹ Scant elements of the palace complex still stand today. As mentioned, the central apartments where Ali Pasha received his guests continued to be used as the provincial palace for the local governor until the 1870s, when the structure burned down.³⁰ The remains of the palace remained essentially undisturbed until excavations were undertaken by the 8th Ephorate of Byzantine Antiquities from 2006 to 2008.³¹

The preliminary reports of these excavations, combined with on-site observations of the physical material and historical sources, make it possible to reconstruct the layout of the palace complex as it stood in Ali Pasha's time (fig. 14). This rare opportunity to conduct such a detailed examination of the architecture and inner workings of a provincial governor's palace will greatly enhance our understanding of how this kind of complex functioned on a daily basis.

The citadel could be accessed from a number of entrances, including a water gate opening onto the lake. Yet the gate on the northern side of the fortification walls (no. 1 in fig. 14) served as the primary point of entry for guests of note, both local elites and foreign visitors, as well as for ceremonial processions (fig. 15). Upon approach, this monumental portal stands apart visually from the rest of the exterior fortification walls surrounding the complex. This stark contrast is achieved primarily by the gate's white limestone, which is lighter in color than the stone used in the other parts of the wall circuit. The portal also strikes the eye with its elegant double-arch design, fashioned with courses of masonry that are more carefully and uniformly fitted than the stones in the fortification walls flanking the entrance. It should be kept in mind that this entrance would have been surmounted with a kind of observation kiosk or belvedere that no longer survives but can be seen in the background of an early nineteenth-century traveler's sketch (fig. 16). A similar configuration was found in one of the main gates to the walled city of Preveza, also built by Ali Pasha (fig. 17).

This portal and its vaguely classicizing design can certainly be situated within an

FIGURE 13 (*opposite*) Jean-Denis Barbié du Bocage, map of the city of Ioannina, 1820. Bibliothèque nationale de France, Paris, Cartes et plans, GE D-14472. (1) Ali Pasha's palace in the southeastern citadel; (2) Ali Pasha's palace on the Litharitsa hill; (3) palace of Veli Pasha; (4) palace of Muhtar Pasha; (5) Ali Pasha's garden palace; (6) tekke; (7) tekke; (8) Church of Agios Nikolaos Kopanon; (9) Church of Agia Ekaterini; (10) Church of Agios Nikolaos Agoras; (11) Metropolitan Church of Agios Athanasios; (12) Church of Agia Marina; (13) Church of the Dormition; (14) Monastery of Agios Panteleimon; (15) Monastery of the Prophet Elias; (16) Monastery of the Transfiguration of the Savior; (17) Stratigopoulos or Dilios Monastery; (18) Filanthropinos Monastery; (19) mosque; (20) mosque; (21) *medrese*; (22) Mosque of Arslan Pasha; (23) Fethiye Mosque; (24) mosque; (25) Mosque of Veli Pasha; (26) mosque; (27) mosque; (28) mosque; (29) Kaloutsani Mosque; (30) synagogue.

FIGURE 14
Ali Pasha's palace complex in the southeastern citadel of Ioannina. Plan by Matthew J. Jacobson. (1) northern gate; (2) guardhouse and barracks; (3) courtyard; (4) reception area of the palace; (5) private quarters of the palace; (6) Fethiye Mosque; (7) mausoleum; (8) kitchens; (9) lake pavilion; (10) military garrison and defensive works; (11) modern Byzantine Museum.

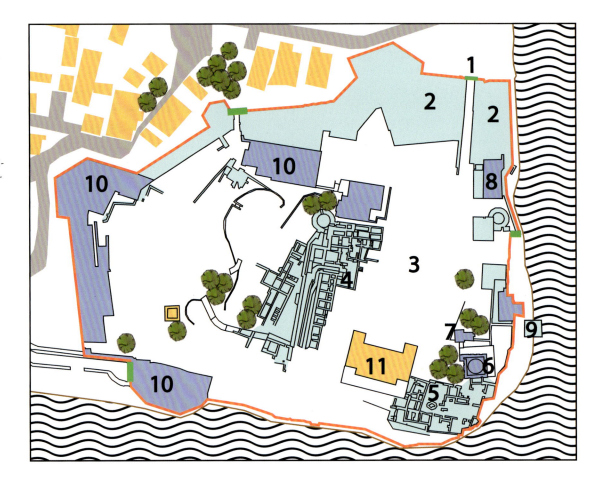

Adriatic sphere, especially when compared with the several examples of monumental gateways of Venetian fortifications. Yet the combination of portal and belvedere also recalls the main entrance of the great showpiece of Ottoman palatial architecture, the Topkapı Palace in Istanbul; it can be deduced from archival and visual records that the portal facing the Hagia Sophia once included a belvedere with grilled windows looking out onto the square. Gülru Necipoğlu has argued that this belvedere participated in a wider architectural rhetoric that attested to the sultan's omniscience, reminding the populace of the sovereign's perpetual gaze over the city.[32] In a similar fashion, the main portal of the Ioannina citadel could be interpreted as part of a distinctively Ottoman conception of palatial design, whereby the purpose of the central entrance is not only to impress the viewer as a staging area but also to convey the sense that the visitor or inhabitant is under constant surveillance. This evaluation is supported by the fact that the entrance is defended by a dense concentration of guardhouses and barracks (see fig. 14, no. 2), along with cannon embrasures in the outer bastion to the immediate west, which directly bear down on any visitor approaching the gate. In other words, pomp and grandeur are balanced with a healthy dose of intimidation.

FIGURE 15
The main entrance to Ali Pasha's palace complex in the southeastern citadel of Ioannina, exterior view looking south. Photo by author.

FIGURE 16
Henry Edmund Allen, *The Serai and Tomb of Ali Pasha, Ioannina* (in the courtyard of the southeastern citadel, looking north), 1833. Pencil on paper, 35.2 × 53.7 cm. © Victoria and Albert Museum, London, SD.18.

FIGURE 17
Ernest Hébrard, photograph of the main gate to the walled quarter of Preveza, ca. 1920. Courtesy of Actia Nicopolis Foundation, Preveza, Greece.

Upon passing through this main portal, visitors found themselves in a wide, open courtyard (see fig. 14, no. 3, and fig. 16) that constituted the heart of the residential complex. On the western side of this enclosure was the public reception area of Ali Pasha's palace (fig. 14, no. 4), accessed from a projecting staircase on the northern side of the structure. Both traveler accounts and historical drawings of the palace confirm that these central apartments were an elaborate version of the *konak* house ubiquitous in the Eastern Mediterranean. That is, Ali Pasha's palace consisted of a two-story structure, the ground floor sturdily constructed of masonry and reserved for storage and other service functions, while the living and reception rooms were on the upper story, built with a lighter wattle-and-daub technique and covered with painted plaster (see the building to the left in fig. 16).

The public apartments seem to have been connected by a covered gallery to the more private quarters of the palace, commonly referred to in Ottoman palaces as the harem (see fig. 14,

FIGURE 18
William Haygarth, *View of Jannina* [Ioannina] (with the Litharitsa hill in the foreground and walled city in the background), 1810. Ink on paper, 27.5 × 40.5 cm. No. 25, Gennadius Collection. American School of Classical Studies at Athens, Gennadius Library.

no. 5), where the women and children of the household resided. On the southeastern side of the courtyard is the Fethiye Mosque (no. 6), once the metropolitan church of the city, which was first converted into a mosque at the very end of the sixteenth century.[33] As discussed further in chapter 3, it seems that the mosque was almost completely reconstructed and decorated in a vernacular baroque style in the second half of the eighteenth century, just before Ali Pasha came to power. Nevertheless, as the governor's new palace complex rose up around this mosque and Ali Pasha had a mausoleum added to house the remains of his family (no. 7), the Fethiye was immediately drawn into this new spatial configuration, bridging the new governor's claim to both religious and military authority. While the eastern half of the citadel revolved around the functions of the court, the entirety of its western half was devoted primarily to military defense: barracks, gunpowder magazines, and cannon works (no. 10). With this kind of investment in security, it is no wonder that Ali Pasha managed to keep the sultan's troops at bay for almost two years during his resistance to the Porte. In a later account, one of the Ottoman soldiers sent to Ioannina for this siege described the citadel as "inaccessible" (*şarp*) and "immensely solid" (*gâyet metîn*) in its construction.[34]

After Ali Pasha had put the finishing touches on his *saray* in the Ioannina castle, he began building another fortified residence beyond the walled city and south of the bazaar area on a natural rocky outcrop (fig. 18 and fig. 13, no. 2).[35] This hill was named Litharitsa, and it afforded an even better view of the surrounding region. Almost nothing of the Litharitsa palace remains; the majority of the upper stories were lost to fire during the sultan's siege of Ioannina (see fig. 6). From travelers' descriptions and Barbié du Bocage's map, we can discern that

FIGURE 19
The southern entrance to the Tepelena citadel. Photo by author.

visitors approached the palace complex from the northwest, now a municipal park. Here, an initial gateway led into an open courtyard where guards and petitioners gathered, while a second gateway opened onto a flight of stairs that brought visitors up to a large reception chamber that provided a magnificent panorama of the area. As can also be seen in the Barbié du Bocage map, Ali Pasha's sons Veli and Muhtar Pasha eventually completed their own residences in the middle of the city at the foot of the Litharitsa complex (see fig. 13, nos. 3 and 4).[36] Muhtar Pasha's palace was obliterated by Ottoman authorities in the late nineteenth century to make way for modern military barracks and a clock tower, and nothing survives of Veli Pasha's residence except the kitchens and the adjacent mosque and *medrese* (theological school) that Ottoman records show he endowed in 1804.[37]

In addition to the palaces at Ioannina, Ali Pasha constructed a large urban residential complex in his hometown of Tepelena, in what is today southern Albania. The governor again commissioned the master architect Petros for the task, and work was completed by 1804.[38] This palace was likewise situated within the walls of the citadel, the construction of which also seems to have been initiated by Ali Pasha around the same time.[39] The whole complex overlooks the Vjosa (Gr. Aoos) River (see fig. 5), and was described by William Leake as "one of the most romantic and delightful country-houses that can be imagined."[40] As in Ioannina, none of the buildings from the palace survive, although they were still standing in ruin at the beginning of the twentieth century.[41] Because the citadel of Tepelena is not a protected heritage area and continues to function as a residential neighborhood, tracing the archaeological remains of these structures is difficult. Nevertheless, primarily from the descriptions of Lord Byron and his traveling companion John Hobhouse, we know that the complex resembled the main palace in Ioannina.[42] The collection of buildings was situated around a wide, open courtyard and included a large two-story residence with public reception areas and private living quarters, along with a garden and adjacent Friday mosque. The main entrance to the palace in the citadel was a monumental gateway facing south toward the market district (fig. 19). The formal architectural vocabulary of a double-arched portal strikingly resembles the main entrance to Ali Pasha's palace in the Ioannina citadel (see fig. 15), evidence that the same team of masons moved from one site to the other. The visitor then progressed through an elaborate bent entrance and emerged in the enclosure of the court.

The only image of Ali Pasha's palace in Tepelena comes from Edward Francis Finden's illustrations in the *Works of Lord Byron* (see fig. 12). This engraving is based on a drawing by the artist William Purser, who did travel to the region, but it is not clear whether he visited Tepelena.[43] The depiction of Ali Pasha's residence and the adjacent mosque reflects the basic elements of the local architectural vocabulary in its broadest strokes, the central apartments being a two-story konak with ground floors in stone and a lighter upper story faced with an arcade. Yet the scale of the mosque and the palace is almost certainly exaggerated in this image. Additionally, it seems unlikely that the palace's arcade would have been decorated with Ionic columns and trilobed arches straight from Córdoba—the standard signifier deployed by Western Europeans in this period to indicate an "Oriental" setting, regardless of the specific geographic context. This image is best understood, therefore, as the work of an artist who was generally familiar with the palatial and religious architecture in the region and had surely read travelers' written descriptions of the place, all filtered through an Orientalist lens that privileges grandeur over accuracy. Elisabeth Fraser argues that these kinds of large-scale illustrated publication projects in France and Britain, which were the result of teams of authors, engravers, and artists, must necessarily be considered "plural" or "multivocal" in nature, and not reflective of a single vision or voice.[44] This point is not to discount, however, the image's ability to convey the dramatic character of Ali Pasha's palace in Tepelena that is evoked in Byron's poetry and Hobhouse's diaries. The view flattens the mosque and reception rooms of the palace like a stage backdrop, capturing the essence of the complex at Tepelena as a space in which Ali Pasha's religious and political authority converged.

The third urban center where Ali Pasha built multiple palaces was Preveza, a former Venetian dependency that, after a brief French occupation, ultimately fell under the governor's direct jurisdiction in 1806. Upon taking control of the city, Ali Pasha first inhabited what is described as a "Château" in a contemporary French map (fig. 20). The buildings were located within a fort named Agios Andreas and were probably existing structures that had been used by the previous Venetian and French administrators.[45] An 1808 memorandum in the archive of Ali Pasha's chancery notes that this "serayi" was undergoing renovations after being damaged in a storm.[46] A few years later, in 1812, the traveler Henry Holland witnessed the construction of a new, larger palace at the narrowest part of the peninsula where the strait opens to the sea, referred to by locals as Bouka after the Italian term *bocca* (mouth).[47] Labeled the "Sérail" on the 1820 French map (fig. 20), this palace complex on the point seems to have been located directly above or nearby the ruins of an earlier fortress that constituted the heart of the early modern city, represented in an early eighteenth-century Venetian plan by Vincenzo Coronelli (fig. 21).

It is unclear to what extent Ali Pasha's new palace construction reused material or followed

FIGURE 20
Jean-Guillaume Barbié du Bocage, detail of a map showing the town of Preveza and its surrounding area, 1820. Courtesy of Actia Nicopolis Foundation, Preveza, Greece.

FIGURE 21
Vincenzo Coronelli, map of Preveza that shows the ground plan of the Ottoman-Venetian fortress to the right, 1707. Courtesy of Actia Nicopolis Foundation, Preveza, Greece.

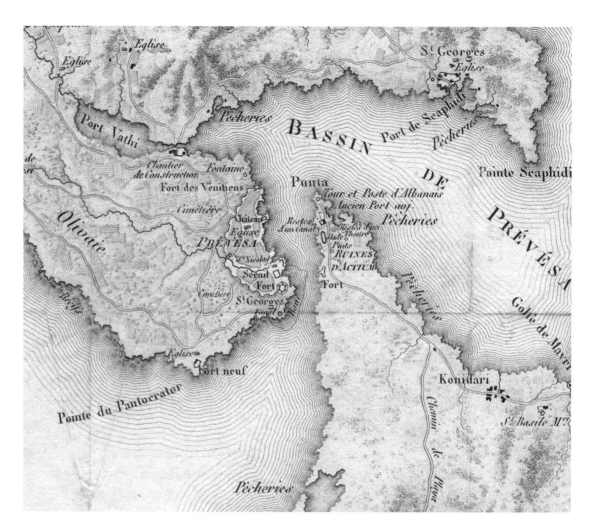

the layout of this earlier fortification, because none of these built elements survive today. This particular area has managed to avoid the urbanization of the modern city and now consists of an open field and park. Large blocks of cut masonry that are still discernible in the vicinity of the Bouka palace suggest that this site may be a profitable candidate for future archaeological excavations, which could reveal the intricate early modern palimpsest located just below the surface. A rare photograph suggests that some basic elements of Ali Pasha's palace complex on the peninsula were still intact as late as 1913 (fig. 22), and contemporary visitors describe a format that is by now familiar: a series of structures including reception apartments, private quarters, guardhouses, kitchens, gardens, and a bathhouse surrounding a large courtyard and protected by high walls.[48] The most distinctive features of this complex include an access point to the water for launching boats directly from the palace, the court of which also served as a kind of shipyard.[49] The palace was also complemented by a battery of cannons just at the tip of the peninsula, serving as a counterpoint to the triangular Fortress of Aktion, which was located directly across the strait, less than a kilometer away (labeled "Fort" in fig. 20).[50]

This overview of Ali Pasha's palaces in the three largest cities under his control—Ioannina, Tepelena, and Preveza—reveals that the governor elected to build his residences in fortified locations that, while well defended, still afforded prime views of the surrounding areas. The palaces in Ioannina and Tepelena were elevated on natural promontories, while Ali Pasha's residence in Preveza commanded a panoramic view of the straits and the city's harbor. Anyone making an approach to these cities, whether a villager from the surrounding

FIGURE 22
Frédéric Boissonnas, photograph showing the location of Ali Pasha's "Bouka" palace in Preveza, May 1913. Courtesy of Actia Nicopolis Foundation, Preveza, Greece.

hinterland or a foreign traveler, would have been confronted with a clear vista of the governor's palace. All of these residences were urban complexes, their campuses located in the middle of the city, but were still defended by massive walls and physically removed from the rest of the population.

A clear model for this urban-yet-separate pattern can be seen in the Topkapı Palace in Istanbul (fig. 23). Although architectural historians tend to place more emphasis on the horizontal expanse of this complex, hierarchically defined by a series of increasingly secluded courtyard spaces, it is equally notable that the Topkapı is located on a promontory. The sultan's residence stands protected behind multiple layers of outer walls. Yet, because of its vantage point, it can still be clearly observed from the Bosphorus and Golden Horn. By way of comparison, when describing Ali Pasha's palace at Litharitsa in Ioannina, Leake writes that the building, "though not so spacious as the Sultan's palaces on the Bosphorus, deserves still greater admiration in respect of the surrounding scenery. Standing upon the summit of a fortress which now incloses the hill of

Litharítza, it forms by its light Chinese architecture a striking contrast with the solid plainness of the basis on which it rests. The parapets of the fortress are armed with cannon, and the lower part of it consists of casemated apartments, so that it may stand a siege after all the upper structure is destroyed."[51] That Leake casually flits from the Bosphorus Strait to the walls of the Forbidden City in describing Ali Pasha's palatial architecture points to the extraordinarily wide currency of the walled urban palace as an architecture of imperial power in the early modern period.[52] The mutual acts of self-presentation and surveillance, of seeing and being seen, that are at work in all of these buildings—from Istanbul to Beijing—are similarly in operation at Ali Pasha's main palaces, these structures being situated in central locations that proclaimed the governor's ascendance in the city. It should also be noted, however, that even in its conception, the palace at Litharitsa equally anticipated the governor's potential downfall, designed from the beginning as a site for a desperate last stand.

Ali Pasha's decision to occupy the high ground in these cities was a marked departure from the settlement patterns of previous government administrators. The chronicles of Evliya Çelebi, who passed through the Epirus region in 1670, offer a glimpse of these provinces a little more than a century before Ali Pasha came to rule. In most of the major towns of the region—Tepelena, Gjirokaster, Ioannina, Arta, and Preveza—Evliya describes a firm division between military and civic power that was expressed architecturally within these urban centers. Typically, the *dizdâr ağası* (castle warden, similar to a sheriff) and his garrison of soldiers occupied the inner citadel, while the provincial governors resided in large palaces located outside the citadel and in the heart of the city, amid the public institutions, such as mosques, tekkes, markets, schools, and imarets, that formed the nuclei of Ottoman neighborhoods. For example, according to Evliya, the southern citadel of Ioannina, which would later become Ali Pasha's primary seat of authority (see fig. 14), was occupied only by the castle warden and the head of the local Janissary corps, while Mustafa Pasha, the provincial governor at the time, resided in what Evliya describes as a "magnificent palace," still within the walled city but outside the inner citadel.[53] Even a cursory survey of some of Evliya's travels reveals that this geographic separation of power was seen in many provincial districts throughout the empire. The generalization is supported by a comment Evliya makes about the political situation in Diyarbakır: "nowhere else [in the empire] is it customary for pashas to enter the citadel—let alone to reside there—except here in [Diyarbakır]. Here all the viziers take up residence in the citadel."[54] Evliya thus stresses that this kind of arrangement is the exception rather than the rule.

The bifurcation of armed muscle and civic bureaucracy reflected wider developments in the transition of cities from the Byzantine/Despotate period to Ottoman rule. Essentially, the citadel, which had once been the fortified Byzantine settlement, was transformed in the Ottoman period into an area used principally as a military garrison, while the cities themselves grew beyond the fortification walls and into the adjacent countryside. The Ottoman tendency in Epirus to expand beyond the Byzantine town is highlighted in Evliya's account of Arta, in which, he reports, the *dizdar ağası* occupied what was the former Byzantine residence in the citadel, referred to as the old "royal palace" (*kıral sarayı*), while the official residence of the *şehir ağası* (town administrator) Yusuf

FIGURE 23 (*opposite*) Matrakçı Nasuh, *View of Istanbul* (with the Topkapı Palace in the top left corner). From the *Beyan-i Menazil-i Sefer-i Irakeyn* (Description of the halting stations along the journey to the two Iraqs), 1537. Istanbul University Library, MS 5964. Photo: Istanbul University Library.

Pasha was located due south of the walls within the new city center.⁵⁵

More than a century after Evliya's travels, Ali Pasha broke with this established tradition of spatially separating civic and military power by placing his palace complexes in the cities of Ioannina, Preveza, and Tepelena within the inner citadel, situating the administrative structure of the city back behind the walls. This move to integrate resources was not only highly symbolic but also strategic: Ali Pasha seemed to anticipate armed attacks from foreign invaders, rival governors, and perhaps even Istanbul itself (rightly so on all three counts, as it turned out). Ultimately, the reclamation of urban spaces that had previously served exclusively as army garrisons signaled a consolidation of Ali Pasha's military and political authority. That this configuration looks more to examples of royal palatial architecture than to provincial seats of Ottoman administration is an important gesture to the governor's grand ambitions.

THE ITINERANT COURT: ROADS AND INFRASTRUCTURE

While Ali Pasha participated in the established tradition of an Ottoman governor's maintenance of a palace in an appointed district, he also improvised upon this convention by initiating in a matter of years the construction of multiple residences throughout his territory and pursuing a policy of continuous mobility between them. Beyond the major complexes in Ioannina, Tepelena, and Preveza, he also maintained a wide range of other dwellings, including smaller administrative seats in towns such as Gjirokaster and Arta.⁵⁶ Ali Pasha's sons, Veli, Muhtar, and Salih, who were appointed as governors of neighboring districts, maintained their own residences in Berat, Larissa, Trikala, Nafpaktos (Lepanto), and Tripoli. Veli Pasha was known, for example, to preside over the district of Tırhala in a large mansion in the village of Tirnavos outside Larissa named "Gülbahçe" (Rose Garden) in Ottoman sources, which the French artist Louis Dupré visited and described as being outfitted in "barbarous magnificence."⁵⁷ All of these urban or suburban palaces made it possible for Ali Pasha and his court to progress through the territory with ease and establish physical loci of power in every corner of the realm.

Ali Pasha proved keen to build houses in strategic or symbolically charged locations as part of his ongoing endeavor to expand his geographic reach. Whenever he secured the allegiance of a new area, his first act was typically to renovate or construct a residence to maintain an official presence there. Upon wresting the district of Delvine from his peer İbrahim Pasha, for example, Ali Pasha's workers set about building a new residence in the citadel of Gjirokaster, one of the most important towns in the region.⁵⁸ For this construction project they were said to have reused wooden beams pilfered from the large houses of Gardik, which, as will be discussed in chapter 4, was a nearby village whose population had been eradicated because of their alliance with the French and with the vizier's rival İbrahim Pasha. In a blatant act of spoliation, Ali Pasha seized the very skeletons of the fine houses that had broadcast the financial success of his enemies and used the material in his own palace. A British consul reported that in 1820, when Ali Pasha finally negotiated successfully for Parga, one of the former Venetian mainland dependencies under protection of the British Crown, he appropriated the residence of the former commanding officer. With "a great metamorphose," Ali Pasha transformed the structure into a large mansion: "In a few months but a few vestiges will be left of what it was."[59] This same house appears in an Ottoman register dated just a few years later listing Ali Pasha's properties; the residence is described as a konak inside the fortress with a stone cistern and fifteen rooms—huge by the region's standards.[60] Ali Pasha thus would not simply occupy the residence of a former administrator but preferred either to build an entirely new construction or to renovate the existing structure.

The governor's palaces were in and of themselves significant infrastructure projects, evidence of his ability to gather considerable resources in terms of physical labor and materials. For example, in a series of documents from Ali Pasha's chancery, we learn of a team of workers employed in constructing a palace for the governor in the suburbs of Tepelena, in the village of Veliqot.[61] This residence, which no longer survives, was evidently a large construction, as the workers who were led by a Master Panos and Vasilis toiled for at least twelve months on the project.[62] Meanwhile, the traveler Thomas Hughes mentions that the poor in Ioannina suffered in winter for lack of fuel, because the vast woods covering the nearby mountains had been stripped bare to fuel the increasing growth of the city, including "the large and numerous serais which Ali and the other members of his family have built."[63] In the construction of palaces, Ali Pasha, for better or worse, made a lasting impact on the cities that he governed and on the ecology of their surrounding environments.

All of Ali Pasha's residences, from the citadel in Ioannina to his seat in Gjirokaster, are best imagined as a connected network of staging points, facilitating the governor's itinerant court. Ali Pasha was always on the move and declared to one of his visitors that "he had passed and repassed over all parts of [his country] in every season of the year."[64] It is even something of a trope in the numerous European travel accounts and diplomatic reports that no one can ever seem to find Ali Pasha. When the British consul John Morier arrived to take up his post in Ioannina, Ali Pasha was in Tepelena; when Leake traveled to Tepelena, the governor was in the nearby Premeti; in Ioannina, John Hobhouse received the pasha's apologies for not being in the city to welcome him because "a small war" (*une petite guerre*) in a nearby province was taking a few more days than expected.[65] Under Ali Pasha's administration, the governor maintained the complementary dyad of having fixed capital cities and frequent peregrinations, creating movable and interconnected bases of power. He was constantly on the road to oversee his various obligations, from conducting military campaigns to, even more crucially, collecting taxes. William Goodison remarked that Ali Pasha made an annual journey to Preveza accompanied by a large body of troops to claim the revenues due to him, and it stands to reason that he may have made similar trips to the other districts under his jurisdiction.[66]

However tempting it may be to ascribe Ali Pasha's high degree of mobility to his more adventurous days as a young mountain warrior roaming the mountain passes of Tepelena, frequent journeys throughout such a wide territory demanded a great deal of coordination and planning. Ali Pasha's peripatetic movements followed established routes from one city to the next. To facilitate his continual movement throughout the districts under his command, Ali Pasha saw to it that resources were invested in maintaining and building up the infrastructure that defined this network—a type of interstitial architecture that included roads, bridges, fountains, and way stations. The major roads connecting the main cities in the region were constantly under repair, and there were also several improvements in bridges and embankments, which were crucial when navigating the rivers and streams found throughout this mountainous territory.[67] Architectural historians have even identified a distinctive typology of bridge construction during Ali Pasha's rule that consists of a large semicircular main arch (often reinforced with smaller arches on either side) and regular courses of cut masonry.[68] That this type of bridge can be found across a relative broad geography, from the Saranda-Delvina road to the Zagori mountains just north of Ioannina, suggests that a group of masons with specialized engineering knowledge were deployed to these different areas. Foreign travelers were often impressed with the high quality of the roads in Ottoman Epirus, noting that a person could maneuver the region's treacherous mountain passes and marshy swamps along paved causeways.[69]

Along these roads were also inns (*hân*) positioned a day's travel apart, which served as way stations for travelers, merchants, and messengers. In several locations in the region there are still remains of large *hans*, the best apartments of which were always reserved for the governor. In the case of Salaora, an outpost on the northern shore of the Gulf of Arta, which documents from Ali Pasha's chancery reveal to be a bustling shipping station, Holland writes that at the principal building there was "a small palace of the Vizier's, employed as a place of occasional repose when he is travelling between Ioannina and Prevesa.... The habitable rooms form wings to the central gallery; but two apartments only are fitted up for the reception of the Vizier and his great officers. These we were not permitted to occupy."[70] By far the most impressive example of Ali Pasha's roadside architecture that can still be seen today is the fortified palace at Pente Pigadia, or the "Five Wells" (fig. 24).[71] The site is located in a small village approximately halfway along what used to be the main road from Ioannina to Arta.[72] Given that the structure was badly damaged in the Ottoman sultan's campaign against Ali Pasha, the central building remains in relatively good condition.[73] Cruciform in plan, the *han* features slanting walls built with masonry techniques resembling Ali Pasha's fortifications in Ioannina and Preveza, suggesting the presence of the same group of engineers. A more compact version of the governor's urban residences, the *han* at Pente Pigadia has two main levels, the bottom story being used for storage and stables and the top floor serving as the apartments. While only the exterior walls survive, an Ottoman document describes the complex as including twelve guest rooms and two "*divânhâne*," or meeting chambers, suggesting that this site was able to host a large retinue.[74] Unlike the reception rooms in Tepelena or Ioannina, however, the second story here is made of stone, not wood and plaster, lending a more martial sensibility to the structure. The *han* is not only conveniently located along the road but also commands a breathtaking view of the Louros River Valley.

The fortified character and positioning of the *han* at Pente Pigadia illustrates another crucial point about Ali Pasha's peripatetic movements and his construction of roadside architecture: the significance of his position as the *derbendler başbuğu*, or commander of the passes. The wider Ottoman province of Rumeli was topographically defined by a series of mountain chains and river valleys, where passage from one area to another is funneled through natural choke points. As mentioned in the introduction, the job of the *derbendler*

FIGURE 24
The fortified way station at Pente Pigadia. Photo by author.

başbuğu was to fortify, maintain, and defend these points, and one of Ali Pasha's major political coups early in his career was his appointment to this position. Such a move made the governor quite powerful, as whoever controlled the mountain passes, at least in Epirus, controlled the territory at large. In an Ottoman register describing the architecture at Pente Pigadia, the *han* is reported as "being positioned above the Ioannina pass [*derbend*]," emphasizing the special designation of this site as one of the key points of passage that the governor was under obligation to protect.[75] Not only did Ali Pasha make use of and build up a road network, but it was also his responsibility to monitor these way stations, especially at the mountain passes, with the expectation that he would be able to quash any threats to security with a firm hand.

Registers of the landed property of Ali Pasha and his sons Veli and Muhtar Pasha now at the Ottoman archives in Istanbul further attest that, in the hundreds of farming villages (*çiftlik*) recorded as being in their direct possession, the governor and his family sometimes kept a residence as part of the estate, to be used when passing through that particular area.[76] The scale of this architectural network only begins to emerge when examining, and mapping, this immense archival source, invaluable because none of these structures survive. For example, among the *çiftliks* found in the districts of Yanya and Delvine, Ali Pasha and his sons maintained more than a dozen konak residences of various sizes (fig. 25). The Ottoman register also records the *hans* located in these villages, which not only were available for the governor's use but also generated revenue by offering lodging

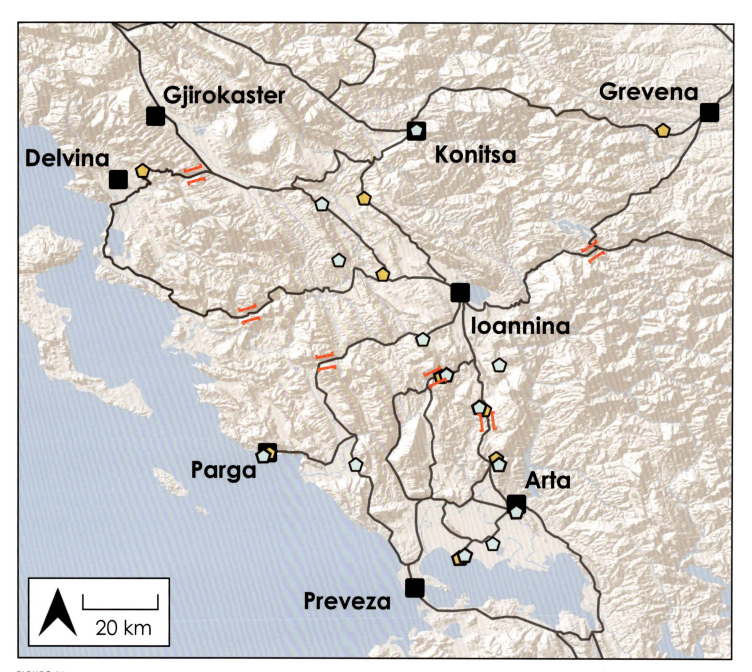

FIGURE 25
The *hans* (*yellow*) and residences (*blue*) in the *çiftliks* of Ali Pasha and his sons in the provincial districts of Yanya and Delvine. Visualization of data drawn from an Ottoman property register (BOA, Istanbul, MAD. d. 9767). The major mountain passes (*derbend*) in the region are also indicated in red. Map by Matthew J. Jacobson.

to other travelers. The map in figure 25 represents my efforts to geolocate the data found in this register to visualize how these different properties were situated in the broader territory. In the process of what digital humanities scholars describe as "iterative mapping," I gradually realized that, while many of the *çiftliks* owned by Ali Pasha were in more rural locations, all of the villages where he maintained a residence or *han* were positioned directly along the main road arteries connecting his court cities of Ioannina, Tepelena, and Preveza.[77] Even though these residences are located in farming settlements, these houses could be considered less a part of a *villa rustica* tradition—i.e., countryside hubs for large agricultural estates—than as prominent nodes along a wider transportation network.

The appearance of these large residences and inns along the region's road system also points to the fact that the governor did not make these journeys alone but was usually accompanied by large retinues of soldiers and court officials. Ali Pasha often preferred to travel not on horseback but in his carriage, reportedly outfitted with gold trappings and of Italian manufacture; this preference for wheeled transportation was a boast about the quality of the road system in Epirus.[78] William Haygarth observed one such impromptu expedition: "The society [in Ioannina] is more civilized than in any other town in Greece. The Pasha, though illiterate himself, is fond of conversing with learned men, and keeps them constantly about his person. Ali left Ioannina before my departure, and crossed the Pindus with a considerable body of troops, in order to have an interview with his son in Thessaly. I overtook him in Triccala, and found that he had brought all the literati of his capital with him, though he intended to be absent only a very short time."[79] In the early modern period, sovereigns often traveled through their territories to ensure that local centers were tied to an ideology of empire. For example, the Safavid ruler Shah Abbas, intent on rotating the site of his court, progressed throughout his realm, which was dotted with dozens of small but luxurious residences for this purpose.[80] In the same way, Ali Pasha sought to parade his authority in various regional centers through the construction of palaces and his perpetual migration from one to the next. Yet investment in infrastructure technology such as bridge construction and paved roads, which greatly improved the ease and speed of travel, must also be understood as a deeply modern impulse, anticipating projects like the development of rail networks across the empire on behalf of the Ottoman state at the end of the nineteenth century.[81] This network or constellation of palaces introduces one of the most notable shifts in how space was controlled and defined in the Ottoman provinces during this period. As mentioned above, Ali Pasha was particularly successful among his contemporaries in negotiating his appointment to multiple provincial districts, and then extending his political influence even further by having his sons placed in adjacent administrative units. In previous centuries of Ottoman rule, it would have been unusual for one individual to maintain so many residences in such a broad territory and have the right to move freely among them. Ali Pasha's endless circulation between his palaces thus tested the boundaries of what was acceptable for a man of his office and also spoke to the fragility of his power base, which constantly had to be renewed and reestablished through the spectacle of ceremonial processions performed by a cadre of court officials.

STAGING RITUAL, CEREMONY, AND LEISURE

Both the urban palaces and roadside residences of Ali Pasha could be understood as a drama of strongman architecture, built to persuade visitors of the governor's ability to maintain a firm hold over the affairs of his territory. The art historian Maximilian Hartmuth has discussed one striking example of how this process of self-aggrandizement worked through a series of murals once found on both the exterior and interior of Muhtar Pasha's palace in Ioannina.[82] According to a number of contemporary travelers, these wall paintings, now lost along with the rest of the building, depicted Ali Pasha's son, surrounded by his own officers, witnessing the execution of two unidentified men "whom the hangman is tying to a gibbet with the same rope: others exhibit decapitated trunks with the blood spouting out from the veins and arteries."[83] Hartmuth argues that these grisly images stand as evidence for the "acute sense of visuality"—to say the least—of Ali Pasha and his sons.

These palaces provided opportunities for the governor and his family to stage not only conspicuous acts of violence but also their conspicuous consumption of luxurious objects, which were displayed in ostentatiously decorated reception areas. Many of the foreign travelers who visited these houses were quick to draw an explicit connection between these two themes—violence and decadence—in order to demonstrate the base character of the governor himself. Thomas Hughes provides an extensive report on Ali Pasha's palace in Preveza, a "magnificent new seraglio which the vizier has built at the entrance to the bay." Hughes describes the complex's richly appointed state apartments and long galleries with views to the sea, and characterizes the exterior as "built of wood, upon a basement of stone, painted in the most gaudy colours."[84] As noted above, it was common in the region for the more elite konak-style houses to have both the interior and exterior of the upper stories embellished with fantastic baroque designs in paint and plaster. Sketches of Ali Pasha's palace in Ioannina (fig. 26; see also fig. 16) and a contemporary example of a mansion from nearby Gjirokaster, the so-called Zekate House (fig. 27), provide an idea of the elaborate designs painted in "gaudy colours" that Hughes encountered.[85] Hughes's analysis of the Preveza palace is followed by a broader reflection on the nature of Ali Pasha's residential architecture in comparison to buildings produced by earlier civilizations that had once ruled the same region:

> Of all arts architecture gives us the most decided character of an age. In the ruins of ancient Greece we discover the grandeur of a generous and free people by the remains of magnificent edifices destined equally for utility and decoration: in the modern buildings scattered over the same tract we observe inelegant and gaudy structures, framed of the most perishable materials, and built only to last during the life of their possessors. Thus the buds of genius are withered by the breath of despotism, and insecurity, contracting the mind, forbids it to look forward into futurity.[86]

Steeped in a British classical education, Hughes draws upon the Vitruvian ideals of *firmitas*, *utilitas*, and *venustas* (stability, utility, beauty) as his key criteria for the assessment of this architecture.[87] When compared to the monuments of Greek antiquity, Ali Pasha's palaces are found to be lacking in both permanence and elegance. Hughes's repugnance for the "modern

FIGURE 26
William Haygarth, *Presentation to Ali Pacha at Joannina* [Ioannina], 1810. Ink on paper, 24.5 × 42 cm. From scrapbook in Gennadius Collection, p. 2. American School of Classical Studies at Athens, Gennadius Library.

FIGURE 27
Interior of the Zekate House in Gjirokaster, ca. 1811–12. Photo by author.

buildings" of Greece aligns with the neoclassical movement (often referred to as the Greek Revival) in Britain, which advocated both sobriety and minimal color in architecture, emphatically turning away from the more boisterous Palladianism and continental baroque styles.[88] In Hughes's eyes, Ali Pasha's palaces—hodgepodge, asymmetrical structures decked out in bright floral painting and lively baroque flourishes—were bound to fall short. The loaded narrative of democracy versus despotism is difficult to escape when discussing Ali Pasha's palatial architecture. This is especially the case because almost all the textual descriptions that we have of these structures come from Western European visitors steeped in an intellectual tradition that considered taste to be a matter of moral character. How, then, to approach these "gaudy" interiors, the piles of weapons and carpets, the murals of harsh justice being served?

Understanding Ali Pasha's architecture through the lens of theater reframes these

"AMIDST NO COMMON POMP" 51

buildings as born out of strategy, not shortcomings. Again, Hughes describes the ephemeral nature of the governor's palaces, their being made of the "most perishable materials, and built only to last during the life of their possessors." Rather than aim for structural permanence, Ali Pasha built his residences to present himself as the Ottoman governor par excellence to multiple audiences in his own day. Although Western travelers comprised only one of these audiences, their detailed descriptions of these cross-cultural encounters lend valuable insight into the rituals and routines that enlivened Ali Pasha's court. Meanwhile, within the local context, the governor's palaces are inextricably linked to the idea of the *otzaki* (οτζάκι, Ott. *ocak*), a word that denotes a hearth but metaphorically refers to the dynastic line of a great family. In this more symbolic sense, the term comes close in meaning to the ancient Greek concept of *oikos*. This theme comes up again and again in the corpus of poetry commissioned or immediately inspired by Ali Pasha himself. For example, in one public inscription, the governor's family is referred to as "the Moutzohousatic otzaki" (Οντζάκι Μουτζοχουσάτικον), a nod to Ali Pasha's great-grandfather, Moutzo Housso.[89] Ali Pasha's palaces translated the notion of the *otzaki* into stone and plaster, as they served as central gathering places and justified the governor's dynastic legitimacy. This idea is most evident in Ioannina, in the cluster of Ali Pasha's palace on the Litharitsa hill and the residences of his two sons Muhtar and Veli situated directly underneath, establishing genealogies in the topography itself (see fig. 13, nos. 2–4, and fig. 18).[90] What's more, a key focus in the majority of the main reception rooms in the governor's palaces was a large fireplace with an elaborate conical hood—a literal *otzaki* (see fig. 26). Tellingly, these fireplaces were often nonfunctional and purely decorative, serving as potent symbols of the owner's hospitality and beneficence.[91]

Within these palaces, ritual and ceremony contributed to the notion of Ali Pasha as a capable and legitimate administrator. These rituals, which were often lavish in terms of the display of luxury goods and the size of the attending court, can be observed in dozens of examples from European travel accounts. In the common case of foreigners' being summoned to one of Ali Pasha's palaces for an official audience, the occasion typically began with an ostentatious procession through the city. When Henry Holland visited Ali Pasha at the Litharitsa palace in Ioannina, "two white horses, of beautiful figure, and superbly caparisoned in the Turkish manner, were brought to us from the Seraglio; conducted by two Albanese soldiers, likewise richly attired and armed. Mounting these horses, and a Turkish officer of the palace preceding us, with an ornamented staff in his hand, we proceeded slowly and with much state through the city, to the great Seraglio."[92] Such processions must have been quite the pageant for the local inhabitants of the city. Unfortunately, there is no way to recover the reactions these rituals elicited from the populace, save for one description from John Hobhouse of a small parade led by Mahmud Pasha, the son of Veli Pasha and grandson of Ali Pasha: "As the young Pasha passed through the streets, all the people rose from their shops, and those who were walking stood still, every body paying him the usual reverence, by bending their bodies very low, touching the ground with their right hand, and then bringing it up to their mouth and forehead. . . . The Bey returned the salute by laying his right hand on his breast, and by a gentle inclination of his head."[93] In this passage, the spectators are active participants in the ritual, expected to stop their daily activities in acknowledgment of the passage of the pasha or one of his extended family, with an exchange of deferential bows and salutes.

Once the special guests arrived at the palace in question, distinguished by the monumental arched entrance, they would dismount their charges within the inner courtyard and make their way upstairs into the apartments dedicated to holding audiences. Guests would usually be made to wait for some time in an adjacent antechamber before being led into the central apartment (*selâmlık*) for their meeting with the governor. Many visitors note in their accounts that most of the interior spaces in these palaces were plain and perfunctory, with the rich painting and furnishings being almost exclusively dedicated to the main audience chamber. These rooms were filled to the brim with jeweled weapons, large carpets from both Persia and France, and Venetian plateglass windows.[94] When he was still in the service of the Russian emperor, the famed Greek politician Ioannis Kapodistrias visited Ali Pasha's palace in the Ioannina citadel and was impressed by the sumptuous interior, including a "carpet of Gobeline manufacture lying on the floor of the divan."[95]

Upon entering the apartment, visitors would find Ali Pasha at the far end of the room, seated in the place of honor: in the corner furthermost from the door and closest to the fireplace, the *otzaki*, with its colorful decoration. The guests would then be invited to sit with the governor on a long row of cushions, the divan. Although none of Ali Pasha's palaces still stand, we can gain an approximate idea of this kind of scene from a sketch by William Haygarth, who recorded his own visit with the governor in Ioannina in August 1810 (see fig. 26).[96] In this drawing, the artist has captured the different stations and duties of the participants in such a meeting, Ali Pasha in the center and the visitor seated to the left, while the Christian dragoman Spiros Kolovos stands nearby to facilitate communication, in this case translating Ali Pasha's Greek to Italian. Just behind the translator, a turbaned man is seated on the floor; this is one of Ali Pasha's Muslim secretaries, drawing up in Ottoman Turkish what was commonly referred to as a *buyuruldu*, or the requisite letters that travelers would need to carry through the governor's territory to prove that they were under the protection of the vizier. In the opposite corner, a group of courtiers in different costumes indicating their rank and confession drink coffee and observe the proceedings. The variety of activities and the diversity of individuals found in this audience hall—reminiscent of Byron's comment about "men of every clime" in Ali Pasha's court—highlight the fact that these palaces were not private residences in the modern sense. Rather, they were gathering spaces where Ali Pasha conducted his diplomatic affairs in full view of local notables.

One of the most striking aspects of the Haygarth sketch is how crowded the scene is. Ali Pasha's palaces were populated with an extensive retinue of soldiers, officers, scribes, and religious leaders. An unusual archival source providing a better sense of the makeup of these retinues are several registers found in Ali Pasha's chancery. Multiple documents from different dates throughout the governor's tenure record the loaves of bread required to feed Ali Pasha's court. One of these registers, dated 1801, lists approximately 250 people who needed about three thousand loaves of bread for only a few days.[97] Included in this list are military officers, scribes, stewards, and Sufi dervishes. That Ali Pasha could provide sustenance for this number of people on a daily basis also speaks to his munificence, which is expressed in the architecture of the Ioannina citadel. The kitchen is one of the first buildings seen from the main entrance and stands in a prominent position in the palace courtyard (fig. 14, no. 8). Similarly, the imperial kitchen holds pride of place in the second courtyard of the Topkapı Palace in Istanbul.[98]

Of particular importance for these audiences in Ali Pasha's palaces is the priority placed on the governor's own gaze. The main audience chambers in these complexes were designed to provide a vantage point from which Ali Pasha could monitor the surrounding landscape and military exercises taking place in the courtyard. Foreign travelers often noted the view from the reception area in accounts of their visits with the governor. On the occasion of Hughes's visit to the palace in the Ioannina citadel, after the customary coffee and tobacco pipe, the governor took his guest to the balcony to watch a game of *jereed* in the courtyard, a lively military exercise involving a simulated fight between two parties on horseback, hurling blunt yet dangerous wooden javelins at the opposing team (the *jereed* can be seen in the foreground of fig. 16). Hughes was then immediately conducted to a small "treasury" adjacent to the palace, which held the standards of the vizier, long poles bearing three horse tails, that were carried before Ali Pasha in battle.[99] These standards represent the governor's high rank in the Ottoman military as a "pasha of three tails." All of Ali Pasha's main palaces were thus sites for the demonstration of his sense of justice and military prowess.[100]

Besides his main palace complexes, Ali Pasha also invested in smaller recreational pavilions and kiosks for the performance of leisure, an essential component of any refined individual of the period. This included a hunting lodge in the marshes of Butrint and a boating kiosk (see fig. 14, no. 9) and suburban garden pavilions in Ioannina. In fact, one of the most famous images of Ali Pasha depicts him fowling in the lake at Butrint (fig. 28). The artist Louis Dupré visited the governor there in 1819 and was inspired to capture the excursion. In the image, Ali Pasha, seated at far right, reclines on a wine-red cushion. Draped in fine silks, gold embroidery, and a fur-lined coat, he smokes from a long pipe as a thirteen-man entourage drives the boat and readies his silver-chased rifle. According to Dupré's account, the hunt was less an expedition than a large open-air party on the water. Ali Pasha was accompanied by several other boats carrying members of his court retinue, foreign guests, and a band of musicians, and after firing off a couple rounds, all indulged in a feast of fish and pilaf.[101]

Meanwhile, the garden palace complex in Ioannina was located at the northern edge of the city, next to the Jewish and Muslim cemeteries. Removed from the claustrophobic bustle of the city center, this palace quarter sprawled over an expansive area, with a view of the lake from a slight promontory.[102] In the Barbié du Bocage map of Ioannina (see fig. 13, no. 5), this complex includes what is labeled a walled "Jardin neuf" with a *saray*, next to the "Kato Baktchi" (low garden) with the "old saray." Immediately to the west of the gardens was a "deer park on the mountain." This was a walled menagerie of sorts, populated, as one traveler observed, with "a few large deer and antelopes."[103] The terms "old" and "new" used in the map imply that the creation of this garden palace area was a gradual process, as different features and structures were developed over time.

The governor enjoyed using this garden palace for entertaining guests, and as a result

many travelers were taken there during their visits in Ioannina. John Hobhouse found a garden "in a wild and tangled state" but "abounding with every kind of fruit-tree that flourishes in this favoured climate—the orange, the lemon, the fig and the pomegranate."[104] Most impressive to visitors, however, was the pavilion built in the middle of the garden, an octagonal salon with a marble floor and seating areas on four sides with gilt latticed openings. Charles Cockerell sketched a series of drawings and a plan of this building when he came to the palace in 1813–14 (fig. 29).[105] The artist depicted a light and airy interior with a central domed chamber supported by arches and thin columns. Cockerell's flourishes on the ceiling and upper registers of the four seating areas indicate that the upper zone of the pavilion was decorated with elaborate baroque painting and woodwork. For visitors, the most memorable feature of this pavilion was the large fountain in the center of the chamber. Cockerell described the fountain as a series of tiered basins placed in a pool sunk into the marble floor. This base of the fountain is probably what Hobhouse was referring to when he mentioned "a pretty model, also in marble, of a fortress, mounted with small brass cannon, which, at a signal, spout forth jets of water into the fountain, accompanied by a small organ in a recess, playing some Italian tunes."[106]

When foreign visitors saw these garden areas, they invariably insisted that these pavilions were evidence of Western European

FIGURE 28
Louis Dupré, *Ali Pasha of Ioannina Hunting on the Lake at Butrint in March 1819*. From Dupré, *Voyage à Athenes et à Constantinople* (Paris: Dondey-Dupré, 1825), plate 8. American School of Classical Studies at Athens, Gennadius Library.

FIGURE 29
Charles Cockerell, *View of the Interior of the Kiosk in Ali Pasha's Garden Palace in Ioannina*, 1813–14. Pencil on paper, 12.5 × 20.2 cm. British Museum, London, 2012,5001.114. © The Trustees of the British Museum.

intervention or influence in the region. In Ioannina, Hobhouse wrote, "the pavilion and its gardens bespeak a taste quite different from that of the country, and probably the Vizier was indebted to his French prisoners for the beauties of this elegant retirement. We were told that it was the work of the Frank."[107] Yet these garden complexes and pavilions can also be seen as participating in the widespread Ottoman tradition of the *ṣayfiye*, a retreat to summer homes during the hot months from around May to September. In the eighteenth century, the Ottoman court began to decamp en masse to the shores of the Bosphorus, and this resulted in an explosion in construction of new summer palaces along the strait.[108] Like these palaces on the Bosphorus, Ali Pasha's garden complex in Ioannina functioned as a space for relaxation and leisure.

In general, information about the ceremonies and rituals that took place in Ottoman provincial palaces throughout the empire remains limited. Evliya Çelebi, for example, tends not to dwell on these kinds of details in the accounts of his travels. The occasional descriptions of court life in the provinces that do exist indicate that the activities staged in Ali Pasha's palaces were in line with the customs of other provincial governors, in the sense that an individual of such rank was expected to show a certain level of hospitality to both guests and clients. In the case of the Çapanoğlu family in central Anatolia, contemporaries of Ali Pasha, the British traveler John Kinneir reported that he was received in the governor Süleyman Bey's urban palace complex "with politeness and dignity, in a magnificent apartment surrounded with sophas made of crimson velvet, fringed with gold, and opening into a garden of orange trees ornamented with a marble basin and jet d'eau."[109] All of the fundamental architectural elements seen in Ali Pasha's palaces can also be found in Kinneir's description of another outpost of empire, from the ostentatiously decorated audience chamber to a pleasant garden hideaway. Yet it was the siting, scale, and number of Ali Pasha's residences that elevated these spaces into settings for pageantry. And beyond the architecture itself, a key component of the performances that activated these spaces were the costumes and props: movable objects that in Ali Pasha's case would eventually become, quite literally, the stuff of legend.

ALI PASHA'S TREASURE

The vizier's palaces also served as repositories for Ali Pasha's considerable material wealth, which far exceeded the revenues of provincial governors in previous centuries. This financial prosperity was put on display for visitors in the form of luxury goods, such as embroidered textiles or weaponry embellished with silver filigree and gemstones. Both textual and visual representations of these palaces by European travelers describe Ali Pasha's reception areas essentially as showrooms: the Haygarth sketch discussed above (fig. 26) incorporates a range of fine objects, including wooden pipes, a glass *nargile*, a silver coffee service, and two long sabers hung on the wall directly behind Ali Pasha. And if the people in the governor's court were itinerant, these kinds of objects were also frequently on the move. During his visit with Ali Pasha in Butrint, Louis Dupré noted that the otherwise humble reception area—by all accounts a simple wooden pavilion—was enriched by the presentation of pipes, coffee served in porcelain cups and silver saucers, and "weapons of an admirable polish placed near [Ali Pasha] just within his reach: these consisted of a rifle, a long dagger and two pistols adorned with precious gemstones. Nothing besides these [arms] and his sumptuous and magnificent costume announced the high rank that he held."[110] In the same way that Ottoman sultans of earlier centuries would pack up their palaces and take their regalia with them on military campaigns, it seems that even for short excursions Ali Pasha always brought along a host of fine goods, especially an array of weaponry, to broadcast his status.

The objects on view in the governor's palaces embodied his power and wealth so successfully that they inspired an entire mythology around Ali Pasha's "treasure." After the governor's execution in Ioannina at the hands of the sultan's men in 1822, rumors began to circulate about the whereabouts of all those fabulous riches. Suspicion soon turned to Ahmet Hurşid Pasha, the leader of the Ottoman forces who killed Ali Pasha. Hurşid Pasha was an important government stakeholder in his own right, having served as grand vizier (*şadra'zam*) before being appointed head of the Ottoman military (*serasker*). After Ali Pasha's execution, it seems that Hurşid Pasha's enemies in Istanbul accused the general of embezzling choice pieces from the governor's palaces in Ioannina. Three memoranda from the sultan's imperial council (*hatt-ı hümayun*) charge Hurşid Pasha with keeping "for himself in secret" a hoard of gold coins, a large diamond ring and treasure chest, and a pair of jeweled pistols and a large dagger of exquisite workmanship.[111] Whether or not these indictments were true, it is significant that the fame of Ali Pasha's riches was already so widespread in his own day that it could cause the downfall of a political figure in the highest echelons of the empire. Hurşid Pasha died just a few months after this scandal, allegedly by suicide.

The obsession with Ali Pasha's treasure continues to the present day. It permeates popular culture in Greece and Albania, from online treasure-hunting forums to history programs broadcast on major television networks.[112] During my fieldwork, personnel of the Greek Archaeological Services in Ioannina told me of ongoing issues with looters digging holes in the historic Ottoman bridges of the region, owing to a widespread belief that Ali Pasha had hidden some of his treasure in the foundations.

It is tempting to dismiss the myth of Ali Pasha's treasure, which evidently has the potential to topple political careers and heritage monuments, as just that, a fanciful story about the piles of riches stored in his many palaces. Even contemporary sources are difficult to take at face value. In January 1822, during the governor's final days in Ioannina, the British consul William Meyer observed that "the state of Ali Pasha is now most curious. He has shut himself up in a small well-secured casemate, with two of his doormen. There he sits enthroned on barrels of gun powder, with all his treasures, ready to destroy himself on any dangerous emergency."[113] This dramatic image sounds like a scene from a play rather than the grim reality of siege warfare, especially coming from an on-the-ground observer—evidence of the power of rumor even as events continue to unfold.

Within the context of the early nineteenth century, the striking image of a ruler who would rather destroy himself and his riches than be captured may call to mind one of the best-known examples of French painting from the period: Delacroix's *Death of Sardanapalus* (fig. 30). The work was executed in 1827, five years after Ali Pasha's death. It is already established that the painting was at least partly inspired by a play on the same topic written by Lord Byron and published in 1821, at the height of the Ottoman blockade of Ali Pasha's fortified palace in the citadel.[114] As discussed above, Byron had met the vizier years before and had already drawn upon that experience for inspiration in his work. It is thus plausible that the siege of Ioannina, which Byron no doubt followed closely from his perch in Ravenna, could have informed his dramatization of the final days of Sardanapalus. What's more, there is circumstantial evidence that Delacroix himself—also a noted philhellene—was directly aware of the story of Ali Pasha.[115] In addition to frequent discussion of the developing political situation in Greece in French periodicals, a theatrical performance in Paris in July 1822 (just a few months after the governor's death) concluded with Ali Pasha's choosing to destroy himself, along with his "immense treasure," by setting alight barrels of gunpowder.[116] Beyond this general cultural milieu, Delacroix owned one of Louis Dupré's original watercolors of Ali Pasha at Butrint (see fig. 28), which he probably acquired in 1824, when both artists were exhibiting at the salon, and seems to have made a copy of the portrait in his own sketchbook shortly thereafter.[117] The rise and fall of a modern Sardanapalus in Ottoman Greece may have been percolating in the mind of the French artist when he set about composing his own work in 1827.

In her foundational article on Orientalist painting, Linda Nochlin writes about *The Death*

of Sardanapalus: "But of course, there is Orientalism and Orientalism.... The Near-Eastern setting of Delacroix's *Death of Sardanapalus* . . . does not function as a field of ethnographic exploration. It is, rather, a stage for the playing out, from a suitable distance, of forbidden passions—the artist's own fantasies (need it be said?) as well as the doomed Near-Eastern monarch. Delacroix evidently did his Orientalist homework for the painting . . . but it is obvious that a thirst for accuracy was hardly a major impulse behind the creation of this work."[118] Significantly, Nochlin chose Delacroix's painting above all others as an example of an Orientalist fantasy world that is so exaggerated and shocking that it is impossible for

FIGURE 30
Eugène Delacroix, *The Death of Sardanapalus*, 1827. Oil on canvas, 3.92 × 4.96 m. Louvre Museum, RF 2346. Photo: Franck Raux. © RMN-Grand Palais / Art Resource, New York.

anyone to take it seriously as "ethnographic exploration." And yet it is impossible to ignore how this precise theme of a ruler choosing to die among all his wealth and possessions in the face of imminent capture so neatly maps onto the stories circulating about Ali Pasha's last stand in Epirus, which was not a distant fable from ancient times but a contemporary news event.

That certain aspects of Ali Pasha's biography clearly draw upon, or perhaps inspired, Orientalist themes and stereotypes (which are easily dismissed as such) warrants an investigation into the basis of these stories. Traces of Ali Pasha's treasures can be found not only in European travel accounts but also in modern museum collections and the Ottoman imperial archives. Such documents serve in their own way as a kind of treasure map, offering a glimpse of the material reality that gave rise to these legends of wealth and influence.

Perhaps the most significant such resource is a collection of archival registers housed in the Ottoman archives in Istanbul. They offer a good deal of information about the accumulation, storage, and dispersal of Ali Pasha's material properties in Ioannina. When the governor was killed by the sultan's forces in 1822, all his property was seized for the imperial trust. In order to keep track of this process, scribes produced two registers that inventory in painstaking detail all of the objects found in the vizier's palaces.[119] These documents are essentially probate registers, typically referred to as *tereke* or *muhallefât* in Ottoman Turkish, which were an increasingly common legal record in the eighteenth and nineteenth centuries.[120] Several economic historians have used these kinds of registers to analyze shifting patterns of consumption and wealth accumulation in the Ottoman Empire.[121] Of course, what ultimately makes these specific documents so fascinating is their connection to Ali Pasha. The front cover of one of these registers bears the title "Inventory of the Materials Seized in the Ioannina Kastro Belonging to the Slain, Defeated Tepedelenli Ali Pasha" (fig. 31). Both registers are dated May 1822, a few months after the governor's death, and are signed and sealed by multiple officials, including the same Hurşid Pasha who led the siege on Ali Pasha's palace and died himself just a few months later. It is important to note the phrase "slain, defeated" (*maḳtûl maḳhûr*), which describes the deceased Ali Pasha every time he is named in these documents. The typical epithet in Ottoman probate inventories for someone who has died is *merḥûm*, a positive term that means "one who has received God's mercy." Ali Pasha is given no such consideration here, subjected instead to a harsh condemnation that is belied by the delicate piece of *ebru* paper upon which the title of the inventory is written, a common feature of such registers. This emphasis on the governor's treason within the quotidian material apparatus of Ottoman bureaucracy, and its redundant repetition throughout the two registers, works to both legitimize and rationalize the seizure of what was a considerable amount of material property from the governor's next of kin in the midst of a chaotic situation.

The two registers create a clear picture of what the sultan's troops found when they entered the vizier's palace in Ioannina. In short, they discovered a lot: register no. 13344 lists more than 250 individual objects, and register no. 13346 has almost four thousand entries. The methodical recording of these items in a rigid matrix arrangement in register no. 13344 (see fig. 31) visually conjures the overwhelming heaps of stuff encountered by the Ottoman officials. While the inventories do

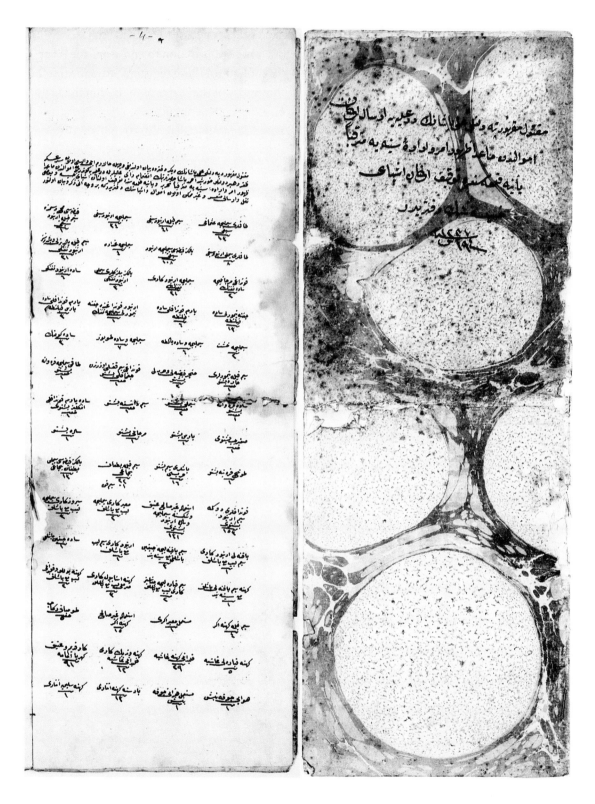

FIGURE 31
The first page and front cover of an Ottoman register listing Ali Pasha's property seized by the sultan's troops from the palace in the Ioannina citadel, 1822. BOA, Istanbul, D.BŞM.MHF. d. 13344.

not seem to overlap (the two registers appear to be divided by value: luxury wares versus more everyday household goods, respectively), they are organized according to the same general categories of objects. Both begin with hundreds of different kinds of weaponry, mostly swords and pistols, chased with silver filigree in the local manner that made Epirus famous throughout the Mediterranean. These are precisely the kinds of weapons that can be seen in the drawings by Haygarth and Dupré (figs. 26 and 28). Beyond weapons, both registers inventory domestic items related to palace life like tobacco pipes and ornamental trappings for ceremonial or recreational riding. Then there are fine serving dishes and luxury textiles, including furs, silks, and embroidered velvet. The list of objects seems to have been divided by gender, with items such as pistols and pipes in the first half of the list, while the second half consists of material normally found and produced in the private apartments of the inner household, especially women's clothing and textiles for the home such as embroidered cushions and bedding. Indeed, one of the registers explicitly states that some of these goods were the property of Vasiliki, Ali Pasha's Christian wife, who survived the siege of Ioannina and was taken into custody by the Ottoman military.[122]

Another notable feature of the objects in this list is their geographic diversity. The accountants took care to record whether a textile or bowl, for example, was imported. Here we see a preference for European luxury items such as gilded table clocks, jeweled pocket watches, pistols and rifles, glass panes for windows, and Austrian tableware, along with objects acquired from eastern trade connections such as Kütahya ceramics, shawls from Lahore, and large jugs from Myanmar—a direct result of the trading networks fostered by Ali Pasha's stewardship of both port cities and land routes.

The great distances that some of these objects traveled remind us that Ali Pasha did not, of course, exist in a vacuum, and raise the question of the audiences anticipated within these palaces. Again, during the tenure of Ali Pasha's career, several foreign governments established their own consulates in Ioannina, most notably the French and the British. Ali Pasha also enjoyed frequent communication with officials on the Ionian Islands through envoys and elaborate receptions. Most notably, Ioannina boasted a community of local Christian elites, many of whom had been educated abroad in Venice and Vienna and maintained close connections to those places through economic or intellectual channels. The accounts of European travelers, who were often hosted by these Christian notables, offer detailed descriptions of their residences and the objects found there. Such texts reveal that these individuals likewise favored imported items like table clocks and pocket watches from Britain and France, velvets and brocades, and printed books.[123]

While the western coast of Ali Pasha's territory was technically an imperial boundary between Europe and Ottoman lands, the governor and his court participated in a visual and material culture shared throughout the Adriatic. In much the same way that a recent volume edited by Alina Payne posits the Dalmatian littoral as a hybrid space of exchange, the coasts of Epirus further south may also be considered a productive zone for examining mechanisms of transnational mobility.[124] The Christian communities in Epirus served as cultural mediators who facilitated the flow of fashionable items into Ali Pasha's territory and the surrounding region. Examples of the materials described in the Ottoman registers and European accounts can be found today in various museums in Greece, including the Benaki collection in Athens and the Museums of Byzantine Art and Silversmithing in the Ioannina citadel. Bringing these contemporary museum collections and European travel accounts into dialogue with the Ottoman property registers in Istanbul clarifies the image of Epirus as a place with a robust mercantile economy and a renowned local craft industry supported by Ali Pasha and the members of his court, regardless of religious confession.

In some cases, the encounters and rituals that took place in the governor's palaces generated hybrid objects that were in turn put on display in the same spaces. For example, there is a rifle today in the collection of the Benaki Museum that bears an inscription in Ottoman Turkish: "The English king presented this gun to the foremost vizier of great renown, his excellency Ali Pasha, 1226 H (1811–12 CE)" (fig. 32). This text in gold has been inlaid next to a stamp confirming that the rifle mechanism was produced by the London firm of Joseph Manton. Putting all this information together, it seems that an agent of the British sovereign, probably the consul in Ioannina, gifted the rifle to Ali Pasha, who handed it over to local craftsmen with instructions to embellish the gunstock with the commemorative inscription and baroque silverwork that made the region famous in the Eastern Mediterranean.[125] The final touch by the Epirote silversmiths is the depiction of a mosque in gold on the barrel of the gun. This motif could be a generic architectural type, but it does bear a passing resemblance to the Fethiye Mosque in the Ioannina citadel, which was incorporated into Ali Pasha's palace complex (see fig. 52). Therefore, with its multiple layers, this rifle—truly a product of life in a contact zone—attests to the diplomatic and transcultural exchanges that took place in the governor's various palaces, the expertise of local artists who lent credibility to the legends of treasure on display in these spaces, and Ali Pasha's agency in crafting his own image. After all, it was the artisan employed by the governor himself, and not those working for King George, who proclaimed Ali Pasha the "foremost vizier of great renown."

PALATIAL ENVIRONS AND IMPERIAL SELF-FASHIONING

Whether understood as stages for ritual or staging points to facilitate court mobility, Ali Pasha's residences innovate upon the tradition of the governor's palace and its form and function in the Ottoman realm. In Ali Pasha's mansions, the *saray* is a particularly attractive environment in which to recirculate and improvise upon cultural memories of power and justice. During the age of revolution, the centralizing role of the imperial palace was echoed and at times challenged by the residences of local notables, who often proved to be mercurial in their relationships with these regimes. Looking beyond Epirus, the Shubra palace of Mehmed Ali Pasha in Cairo featured elaborate chambers for the reception of foreign dignitaries, decorated with calligraphic medallions bearing the name of the governor and his sons, while the name of the sultan is nowhere in sight.[126] At the same time that these *ayan* notables were consolidating their authority in palace structures throughout the Ottoman

FIGURE 32
Details of a rifle of British manufacture that was gifted to Ali Pasha and then decorated with gold and silver by local craftsmen, 1811–12. Benaki Museum, Athens, GE 5679. © 2025 by Benaki Museum, Athens.

Empire, emerging provincial power holders in other parts of the globe also concentrated on conveying their hard-won status in the form of grandiose houses. As noted in the introduction, the Nawabs of Awadh governed what is now the state of Uttar Pradesh in northern India and asserted their control in the face of the waning Mughal Empire by constructing several fantastic palatial complexes. A striking parallel to Ioannina is the Nawab capital of Lucknow, which witnessed the construction of several palaces in the late eighteenth and early nineteenth centuries, including the Daulat Khana, Panj Mahal, Qaiserbagh, and Chattar Manzil. Manuscript paintings and, later, photographs record the lively cosmopolitan atmosphere in these complexes overlooking the Gomti River, depicting everything from acrobatic performances to water festivals that featured a wooden boat in the shape of a fish, the personal insignia of the Nawab dynasty.[127] Ali Pasha was thus also engaged in a wider phenomenon from the eighteenth to the early nineteenth century in which newly wealthy nobles flaunted their assets in ways that were not necessarily refined but were certainly flashy and impressive. Using these assets to secure his hold over his territory, the vizier commissioned numerous residences as sites for pageantry and ceremony.

Ali Pasha's palaces illuminate the means and motives of the man who erected these buildings and brought them to life, striving to emulate the Ottoman capital and at the same time to distinguish himself from a center that, by comparison with this dynamic new zone of patronage, began to appear peripheral. Among his peers, Ali Pasha was one of the most ambitious in terms of the scale and number of his residences, setting a high standard for other provincial ruling families. Ali Pasha also strove to make manifest his newfound wealth and authority by investing in luxury objects. In 1818, he ordered a portrait from the artist Spiridon Ventouras, a Christian painter from the British-held Ionian Islands who trained in Venice and was famous for his icons (see fig. 3). Ventouras was summoned to the governor's palace in Preveza to draw the image from life. As far as I am aware, this is the only image of Ali Pasha, of the many that survive, commissioned by the governor himself. In the painting, which is approximately life-size, Ali Pasha confronts the viewer with a commanding gaze. Shown as a seated half figure, Ali Pasha sits against a dark ground, his sumptuous fur mantle almost dissolving into the shadows behind him. Calm and confident, the figure depicted here legitimizes his sociopolitical position by not only ordering the portrait but also assembling and presenting several precious objects within. In the painting, the governor is attired in a rich costume, with a vest and black velvet cap embellished with dense gold embroidery. On his right hand, Ali Pasha wears a ring, probably a seal that he would use to officiate documents. This hand rests on a pistol embellished with an outer casing of rich silverwork.

But perhaps the most fascinating aspect of this portrait is the large medal pinned to Ali Pasha's vest, boasting an enormous cut diamond in its center surrounded by fifteen smaller diamonds set in a black enamel casing. During his audience with Ali Pasha in Ioannina in 1814, Thomas Hughes described this medal, remarking, "The dress of the vizir . . . appeared costly but never gaudy; . . . he has bought a diamond from the ex-King of Sweden at the price of 13,000*l.*, which, with a number of others, he has had formed into a star, in imitation of one which he saw upon the coat of Sir Frederick Adam: this he now wears upon his breast, and calls it 'his order.'"[128] Sir Frederick Adam was a military officer who would eventually be appointed British high commissioner of the Ionian Islands, and we learn from Hughes's account that he had at least one meeting with the governor. At such a high-stakes encounter—the British had great interest in Ali Pasha and his ability to curb the French in the region—there is no doubt that Adam would have come in full regalia, including medals awarded by the British Crown. Within this painting there is represented on the very person of the vizier the exchange of both objects and fashions across an imperial border.

This portrait of the vizier, surrounded and enrobed with all his "stuff," suggests that the myths surrounding Ali Pasha's prosperity were generated, first and foremost, by Ali Pasha himself. As discussed above, the vizier could certainly back up his claims to a substantial level of personal wealth, especially in terms

of his land holdings—arguably the real treasure that was seized upon Ali Pasha's demise. By some accounts, the governor was one of the top landowners in the empire, with a combined portfolio of cash and real estate that, as one scholar put it, "haunts the imagination."[129]
In other words, this performance was not all smoke and mirrors, and the sultan's men in Ioannina did not walk away empty-handed. But what was unique to Ali Pasha was his charismatic flair and keen sense of theater. This portrait conveys the extent to which the governor was a real show master and how he externalized his wealth through elaborate costume and luxurious objects. By commissioning this portrait, by piling his reception areas with heaps of valuables, by marking his territory with dozens of large residences, Ali Pasha was playing with and turning to his own advantage the trope of a powerful ruler rich beyond the dreams of avarice. When we examine Ottoman archival records, European travel accounts, fieldwork documenting architecture on the ground, and objects that survive in various museum collections, it becomes clear that the governor worked to engineer this persona in terms of both architecture and material culture, surrounded "amidst no common pomp."

Revising the Rules of Engagement
FORTIFICATIONS ON A LIQUID FRONTIER

CHAPTER 2

The Battle of Lepanto, a deadly showdown off the coast of western Greece between the Ottoman imperial fleet and the combined forces of the Holy League of 1571, unfolded beneath a hot midday sun in early October. Involving almost five hundred warships and approximately forty thousand casualties, it was the most significant naval battle to take place in the early modern Mediterranean.[1] It was also a stunning victory for the Holy League. Even though the Ottoman naval forces managed to rebuild quickly and assert their military dominance, especially in Cyprus and along the shores of North Africa, this event had the long-term effect of Europeans' conceptually dividing "East" from "West" along the axis of the Ionian Sea. This codification of geographic imagination can especially be detected in Western European depictions of the battle, which proliferated after the fact. For example, only a year after the conflict, the pope commissioned the artist Giorgio Vasari to include a visual account of Lepanto in the Sala Regia, then under construction and intended to serve as a diplomatic reception area in the Vatican (fig. 33).[2] In this imagined calm before the storm, the two armadas face each other down, individual ships disappearing into thick forests of masts and banners. The severe regularity of Vasari's composition partitions the scene into two halves, extending down to the allegorical figures below, who represent the two sides and are in turn separated by a cartographic representation of the wider area. The overall effect crystallizes this region as a strict line of division between European and Ottoman, us versus them, here versus there.

More than two centuries later, this same terrain became less about imperial juggernauts flexing the might of the state than about one provincial governor's aspirations to delineate and expand his own territory through the construction of military fortifications—a spectacular case of architecture as local self-definition on the frontier. When Ali Pasha ascended to power as the administrator of multiple Ottoman provinces in Epirus in 1785, he concentrated his energy on the construction of large urban palace complexes in the interior of the region, as we have seen. In the first years of his rule, he had limited access to the sea, as the seven Ionian Islands and most of the ports along the coast were still under Venetian rule. After the Serenissima collapsed in 1797, however, it soon became clear that Ali Pasha had designs on these maritime territories, which had long been used as convenient positions for communicating with the Italian peninsula, Malta, Dalmatia, and the Peloponnese. And the governor was not the only one interested in this newly available real estate. At the turn of the century, the battle for control over this

coast devolved into a frantic melee among British, French, and Russian soldiers, who sought to gain a foothold in the area in frequent skirmishes. As the main power broker in this region, Ali Pasha turned to his own advantage the dizzying rate at which these European powers shifted alliances. While the governor was occupied with pitting the major stakeholders, including the Porte in Istanbul, against one another, he was also securing the maritime frontier through the seizure, maintenance, and reconstruction of fortifications up and down the western coast of Epirus. Ali Pasha's patronage program would come to include almost a dozen individual military installations (fig. 34). This line of military constructions stands as an impressive feat of logistics and mobilizing resources, especially considering that much of this building activity took place in the span of about a decade.

A close examination of these structures reveals the delicate balance of power among various political actors at this time, and how these macrodynamics were expressed spatially along a liquid frontier. The concept of a "liquid frontier" that faces the open sea might at first seem paradoxical: after all, a frontier by definition is a line that separates two sovereign states. But this particular maritime zone, as it stood in Ali Pasha's day, could be considered a frontier because of the unique geographic relationship between the seven Ionian Islands and the shore of Epirus.[3] The islands, especially Corfu and Lefkada, are extremely close to the mainland, at points with only one or two kilometers between them—a razor-thin border between empires, "east" and "west." Yet it was precisely this spatial proximity that resulted in the constant movement of luxury goods, basic supplies, and people, which never ceased, not even when Ali Pasha was busy building fortifications along the coast. In other words, this area was an integrated ecosystem; the islands had always been dependent on the mainland because they could not cultivate sufficient food supplies to survive on their own.[4] This area can therefore be described as "liquid," a term that I have adapted from Fernand Braudel's description of the Mediterranean as a series of "liquid plains," in that the coastline was a permeable membrane that allowed for a high degree of exchange among different communities.[5] As the historian Linda Darling has observed, the notions of frontier and borderland are two different paradigms that can operate in the same place: "the frontier divides one society from another, while the borderland is where they overlap and blend."[6] While Ali Pasha's coastal fortifications bluntly define the expanse of his political territory, these constructions should be interpreted less as proof of the "clash-of-civilizations" model of Christianity and Islam than as a material confrontation that often springs from the uncomfortable intimacy of neighbors.[7] When Ali Pasha summoned the artist Spiridon Ventouras from Lefkada to paint his portrait (fig. 3), this mission was, technically speaking, a journey between two empires. It was also a forty-five-minute trip by rowboat.

Within this border region, a compressed construction schedule and Ali Pasha's reliance on a local team of master masons resulted in a distinctive "brand" of military architecture. No matter the scale or topography, from a small way station at Pente Pigadia defending the mountainous corridor between Ioannina and Preveza (fig. 24) to the massive city walls of Tepelena (fig. 5), these fortifications bear remarkable similarities in terms of stoneworking technique and overall design features.[8] As we saw in the previous chapter, military

FIGURE 33 (opposite)
Giorgio Vasari, *The Battle of Lepanto (The Fleets Approaching Each Other)*, begun 1572. Fresco. Sala Regia, Vatican Palace, Rome. Photo: Alonso de Mendoza.

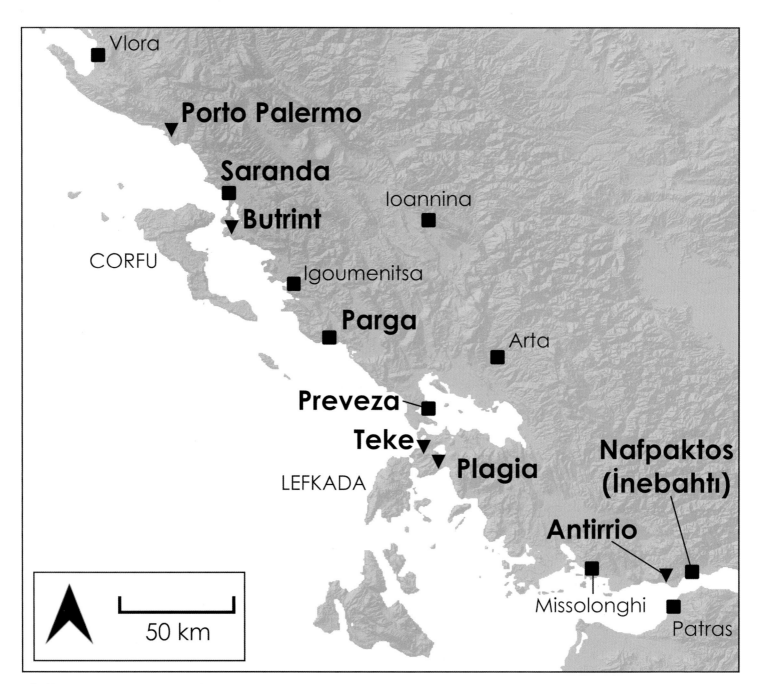

FIGURE 34
The eastern coast of the Ionian Sea, with the major cities (*squares*) and sites (*triangles*) where Ali Pasha commissioned coastal fortifications indicated in bold. Map by Matthew J. Jacobson.

constructions were a key element of Ali Pasha's elaborate network of urban palace complexes and the connecting infrastructure of roads and checkpoints. It is evident that the same teams of masons who were working on the governor's coastal defenses were also employed in the rebuilding of the citadels in Ioannina, Tepelena, and Gjirokaster. These were also important projects, but the governor's line of defense along the coast is instructive in understanding the high-stakes politics of a frontier zone, not only among sovereign states but also, crucially, between imperial center and periphery. Ali Pasha's building activity often alarmed the inhabitants of the Ionian Islands, and this was entirely by design. In the archival record, there are several episodes in which the governor was rebuked either by representatives from the islands or by officials of the Porte itself, as they scrambled to minimize the diplomatic fallout from his provocations.

The expanding literature on Ottoman frontiers has described Ali Pasha's relationship with Istanbul as "contractual," such that the state granted the vizier wide latitude in his affairs as long as he supported the Porte in terms of troops and supplies.[9] An investigation of his building activity on the Ionian Sea provides nuance to the precise nature of this negotiation between Ali Pasha and the state in the implementation of foreign policy. At first, these coastal areas were acquired on the pretext of defending the sultan's well-protected domains, but in the end these fortifications should be understood as expressing Ali Pasha's own vision of territorial expansion and economic success, which at times put him at odds with the Porte. In 1811, the governor sent his agent Said Ahmet Efendi to London to hand-deliver a letter to the Foreign Office demanding that the British turn over the recently acquired Lefkada and Parga, arguing that these places were his by right before their capture by the French. In their response, the British administrators demurred: "It is not likely that his majesty's govt. will on any account be induced to separate any of the seven islands which once formed the septinsular govt. from the rest"—in other words, it would be a shame to break up the set.[10] Nevertheless, it is extraordinary that Ali Pasha felt sufficiently empowered to conduct this kind of negotiation outside the traditional channels of state diplomacy, concerning what was essentially the expansion of the borders of the Ottoman Empire.

In comparison with other provincial power holders of the time, Ali Pasha was by far the most prolific in his production of military constructions. *Ayan* famous for their military prowess, such as Osman Pasvantoğlu in Vidin or Mehmed Ali Pasha in Cairo, were not great fort builders.[11] The only leader who could compete with Ali Pasha in this respect was Zahir al-'Umar in Palestine, who was responsible for the construction or reconstruction of inland fortifications such as Tiberias, Deir Hanna, and Qal'at Jiddin in the mid-eighteenth century.[12] Among the works overseen by Zahir al-'Umar, perhaps the most relevant comparison to Ali Pasha's fortifications is the coastal city of Acre (Ott. Akka) in present-day Israel, whose city walls received a major facelift in the late eighteenth century under Zahir and subsequently under Ahmad Pasha al-Jazzar.[13] In her foundational article on *ayan* architecture, Ayda Arel documents how the Cihanoğlu family, a minor clan active around the Aydın district, created farmstead estates with a fortified character.[14] Most notably, these mansions were surrounded and protected by tall, densely buttressed walls. Looking to the wider tradition of vernacular tower house architecture found throughout the Balkans and Anatolia, however, it should be stressed that these structures were limited to the protection of single farmsteads.[15] By contrast, Ali Pasha's coastal fortifications—an extensive defense network—operated on a more international stage, as the Napoleonic Wars unfolded practically on his doorstep.

CLAIMING THE COAST

The process by which Ali Pasha co-opted the long-contested littoral of the Ionian Sea was incremental. It did not take place with the stroke of a pen but was a painstaking, exacting endeavor that involved the gradual acquisition of the most important maritime stations in the region. And the construction of fortifications at these sites was vital in advancing the governor's claim on the surrounding area. Ali Pasha inherited a complex geopolitical situation on the western coast of his territories. Despite the Ottomans' best efforts, the Ionian Islands had never come under the sultan's direct control, and port cities on the mainland had repeatedly traded Venetian and Ottoman banners throughout the early modern period. By the early nineteenth century, Napoleon's expansionist policy and the end of the Venetian Republic had transformed the Adriatic and Ionian Seas into a hotly disputed zone. In October 1798, the Porte charged Ali Pasha with the task of ousting the French from the four former Venetian dependencies on the mainland: Butrint, Parga, Preveza, and Vonitsa.[16] The governor responded by successfully routing Napoleon's troops at the Battle of Nikopolis, which took place just two weeks after the order from Istanbul was issued.[17] Two years later, in 1800, the Ottoman and Russian authorities agreed that these key coastal properties would be included in a semiautonomous "Confederation of Continental Cities," under direct vassalage to Istanbul.[18] The same treaty formed the Septinsular Republic, a league of the seven Ionian Islands that had once been under Venetian control. Yet with the outbreak of the Russo-Ottoman War in 1806, the short-lived confederation fell apart, and it was then that Ali Pasha was finally able to occupy almost the full extent of the coast.[19] Seizing these territories was not only a matter of military tactics but also granted access to economic resources such as port facilities and fisheries.

Thus, by the beginning of 1807, Ali Pasha and his sons were responsible for maintaining a maritime border that ran the length of the western seaboard of northern Greece and Albania (see fig. 34). This was a 350-kilometer stretch extending from the "gates" of the Adriatic at Vlora in the north all the way to the straits of Lepanto (Gr. Nafpaktos, Ott. İnebahtı).[20] One geographer described the topography of this coast, largely defined and hemmed in by the western flank of the Pindus Mountains, as "bold and inhospitable."[21] In the premodern era, ships navigated the length of this shore by hopping between bays along the coastline, which was steep and rocky to the north and inundated with marshes to the south. From Vlora to Porto Palermo, for example, there is virtually no place to drop anchor, the geography forming a dreaded lee shore that was dangerous to ships in bad weather. Within this environment, it was therefore vital to protect ports that offered refuge to marine traffic.

Perhaps the best way to introduce this network of defenses and to understand how each construction contributed to an evolving strategy of defense and territorial acquisition is to imagine how someone would have encountered these fortifications on the ground (or, in this case, on the water) as they sailed down the coast from harbor to harbor. Re-creating this spatial—and,

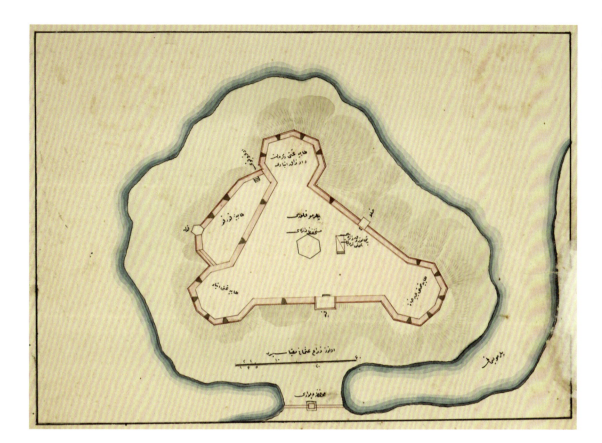

FIGURE 35
Ottoman ground plan of the fortress at Porto Palermo, late nineteenth century. BOA Istanbul, PLK. P. 859.

crucially, visual—experience clarifies the concept of a liquid frontier, especially because all the installations under examination in this study are designed to face the sea and address the Ionian Islands, particularly the capital in Corfu and the highly desired Lefkada. This brief tour will also reveal other key characteristics of Ali Pasha's fortresses, like the fact that many of these posts were not new constructions but rather heavy renovations or complete rebuildings of existing Venetian structures.[22]

Our hypothetical vessel launches from Vlora (Ott. Avlonya), an important port with a large harbor, connecting land routes such as the Via Egnatia to the Adriatic.[23] When Ali Pasha first came to power, Vlora was held by his rival Beratlı İbrahim Pasha. Upon İbrahim Pasha's removal, Ali Pasha's son Muhtar was finally appointed governor (*mutasarrıf*) to the Avlonya district in 1810, thus opening the port to Ali Pasha's use.[24] Exiting the bay, our vessel would make its way around the long peninsula and down to Porto Palermo, the only harbor offering shelter along what is now marketed as the "Albanian Riviera," between Vlora and Saranda. Porto Palermo did not have any kind of permanent settlement but was an outpost for monitoring Corfu and the independent village of Himara immediately to the north.[25] Because of its strategically valuable position, the site of Porto Palermo—the Venetian name, meaning "sheltered port," stuck even under Ali Pasha's control—has long been used for defensive purposes, from an ancient Roman garrison

REVISING THE RULES OF ENGAGEMENT 73

to a World War II submarine dock straight out of a James Bond film, which is now abandoned but almost fully preserved.[26]

The calm water of the harbor is flanked by promontories to the north and south, with a small rocky projection that separates the port into north and south bays. It was on this outcrop that Ali Pasha constructed his fortress, a triangular structure with three polygonal bastions (fig. 35). As discussed in chapter 4, an inscription that was once located above the main entrance includes a date of 1814, but this should probably be considered a *terminus ante quem*, as archival evidence from the National Archives in London suggests that the fortification was initially constructed around 1805.[27] This installation was no doubt part of a strategy to ratchet up hostilities against the people of Himara, who about a year earlier had appealed to the Russian commander of Corfu for protection against Ali Pasha in exchange for mercenary work.[28] Approached by a narrow path from the shore, the fortress stands isolated and has only basic amenities to serve the immediate needs of the garrison stationed there. One of these amenities was a church, which can still be seen today, a feature that suggests that the soldiers under Ali Pasha's command included Christians as well as Muslims.[29]

Leaving the bay of Porto Palermo behind, we continue south to the port of Saranda, a harbor town serving as an outlet for the agricultural production from the Delvina plain and, even further beyond, from the Gjirokaster River Valley (fig. 36).[30] In order to monitor both Saranda's harbor and the narrow channel between Butrint and Corfu to the south, in the summer of 1804 Ali Pasha requisitioned a fortress atop the hill of Likurs, which functioned as a citadel for the port below.[31] The traveler Richard Burgess claimed that the fortress at Likurs was first built by the Venetians and later "renewed" by Ali Pasha, and this assertion is supported by an early eighteenth-century Venetian map that indicates a walled enclosure situated on the crown of the hill.[32] The rounded towers of the fort also resemble the design of other earlier Venetian constructions, such as a triangular fortification just a few kilometers away in the channel of Butrint, suggesting that Ali Pasha's masons reconstructed the defensive structure by building upon an existing trace (fig. 37).

In its dialogue with Saranda, the site of Butrint was one of Ali Pasha's most strategically critical positions. It not only directly faced Corfu Town—the capital of the Ionian Islands—but also protected the nearby fisheries in the eastern lagoon and the arable lands in the Vrino plain to the south. Again, it was in Butrint that the French artist Louis Dupré captured the iconic image of Ali Pasha fowling amid the rushes in the lake (see fig. 28). Unlike Porto Palermo or Saranda, Butrint did not offer anchorage for large vessels. The Vrino channel is shallow and muddy, and at some points narrower than a hundred meters from shore to shore. Butrint was effectively under the control of Ali Pasha as early as 1804, despite multiple requests from the Russians on Corfu that he evacuate, as Butrint was considered part of the semi-independent Confederation of Continental Cities.[33] Ali Pasha refused to leave because Istanbul had granted him a tax farm for the fisheries and he claimed that he had not yet been paid his expenses for expelling the French from the place in 1798.[34]

At Butrint, Ali Pasha's men maintained a network of towers, fortresses, and outposts to hold the area. Opposite the ancient walled city known as Buthrotum, on the southern banks of the Vrino channel, lies the triangular fortress that was originally constructed by the Venetians but was seized by Ali Pasha and needed

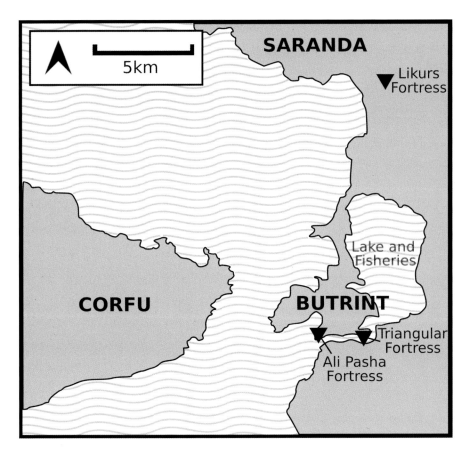

only minor repairs to render it serviceable for direct supervision of the fisheries (see fig. 36).[35] Meanwhile, the main architectural remnant from Ali Pasha's period is a square fortress at the mouth of the Vrino channel looking out to the sea, located on a small island formed by alluvial deposits (fig. 38). The installation is clearly visible from most of the northeastern shore of Corfu, and it controlled the critical choke point for boat traffic moving through the straits, only two kilometers wide at its narrowest (see fig. 11). This fortress was recently analyzed by José Carvajal as part of a survey conducted by the University of Granada in 2009, and his team's research revealed a sequence of building phases.[36] Using the northeast tower of the fortress to propose a general outline of the phasing of the entire structure, Carvajal suggests that the castle was originally constructed by the Venetians, with extensive repairs during the Ottoman period.[37] Carvajal also posits that the first phase of Ottoman repairs probably took place once Ali Pasha took over the area in 1798. Looking at documents from Ali Pasha's chancery, it is possible to further narrow this dating to before 1801.[38]

Sailing away from Butrint, we pass the harbors of Sagiada and Igoumenitsa, where Ali Pasha never maintained a military presence, although he had made plans to do so.[39] The next port of call is Parga, the largest harbor between Butrint and Preveza. Because Ali Pasha finally gained control of the town from the British in 1818, only two years before his deposition,

FIGURE 36
Fortifications in the areas of Saranda and Butrint. Map by Matthew J. Jacobson.

FIGURE 37
Southeastern tower at the Likurs fortress, Saranda. Photo by author.

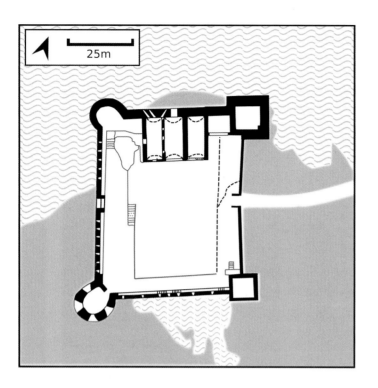
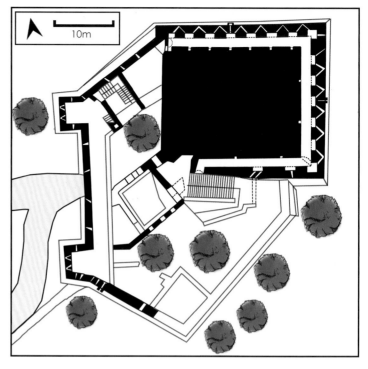

FIGURE 38
Ali Pasha's fortress in the Vrino channel at Butrint. Plan by Lisa T. D. Backhouse. Adapted from Giorgos Smiris, *To diktio ton ochiroseon sto pasaliki ton Ioanninon* (Ioannina: Etaireia Ipeirotikon Meleton, 2004), 265.

FIGURE 39
The fortress constructed at Agia-Anthousa, northwest of Parga. Plan by Lisa T. D. Backhouse. Adapted from Giorgos Smiris, *To diktio ton ochiroseon sto pasaliki ton Ioanninon* (Ioannina: Etaireia Ipeirotikon Meleton, 2004), 226.

he had little opportunity to make any significant changes to Parga's large fortress, which is located on a projecting peninsula dividing the harbor into two bays.[40] Far more interesting for the purposes of this study is a small fortress bearing down on Parga, located about five kilometers northwest of the city (fig. 39). Located next to the hilltop villages of Agia and Anthousa, this fortress was constructed by order of Ali Pasha in 1814, when the residents of Parga were still refusing to accept the vizier's suzerainty.[41] A French reconnaissance map indicates that an earlier "Turkish *palanka*" at Agia was subsequently replaced by this more substantial fort, which may have been built after Ali Pasha was bitterly disappointed to be denied Parga by the French after the Treaties of Tilsit in 1807.[42] The term *palanka* traditionally refers to an earthwork fortification, but by the eighteenth century it could also mean some kind of built structure with a palisade.[43] This fortress at Agia-Anthousa is an ideal example of a military post built by Ali Pasha explicitly to antagonize the residents of a nearby territory that he wished to acquire.[44]

Leaving behind the standoff at Parga, which was only resolved when Ali Pasha secured the city at the very end of his governorship, our vessel arrives at the port of Preveza. This region is particularly significant because it boasted the heaviest concentration of Ali Pasha's military building activity on the Ionian Sea (fig. 40). Topographically speaking, Preveza was the only point along the coast where an enemy could land troops and continue unimpeded inland to Ali Pasha's capital in Ioannina.[45] The other ports along Ali Pasha's coast, such as Vlora and Saranda, were blocked by a series of mountain ranges and thus gave enemy invaders access to the interior only through narrow mountain defiles impracticable for the movement of large battalions and field artillery.⁴⁶ Preveza was a crucial asset because it overlooks the narrow straits, controlling access to towns such as Arta and Vonitsa, essentially the heartland of northwestern Greece, which was very productive in terms of agriculture and fisheries. Finally, the town was the key to the governor's longer-term plans because it directly faces the island of Lefkada, which changed hands many times during Ali Pasha's rule and was a territory upon which the vizier had literally set his sights.⁴⁷

Long before Ali Pasha's day, Preveza was considered a key strategic site by both the Ottomans and the Venetians. It is thus an understatement to say that the history of political rule in Preveza—and likewise its built environment—is complicated. As mentioned in chapter 1, the first major fortification on the strait was the so-called Bouka castle, a walled settlement constructed by order of the Ottoman sultan Mehmed II in 1478 (see fig. 21).⁴⁸ Defended by a moat and seven towers, it was improved by the Ottomans several times in the late fifteenth and early sixteenth centuries, and when Evliya Çelebi visited Preveza in the 1670s, he reported that the Bouka castle was guarded by a large garrison of 250 soldiers.⁴⁹ When the Venetians seized Preveza in 1684, they also repaired the towers of the walled city on the point, but they blew up the same towers of the Bouka castle only a few years later, before surrendering the town to the Ottomans in 1701, as stipulated by the Treaty of Karlowitz.⁵⁰ With the old walled city in ruins, the Ottomans shifted the center of Preveza north by constructing a totally new castle, which is now known as the Fortress of Agios Andreas, today located in the center of the modern town. After the Venetians took Preveza yet again in 1717, they improved the fortifications at Agios Andreas by redigging the moat and constructing a new bastion on the western side.⁵¹

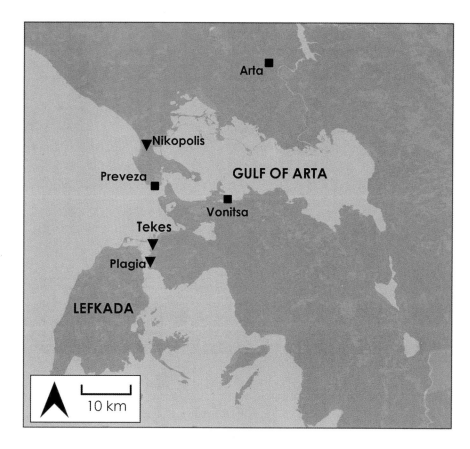

FIGURE 40
Preveza and the surrounding region, with major towns (*squares*) and other important sites (*triangles*) indicated. Map by Matthew J. Jacobson.

This was essentially the situation until 1797, the beginning of a tumultuous period in which one invading force after another occupied Preveza. Again, after the outbreak of the Russo-Ottoman War in 1806, the Ottomans moved quickly to claim the town, and Ali Pasha entered Preveza with his own men in November of that year.⁵² Over the next decade, the governor maintained a robust program of military building activity in the town itself and the surrounding region (fig. 41). This program included the repair of the older fortifications and the construction of two new fortresses defending the city, which was surrounded by a deep, revetted trench and protected by a triangular fortress on the eastern side of the straits.

REVISING THE RULES OF ENGAGEMENT   77

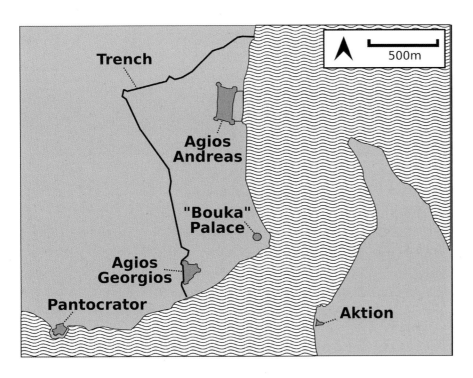

FIGURE 41
The city of Preveza, with the major fortifications that were constructed or renovated in the early nineteenth century indicated. Map by Matthew J. Jacobson.

The first fortification commissioned by Ali Pasha in the city of Preveza was that of Agios Georgios, built de novo in 1807 on the southern end of the city's defensive wall trench (fig. 42).[53] For the cavalry division stationed at the post, three platforms were constructed on the eastern side of the enclosure and equipped with artillery pieces that faced the water and the entrance to the narrow strait. Just a year later, Ali Pasha's workers turned their attention to Agios Andreas, whose quarter would include a residence for the vizier and a mosque. The walls of Agios Andreas were built on the foundations of the earlier, by then dilapidated fortress, but most of the masonry can be dated by an inscription on the southern bastion, with a Hijri date of 1223, corresponding to the years 1807–8. As discussed in the previous chapter, a few years later, in 1812–13, Ali Pasha had another larger palace erected east of Agios Georgios at the tip of the peninsula, where the Bouka castle had stood, defended by a rounded battery. Around the same time, the governor's men constructed a wide trench, lined with stone revetment and surrounding the length of the land side of the city; according to one observer, it was the product of "6,000 labourers daily employed in cutting a ditch of three miles round the walls of the town, 40 feet deep and 40 feet broad."[54] Although the trench has fallen into disrepair over the years, the streets of the contemporary city follow this early modern border, and the outline of the moat system can still be seen in satellite views.

Beyond this trench and further west of Agios Georgios stands the Pantocrator Fortress, Ali Pasha's last large-scale military construction project, completed around 1815.[55] Although it seems strange that the vizier would commission another fortress only about eight hundred meters down the shore from Agios Georgios, the Pantocrator has the advantage of being placed directly on the sea, its battery facing both the entrance to the gulf and any boat approaching from the northern end of the peninsula. On the other side of the strait facing Preveza is the triangular Fortress of Aktion (ancient site of Actium), whose bastions were constructed as early as 1801, but it was repeatedly modified 1812, the date on a plaque fixed above the entrance to the fort.[56] When Ali Pasha first established a military presence on the Aktion point at the turn of the century, its function would have been to intimidate the people of Preveza, who were still part of the independent confederation of ex-Venetian territories. A little later, the post served to monitor the Fortress of Lefkada (It. Santa Maura) across the bay, maintaining a direct line of sight across the water.

As part of this wider defense system for Preveza, Ali Pasha also turned his attention to two fortresses directly facing Lefkada on the eastern shore: Tekes and Plagia (see fig. 40). Both fortresses were under constant repair and reconstruction during Ali Pasha's tenure as governor. As early as 1801, Ali Pasha's workers were not only busy repairing an old tower on the site of Tekes but were also constructing bastions there and at Plagia.[57] These fortifications continued to play an important role in the Russo-Ottoman War of 1806–7, when Ali Pasha's men were stationed there to harass the Russians occupying Lefkada (fig. 43).[58]

Heading south from Preveza, our ship must go around Lefkada, because a causeway connecting the northern tip of the island to the mainland blocks access to the narrow channel at Plagia. After rejoining the coast, our vessel passes the port of Missolonghi and through the strait to arrive at the town of Nafpaktos (Ott. İnebahtı), where Ali Pasha's coastal territory terminated (see fig. 34). Perhaps better known to many historians by its Italian name, Lepanto, this port was the staging area for the Ottoman fleet during the famous battle of 1571. The town itself, which sits just north of the shore on the slope of a hill, boasts its own city walls, with an inner citadel at the summit. To the southwest of this small harbor stand a pair of fortresses, the castle of Antirrio to the north, and Patras to the south, straddling the strait and guarding the Gulf of Corinth.

Like other fortifications in strategic zones, the installation at Antirrio, first constructed in 1499 under orders of the Ottoman sultan Bayezid II, was destroyed and rebuilt several times by different state actors.[59] A late seventeenth-century Venetian map by Vincenzo Coronelli shows a fortress with four round towers at Antirrio, and repair registers from the Ottoman archives attest that the defense works of Nafpaktos were the object of the Porte's constant attention in the eighteenth century after it was restored to Ottoman control by the Treaty of Karlowitz in 1699.[60] Archaeologists working at the site have suggested on the basis of structural evidence that most of the fabric still extant today dates from the time of Ali Pasha.[61] If this is the case, all of that extensive building activity would have taken place after 1797, when Muhtar Pasha was assigned

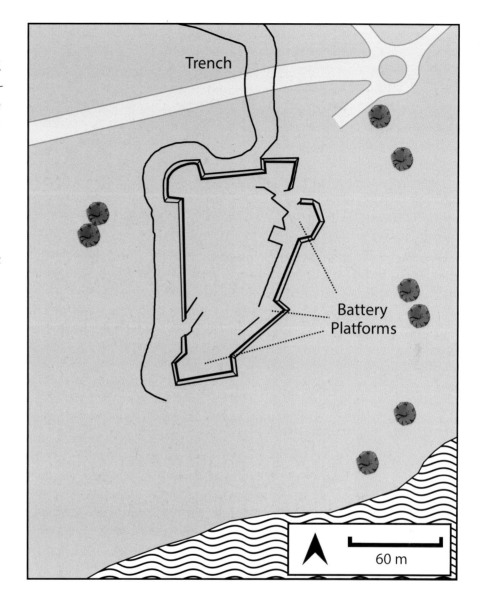

FIGURE 42
The Fortress of Agios Georgios in Preveza. Plan by Matthew J. Jacobson.

FIGURE 43
View from one of the battlements at the Plagia fortress looking north to the town of Lefkada across the strait. Photo by author.

FIGURE 44
View of the Fortress of Antirrio looking southeast toward the strait at the entrance to the Gulf of Corinth. Photo by author.

as governor of the district. In January 1807, Muhtar Pasha wrote to his father from Nafpaktos that both the town's citadel and the Antirrio castle were "all in a ruinous state" and in need of further repair.[62] An additional renovation on behalf of the Porte occurred in 1816.[63] The physical traces of these different construction campaigns are discernible when standing on the exterior of the fortress; the curtain walls are a messy jumble of different masonry techniques, a visible stratigraphy attesting to the ongoing efforts to keep the fort serviceable (fig. 44). With several foreign powers yet again clamoring at the gates to the Gulf of Corinth, Ali Pasha was resolved that there would not be another defeat at Lepanto under his watch.

Unfortunately, it is not always possible to determine precise dates for the different phases of a building's construction—archaeologists, who analyze things like mortar composition and stonework techniques, tend to estimate in terms of centuries, not decades. Nevertheless, as demonstrated above, one can establish an approximate chronology of the fort-building activity on Ali Pasha's coast from fieldwork and archival documents, which provide a general sense of where the governor's engineers were working at a given time. This survey reveals that there must have been at least one team of engineers and craftsmen, maybe more, who were continuously engaged in building or repairing these coastal fortifications from approximately 1800 until 1818. And it was these master masons who played a decisive role in the introduction of a new style of fortification system along the shores of Epirus.

A NEW TYPE OF FORTRESS

The engineers employed by Ali Pasha to build up the coast almost always worked with preexisting fabric. This was especially the case at the ex-Venetian mainland ports that ultimately came under the governor's jurisdiction. Fundamentally, military architecture is often a palimpsest, accruing layer after layer of interventions to keep a particular structure viable and in step with the latest advances in war technology. Fortifications are notorious for being in constant need of repair. Earthworks and ditches are particularly difficult to keep in good condition; in Ali Pasha's own archive there are constant requests for workers to dig out one moat or another.[64] It also stands to reason that military works would frequently be located on top of earlier sites, as topography, sightlines, and ease of access play a large role in determining the most strategic location for a fortress.

The fluid nature of military architecture itself—with structures frequently being updated and adapted, in a perpetual state of becoming—resists the traditional notion in architectural history of giving a fixed date of completion for a building. On the Ionian littoral, where territories repeatedly changed hands in the early modern period, it is somewhat beside the point for historians to classify sites according to specific temporal or dynastic markers. In other words, many fortifications in this region could be understood equally as "Venetian" and "Ottoman." For this reason, my study of Ali Pasha's military interventions relies not only on information gleaned from archival sources and traveler accounts—which are often laconic and frustratingly vague—but also on numerous site visits that I conducted to assess the phasing of structures. It was during this fieldwork that I observed the extent to which the fortifications associated with Ali Pasha shared a typology of similar structural characteristics, even though these sites were spread over a relatively wide swath of territory.

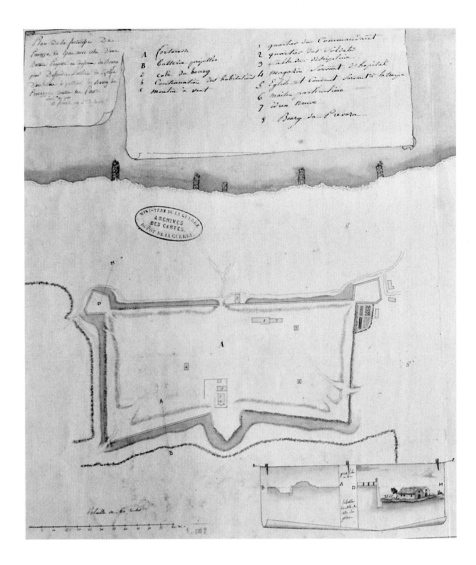

FIGURE 45
French plan of the Fortress of Agios Andreas in Preveza, 1798. © Service historique de la Défense, Vincennes, R-18-4-10-B-202. Photograph courtesy of James Curlin.

The defining feature of the governor's various military works is the use of projecting polygonal bastions. This feature marks a notable shift from the fortifications designed in the same region in the medieval and early modern periods. Byzantine or Despotate-era fortresses, such as the citadel at Arta or the Rogoi Castle near Louros, tend to follow the contours of the topography, with irregular, curving curtain walls punctuated at intervals by tall square or rounded towers. Meanwhile, the most significant early modern innovation in fort-building technology in the area was the introduction of an additional system of outer defenses featuring trenches and star-shaped earthworks, along with lower, rounded bastions suited to housing artillery.[65] Examples of this type of fortification can be seen in the Venetian Fortress of Santa Maura, which defended Lefkada, and the "Bouka castle" at Preveza (see fig. 21).[66] The fortifications built under Ali Pasha innovate further upon this fort-building tradition that was established in the sixteenth and seventeenth centuries by replacing the round or square tower with a slanted polygonal bastion. This defensive feature, which can be found in new constructions and in repairs of earlier forts, is strategically superior because a short, slanted bastion is more capable of deflecting artillery fire than a vertical tower with square or rounded surfaces.

When Ali Pasha's workmen repaired older fortifications, they usually sought to improve upon the earlier design. One of the best examples of this can be seen at the Fortress of Agios Andreas in Preveza. A slightly earlier French map, produced in May 1798, shows the precise state of the fortress before it was extensively repaired under Ali Pasha around 1807 (fig. 45). During the French occupation of Preveza, Agios Andreas had stone revetments only in some areas of the walls, while the rest of the enclosure was defined by earth and loose rocks, constituting potential breaches in the defensive system.[67] In Ali Pasha's time, the fortification's two bastions facing the sea were rejacketed with new revetments, and this masonry was continued around the entire fortification, creating a unified stone enclosure (figs. 46 and 41). Two polygonal bastions were also added to the northwest and southwest corners of the fortress facing the town, along with an outer enclosure wall on the opposite side running

FIGURE 46
The southeast bastion at the Fortress of Agios Andreas, Preveza. Photo by author.

down to the sea, which had its own monumental gateway with a bent entrance (see fig. 17).

The portal at Agios Andreas in Preveza demonstrates that another hallmark of Ali Pasha's fortifications is a particular style of entrance gate, in most cases a rounded arch recessed in a rectangular frame. These portals are typically distinguished from the rest of the monument by their construction in a different kind of stone, often white limestone or marble, making the doorway, set against masonry of contrasting hue, particularly eye-catching (fig. 47). The entrance portal to the citadel in Ioannina shows that such gateways were also a feature of the wall systems built for cities in the interior in Ioannina, Tepelena, and Gjirokaster (see fig. 15). As we shall see in chapter 4, set above these doorways are decoratively carved machicolation and niches for epigraphic inscriptions and figural plaques, some of which survive in situ. These decorative portals bring a sense of refinement to even the smallest and most remote of the coastal fortifications. To gain a full understanding of this shift in presentation, one has only to observe the rather perfunctory entrances to earlier fortresses in the region, such as those at Butrint, Parga, and Vonitsa.

As for the polygonal bastions that define Ali Pasha's fortifications, they also tend to be executed in a very specific manner, their most distinguishing features being a quoin of ashlar blocks at the corners of the polygon design, a gradual slant upward (making the base of the bastion much wider than the top), and a cornice setting apart a necklace of artillery battlements at the top of the wall (fig. 48; see also fig. 35).[68] The quality of the masonry in the external walls of these bastions varies, but

REVISING THE RULES OF ENGAGEMENT   83

FIGURE 47
Main entrance to the Tekes Fort.
Photo by author.

generally this stonework can be divided into two types, the first being a system in which courses of masonry are formed with small rectangular blocks of relatively uniform height with little or no mortar visible (see figs. 37, 46, and 48), and the second featuring an external wall composed of roughly cut fieldstones set in thick mortar, in most cases covered with another layer of plaster or mortar (see fig. 47). A breach in the curtain wall at the Plagia fortress that can be seen today suggests that the walls of these bastions were supported with a rubble masonry infill.

The difference between the two types of masonry outlined above can best be understood in terms of economic pragmatism. The first type of masonry would have been more costly and time-consuming to execute, as the cutting and placement of the ashlars for the revetment of the bastion walls required the employment of a team of more specialized craftsmen. The second type of masonry was easier and faster to produce because workers could erect walls with moderately shaped fieldstone and encase them in mortar. From a defensive standpoint, however, the first type of masonry would have been preferable because the regular courses of cut stone offered increased stability and were more resistant to artillery fire than fieldstone. Ibrahim Manzour, a military advisor in Ali Pasha's court, reports a tense exchange between the governor and Don Santo Montéléone, the engineer behind the Agia-Anthousa fortress, which features the second type of masonry. The vizier was "irritated because at the fortress of Agia the soldiers do not want to stay there because they fear that it will crumble around them."[69]

These different masonry typologies do not follow a neatly delineated timeline. For example, the fortresses at Anthousa and Tekes, whose major building phases were executed about four years apart, both feature the second type of masonry. The most logical explanation for these different styles of stonework in Ali Pasha's fortresses is the presence of different teams of laborers. Given that Ali Pasha had many construction or repair projects running at the same time, we can conclude that some of the more seasoned or adept craftsmen simply did not have the ability to be in two places at once.

But who were these laborers? A document from Ali Pasha's chancery, a register listing workers employed in construction activity at the "kastro" of Ioannina, offers a glimpse.[70] Dated 1801, the register records the reconstruction and enhancement of the medieval wall system surrounding the old city. In terms of design and masonry, the new walls and bastions very much resemble several of the coastal fortifications under discussion, especially the Agios Georgios and Agios Andreas forts in Preveza. The document lists almost two thousand workers—1,815, to be precise. Besides providing ample evidence of Ali Pasha's ability to mobilize a sizeable labor force for the execution of large-scale infrastructure projects, this register also gives a sense of the hierarchy at one of these worksites, divided between skilled and unskilled workers. The overwhelming number of unskilled laborers are classified according to their place of origin: fifty-eight men from Kastoria, thirty-five from the village of Molista, twenty-eight from Metsovo, and so on. It was common practice for Ali Pasha (and indeed for other construction projects throughout the Ottoman provinces) to source workers from nearby towns and villages, usually in lieu of their annual taxes.[71] As for skilled masons, the vizier often covered these expenses himself. That said, in the case of Ioannina, Thomas Hughes reports that no one could escape

FIGURE 48
The south bastion at the Fortress of Agios Georgios, Preveza. Photo by author.

pitching in on the task at hand: Ali Pasha "spared not even the primates, archons, and priests of the Greeks, any more than the beys and agàs of the Turks; nay, he forced the archbishop and his own son Mouchtar to labour. Signore Nicolo's back seemed to ache afresh as he recounted to us the fatigues which he used to undergo in carrying stones and working with the pick-axe."[72]

Apart from the indelible image of Ioannina's construction crew of town notables, most of the anonymous workers in the register can be considered unskilled laborers who were assigned the onerous yet uncomplicated tasks of transporting and breaking up stone and preparing lime for mortar.[73] The register also names a handful of men described as architects (μειμάρης, *mimaris*) or master masons (μαστόρος, *mastoros*) and their own teams of workers: thirteen men under Stathis, the *mimaris*, twenty-four men under Master Lampros, and twenty-three men under Christos, also a *mimaris*. A separate group of roofing specialists (νταβαντζήδες, *tavantzides*) are named as well. It is important to note that these master masons—along with others who appear in Ali Pasha's archive—were all Christians. Muslims do not seem to have been engaged at all in the construction industry in this region, perhaps a simple reflection of population demographics, or evidence of a distinctive labor culture defined at least in part by confession. The smaller groups working under the named expert craftsmen would have been responsible for the more skilled tasks of raising the walls and bastions on the instructions of the master masons, and in laying the courses of the external casing walls to achieve a gradual slope for the enceinte. While the unskilled labor for all of Ali Pasha's construction projects could simply be drawn from the surrounding area, the remarkable consistency in appearance and technique among these fortifications suggests that the smaller groups of more specialized craftsmen moved from site to site.

By examining stone-working techniques in these defensive structures, we thus begin to discern a clearer picture of the masons who worked on these buildings. The question of who was responsible for first laying out or designing these fortifications, however, is another matter. Even a cursory review of the archival sources and available travel accounts reveal that Ali Pasha depended on an eclectic mix of architects and engineers to oversee his various building projects. One gets the impression that the governor recruited anyone with some claim to engineering skills who came his way. In several instances, Ali Pasha hired foreign architects who crossed international borders to work in Epirus, supporting the framing of this region more as a borderland zone that, as Linda Darling puts it, "channel[s]—not . . . prevent[s]—the movement of people, goods, and ideas."[74]

Many scholars have speculated that the men who masterminded the designs of Ali Pasha's fortification projects must have been among the several Western Europeans who were constantly making their way to the governor's court.[75] As we shall see, this was most certainly the case, but it is also clear that Ali Pasha had local architects upon whom he could consistently rely. First among them was Petros of Koritsa (Alb. Korçë), described in a document from Ali Pasha's chancery as the "chief architect of the vizier" (μεήμαρη τού βεζήρ).[76] William Leake refers to Petros with the same title and notes that he "constructed the bridge and seráï at Tepeléni, and has built many others of the Pashá's palaces and castles." The English observer confirms that Master Petros was always on the move from one site to the next, the consummate servant to the governor: "Although Peter is the Vezír's chief architect and engineer, he has served in his present capacity for five years without receiving a pará, although constantly employed in superintending the building of some castle or serái for the Vezír or his sons."[77] Whether or not the claim about the delayed payment was true, we can confirm that Petros was responsible for laying the foundations of Ali Pasha's palace in the Ioannina citadel, and his name in fact appeared in a Greek inscription on the main gate leading to the Fortress of Agios Andreas in Preveza, which no longer stands (see fig. 17). Besides naming Ali Pasha's agents in Preveza, Bekir Ağa and Süleyman Bey, the epigraphic plaque also proclaimed that the fortification was the work of "Petros the architect (αρχιτέκτων)."[78] Petros, a Christian from northern Epirus, probably gained his skills in the manner typical in the region, by working his way up as an apprentice alongside more experienced craftsmen.[79] He would have had ample opportunity to pick up such specialized knowledge in his native area of Korçë. This zone is famous for its vibrant tradition of stone architecture, especially in the town of Moschopolis (Alb. Voskopojë), which saw fourteen new quarters and twenty-two churches constructed in the eighteenth century.[80]

Although it seems that the design and construction of fortresses in the area under Ali Pasha's control were kept in house, so to speak, there were several occasions when the governor received outside assistance. For example, after a meeting with the governor in Ioannina in 1808, the British agent Anthony Baker reported to London that the vizier was "anxious for the assistance of some able engineer who might superintend the works he is constructing at Preveza, and direct other necessary measures of defence about to be adopted."[81] Ali Pasha was keenly aware that the French, British, and Russian forces that were constantly circling his territory kept engineers on hand, and he thus frequently made special requests to the diplomats at his court to lend him these military specialists for his own projects.

One of the best opportunities to observe how Ali Pasha communicated and worked with foreign specialists comes in the form of handwritten reports by two French engineers who oversaw the design and construction of the Fortress of Agios Georgios in Preveza and several other military works in the region. These reports, now housed in the manuscript collection at the Gennadius Library in Athens, are part of the personal papers of General Fréderic-François Guillaume de Vaudoncourt (1772–1845), who first made a name for himself in Italy as an artillery specialist in the French army.[82] In his published memoirs, Vaudoncourt recounts that, in 1806, Ali Pasha pressed François Pouqueville, the French consul stationed in Ioannina, to send for both officers and supplies from Napoleon's troops. This request included military engineers who could assist in the construction of new fortifications in the region, particularly at the newly acquired Preveza and the camps positioned against the Russian troops on Lefkada. Thus, in early 1807, the young Vaudoncourt, at the time a colonel, found himself in the court of Ali Pasha in Ioannina. Although he eventually published his experiences as *Memoirs on the Ionian Islands*, in his book Vaudoncourt mentions the fortifications in Epirus only in passing, and he refrains from indicating the primary role he played in their construction.[83] This omission may be attributed to the fact that, in the end, the general came to resent Ali Pasha's resistance to the proposed designs.[84]

The field reports now in Athens consist of three sections: the first is a miscellany of papers related to various projects, such as a bridge under repair (probably at Tepelena), the "chateau at Litaritza," and large-caliber guns cast for Ali Pasha in Ioannina; the second is a six-page report by a Captain Ponceton outlining his designs for fortifications in Preveza; and the third is the longer report written by Vaudoncourt himself. It seems that Ponceton and Vaudoncourt were sent together to assist Ali Pasha, and during their short tenure they were kept busy in several of the governor's most important urban strongholds. Most pertinent to the present discussion, however, are the final pages of Vaudoncourt's report, which provide a wealth of detail about the circumstances of Ali Pasha's commissioning and construction of the Agios Georgios Fortress in Preveza. Again, this fortress was the first major military work executed by Ali Pasha after taking control of the city. It is today situated on the southern edge of town, set approximately seventy-five meters inland from the beach (see figs. 41, 42, and 48). Vaudoncourt explains that the primary objective of the regiment's mission to Ali Pasha in Epirus was to ensure that Preveza be fortified, or at least sheltered from a sudden, swift attack ("coup de main").[85] After surveying the terrain, Vaudoncourt determined that the best place from which to protect the garrison of the town and to defend the canal was the natural elevation of the Agios Georgios Hill, noting that it would be impossible for any boat to enter the gulf without passing under the fire from its batteries.

Vaudoncourt returned to Ioannina to discuss his plans for fortifying Preveza. He arrived in time to witness Ali Pasha, in the course of negotiating with the French consul Pouqueville, issue "in a very public manner" an order for the construction of a number of flat-bottomed boats to aid in the defense at Plagia.[86] Vaudoncourt was annoyed that Ali Pasha, in looking over the plans for the Fortress of Agios Georgios, expressed concern that it would be too costly, while continuing to add other projects, such as casting artillery, that he wanted the young French engineer to undertake at the same time. Vaudoncourt attributed what he perceived as Ali Pasha's irrational behavior to a "Turkish" tendency "to walk continually in imaginary spaces and magical illusions." Regardless of this Orientalist perspective, it could be argued that Ali Pasha was adopting a pragmatic approach, taking advantage of Vaudoncourt's expertise for as many projects as possible.

Once the choice of location had been made and plans had been drawn up for the Fortress of Agios Georgios, Ali Pasha eagerly arranged a public ceremony: he would come to Preveza to lay the first stone for the fortification, with Pouqueville also in attendance.[87] It was Ali Pasha's intention, Vaudoncourt added, that "his presence [in Preveza] would give weight to the rumors, which [Ali Pasha] himself had spread," that he would dispatch troops to the front lines facing the island of Lefkada. In this way, Ali Pasha used military construction as physical testimony to what had before been only a vague threat. By arranging a spectacle in which he would lay the foundations for the Agios Georgios Fortress, Ali Pasha sought to portray the Russian forces on nearby Lefkada as a legitimate danger to the city, and to present himself as the capable defender of Preveza.

After these events, Vaudoncourt found Ali Pasha to be an exacting patron. Once the designs for the fortification had been drawn up, Ali Pasha wanted to inspect them himself;

upon viewing the plans, he expressed his disapproval that the bastions would not be square, or polygonal ("tours quarrés"), presumably because Vaudoncourt had employed a more irregular design to better accommodate the natural shape of the hill.[88] Ali Pasha also objected to the placement of the fortification a short distance from the sea (40 *toises*, approximately 77.5 meters), and requested that the location be advanced so that the fort would sit directly on the beach, where his forces could establish casemates. Vaudoncourt defended his choices, pointing out that the sandy beach was not suitable for the casemates, whereas the natural elevation at Agios Georgios offered more stable terrain.

Despite Ali Pasha's protests, it seems that he deferred to Vaudoncourt in the end, as the designs that the colonel describes in his report are essentially what can be found on the ground today: an irregularly shaped fortification on the Agios Georgios Hill set slightly inland from the sea. Yet the haggling continued. By the time the first trench had been dug for the foundations of the enceinte walls, Ali Pasha had established his own dwelling ("son domicile de jour") on the beach so that he could personally observe the construction work. This house was probably located on the point of the Preveza peninsula, where a few years later Ali Pasha would establish his walled palace complex. As the work was under way, Ali Pasha berated Vaudoncourt, complaining that under his watch the masons were far too occupied with advance preparations and that at this rate he "would not be able to finish the fort before two years' time, and had to make do with the variables that had been presented to him at the present moment."[89] At this point in the report, Vaudoncourt conjectures that Ali Pasha was impatient to see the speedy completion of the fort because he feared that if there was a sudden conclusion of hostilities between the Russians and the Ottomans, the French would attempt to occupy Preveza once again. If this happened, Ali Pasha "did not know if His Majesty the Emperor and King would indemnify the defenses," i.e., have the right to claim the new fort because the construction had been overseen by French engineers.

Ultimately these fears were never realized. Vaudoncourt had the assistance of Captain Ponceton in outfitting the defensive works, and Ponceton's own report states that he was entrusted with the task of placing munitions at the various batteries defending the entrance to the port. For the cavalry division at Agios Georgios, Ponceton had three platforms constructed on the eastern side of the enclosure and brought some artillery pieces to the battery. Additionally, in the miscellany at the beginning of the dossier in Athens, there is a short document in Italian, the language in which the French soldiers and Ali Pasha's agents communicated. This text was intended to accompany a plan of the Agios Georgios Fortress (unfortunately missing), and provides some additional information about the fort's specifications. Ponceton also records that the entire construction process—including the excavation of the foundations, the erection of the walls and parapet, and the revetment of the dry moat on the western side—took three months and employed three hundred general laborers for moving the earth and two hundred more specialized workmen for the masonry. These are simple, utilitarian notations, yet they reveal a fascinating set of circumstances in which an Ottoman governor independently enlisted French engineers to build a fort with local Christian workers—a transimperial encounter in the borderlands of empire.

We can draw several conclusions from these documents about Ali Pasha's style of patronage. First, he took an active interest in the design and implementation of building plans, sometimes to the point of being overbearing in the eyes of his French contractors. Additionally, while Ali Pasha certainly seemed to value foreign engineers and building specialists, the accounts of the hierarchy of laborers responsible for these constructions destabilizes simplistic designations of these fortresses as "European" or "Ottoman" in design. While the Fortress of Agios Georgios in Preveza was overseen by Guillaume de Vaudoncourt himself, less than a year later, construction began on the other side of the city at Agios Andreas under Master Petros, whom Pouqueville described as "the Vauban" of Ali Pasha.[90] As the masonry techniques are virtually identical at both fortresses, it is clear that the two hundred skilled masons employed at Agios Georgios—who could very well have worked under Master Christos and Lampros years earlier in Ioannina—simply moved over to Agios Andreas to begin what was just the next episode in a seemingly endless round of construction projects on Ali Pasha's coast.

THE RIGHT TO BUILD

By their very nature, military fortifications serve as ideal resources for tracking the shifting geopolitical relationships of a border region. Fortresses are fixed coordinates in a fluctuating landscape, the material embodiment of invisible boundaries that ebb and flow over time. Just like the frontiers that they defend, however, fortifications—and their construction—can also be a matter of intense negotiation.

Several of Ali Pasha's coastal fortifications became sites of conflict, not only in the more traditional sense of military combat but also in terms of diplomatic confrontations provoked by the building of these installations. The potential for tensions between Ottoman center and periphery can perhaps best be framed by posing a simple question: Who has the right to build a fortress? The most recent work on military architecture in the Ottoman Empire—a relatively new line of inquiry in Ottoman studies—usually adopts the underlying assumption that the Porte in Istanbul took the initiative on the foundation and maintenance of fortifications throughout the empire.[91] There are many reasons why this top-down model makes sense as a pattern for military construction: the center, of course, would have a vested interest in expanding or maintaining the boundaries of its sovereignty. Yet it is precisely in the borderlands that local actors often have their own motivations or incentives, which at times diverge from state policy.

The port city of Preveza serves as an ideal place in which one can observe this interplay among state, local, and foreign interests. As explained above, firm control over Preveza presented significant strategic advantages, as the town is located on a peninsula directly facing the island of Lefkada and leading to the Gulf of Arta (see fig. 40). When the Porte ordered Ali Pasha to secure the town after the Venetian Republic dissolved in 1797 and Napoleon's troops moved to occupy the position, its instructions were issued in the understanding that the governor was the servant of the state who was responsible for defending the borders of the Ottoman Empire. Yet when Ali Pasha eventually bested the French troops and his soldiers entered Preveza in October 1798, the townspeople did not welcome their "liberators" with open arms.[92] When the Confederation of Continental Cities was formed in 1800, the inhabitants of Preveza insisted that an administrator be sent from Istanbul, expressly to avoid coming under Ali Pasha's direct authority.[93] It is revealing that Ali Pasha's response to the loss of Preveza, which he felt was his by right after his victory over the French, was to set up a fort: this is when he sent his son to establish a presence on the Aktion peninsula with the triangular fortress that was within cannon range of Preveza and also had a clear sightline to the older Venetian fortress guarding Lefkada (fig. 49).[94]

This new fortress on the peninsula incited panic among the people of Preveza and Lefkada alike. In the fall of 1801, Ali Pasha received a letter from one of his agents in the capital, a Phanariot scribe by the name of Yiankos, who told Ali Pasha that one of the sultan's officials had paid him a visit at his residence in Istanbul, demanding to know the meaning of the governor's construction of a fortification near Preveza: "Yesterday his highness Çelebi Efendi told me that the islanders of [Lefkada] were complaining that a fortress that you built in Preveza would harm them, and he asked me, if I had seen it, what is this fortress? I replied that this fortress was old and that you had just built it anew on top of the earlier foundations. And of course, I said this fortress was necessary there, as it is at the tip [of the peninsula] and it does not communicate easily for your entry into the sea, posing no threat to the people of [Lefkada]."[95] Yiankos concludes by asking Ali Pasha to write him as soon as possible and explain what exactly *was* going on in Preveza, so that he would be better prepared the next time Porte officials came around asking questions.

It is important to note that Yiankos insisted that Ali Pasha was only carrying out extensive repairs on a much earlier fortress that *was already there*, not constructing a completely new fortification. According to the 1718 Treaty of Passarowitz, which the Ottomans agreed to uphold when they established the Septinsular Republic and Confederation of Continental Cities, any construction of a new fortress on the shore of the mainland was strictly forbidden.[96] It is equally important to note that Yiankos was lying—there is no sign of an earlier fortress on the Aktion peninsula in earlier Venetian maps and *vedute*, or even in a French map produced just before the Fortress of Aktion first appears in Ali Pasha's chancery.[97] This fortification therefore appears to have been a new construction, in violation of the recently signed agreement between the Ottomans and Russians.

These treaties were far more than just symbolic documents, signed and then thrown into a cupboard to be forgotten. Ali Pasha, for one, apparently knew these texts by heart. In 1806, for example, there was an incident in which one of the governor's vessels was stopped off the coast of Corfu by Russian officials. In subsequent exchanges, Ali Pasha and the Russians descended into pedantic arguments over the precise terminology of a specific section of the Ottoman-Russian treaty: Ali Pasha agreed that Article 7 forbade "armed vessels," whereas his ship was simply *transporting* guns to Porto Palermo.[98] The British consul to Ioannina, William Meyer, would later complain about Ali Pasha's refusal to abide by the rules of engagement:

> His Highness has chosen to act upon principles peculiar to himself. When it suited his purpose, he utterly disregarded the spirit and the letter of treaties which forbad the erection of forts on the Turkish coasts within a league of the sea, and he erected them in the most offensive situations in defiance of all remonstrances against it. . . . In explanation of such proceedings we are

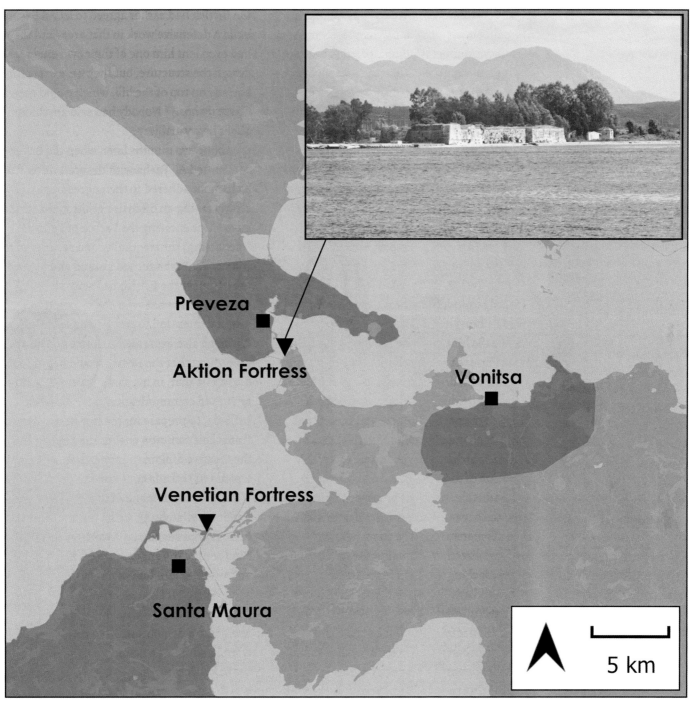

FIGURE 49
Map showing the location of the Aktion Fortress in relation to the territory of the Septinsular Republic and Confederation of Continental Cities in 1801. Map by Matthew J. Jacobson.

told that these ports and places are His Highnesses own conquests, and do not come under the operation of existing treaties, the stipulations of which are inconsiderably looked upon as concessions extorted from weakness and ignorance.[99]

Only a few years after Ali Pasha undertook military works on the Aktion peninsula, Istanbul addressed a memorandum to the governor stressing that because the people of the Septinsular Republic were under Ottoman protection, it was his duty to respect and ensure the security and "repose" (istirâhat) of the sultan's "subjects" (re'âyâ) in Lefkada—as if he needed a special reminder that he was not to provoke anxiety among his neighbors.[100] Ali Pasha did not take the hint. After he finally claimed the city of Preveza for himself in 1806, the governor spent the next decade constructing no fewer than six individual fortifications that both defended the port at Preveza and monitored the water channels leading into the port at Lefkada, which by then had come under the protection of the British.

One fortification that prompted a transimperial clash was the Tekes Fort, located about three kilometers from the town of Lefkada itself and directly threatening the water channel approaching the town from the north (see figs. 40 and 47). In May 1810, a Colonel Lowe stationed in Lefkada wrote to the British high commissioner in Corfu that he had observed several men carrying out work "at the old castle which lies opposite" the port. Colonel Lowe reported that two thousand workmen were rumored to be employed there and that the new fort was supposed to be outfitted for twenty pieces of cannon: "it is the vizier's intention to have it completed six weeks from hence."[101] Further internal correspondence indicates that the British had earlier agreed to let Ali Pasha build a defensive work in that area, and they had even lent him one of their own engineers to design the structure, but they were expecting a barrack on top of the hill, which would merely house troops.[102] Nobody had said anything about heavy artillery.

About two months later, when the British confronted Ali Pasha with the accusation that he had not adhered to their agreement and was clearly taking an offensive position that threatened ships entering the harbor of Lefkada, "menac[ing] the tranquility and security of that island," Ali Pasha turned around and blamed the engineer the British had sent, claiming that he was the one who had deviated from the original intention to erect a simple barrack. Ali Pasha also expressed surprise and disappointment that the British would begrudge him a fort that, in his view, "secure[d] an uninterrupted communication" with his allies on Lefkada, to prepare for the impending attack from their common enemy, the French. Despite the creative diplomatic acrobatics, a General Oswald in Lefkada continued to press the issue. When Oswald demanded that the construction halt immediately, Ali Pasha responded that he could not suspend the work, as this would "undermine the appearance of their friendship, and would injure him to public opinion as well as the Porte." If General Oswald wanted the structure to come down, Ali Pasha would only recognize a demolition order coming straight from London. As evidenced by the presence of the Tekes Fort on the ground today, the general decided not to insist on the matter, and "the works . . . continued with extraordinary diligence."[103]

In the State Ottoman Archives in Istanbul, there is a striking absence of documentation regarding the construction of Ali

Pasha's fortifications. This lacuna is especially noticeable given the abundance of records that appear after Ali Pasha's death and describe the continuous efforts on behalf of the Porte to repair these structures.[104] This silence in the archives suggests that Ali Pasha was constructing these military works "off the grid," organizing the building of fortifications with his own funding, men, and materials—and documents from Ali Pasha's chancery confirm that this was definitely the case. Such an arrangement was hardly uncommon in this period; Istanbul often encouraged local notables to contribute to the costs of construction and maintenance of fortresses under their jurisdiction.[105] But Ali Pasha's building activities are significant because they reveal Istanbul's lack of concern about, or even knowledge of, these structures—until, of course, people started to complain about them. In 1810, the French consul Pouqueville protested to Istanbul that Ali Pasha was conspiring with the British to seize the island of Lefkada. Süleyman Efendi, one of Ali Pasha's agents in the capital, reported that the Porte had rejected this claim and insisted that nothing of the sort was going on.[106] Yet, as can be seen from the episode at Tekes and additional diplomatic correspondence in the British archives, Ali Pasha was indeed trying to enlist the British to help him win the island for himself.[107]

The vizier's staunch independence and his tendency to act first and ask for forgiveness later stand in contrast to the picture we have of military architecture in the Ottoman Empire. Recent scholarship presents compelling evidence, primarily through the examination of Ottoman repair registers (*tâ'mîrât defterleri*), that the center exercised a great deal of control and care in decision making about fortress construction and repair projects, to a degree that some have described as "micromanagement."[108] This emphasis on a competent top-down model of patronage is best understood as a corrective to the long-standing view—frequently rehearsed in the abundant literature on Western European fortifications—that the Ottomans were inept in the construction of defensive works.[109] Ali Pasha's program of military architecture adds nuance to our understanding of the precise mechanisms surrounding the process of building or repairing a fortress in the Ottoman Empire. If anything, the construction of fortifications beyond the direct management of Istanbul serves as the exception that proves the rule. When summoned by Ali Pasha to build fortifications at Preveza, Captain Ponceton wrote that he felt a great deal of anxiety about the mission because his team was "unsure in being considered favorably by the authorities, as they had no *firman* [order] from the Ottoman court, which was at a considerable distance from the confines of the Vizier Ali Pasha's country."[110] This statement implies that Ali Pasha's inviting French engineers to construct defensive works in his territory without permission from Istanbul may have fallen outside established norms for building a fortress within the Ottoman Empire.

The construction of fortifications as a potential source of conflict between center and periphery points to the related issue of internecine tensions between rival governors, which state officials in this period often sought to quell for fear that the situation could explode beyond their control. While the Porte tended to support Ali Pasha in his suppression of rebellious mountain communities like Souli, missives from Istanbul condemned in the harshest terms his long-standing rivalry with his counterparts to the north, Mustafa Pasha of Delvina and İbrahim Pasha of Berat.[111]

As part of these rivalries, acquiring artillery was a pressing concern in efforts to ensure that the fortresses continued to deter potential attackers. While there is documentation that the Porte provided Ali Pasha with guns, there is also ample evidence that the vizier was remarkably self-sufficient in amassing the firepower he needed for his new military constructions on the coast.[112] For example, the governor established a foundry for this purpose in Bunila, a village just southwest of Ioannina.[113] In a letter dated 1801, Athanasios Psalidas—primarily known today as a luminary of the Greek Enlightenment but also an agent of Ali Pasha's court—wrote Ali Pasha from Corfu after being sent there to acquire military supplies for the newly constructed fortress at Butrint.[114] He reported that he had purchased four nice cannons of seven-pound caliber, one hundred cannonballs, thirty sacks of grapeshot, and a pile of hand grenades. As for the gunpowder, Psalidas gloated that he managed to outbid not only Ali Pasha's rivals in Souli and Parga but also the men representing Mustafa Pasha in Delvina, "who are mad at me because they were not able to take even a third" of the powder. This document is remarkable in revealing that, at the turn of the century, Corfu was operating as an open arms market where military supplies went to the highest bidder. What Psalidas describes is a situation in which agents from opposing sides (the rebel communities of Souli and Parga against Ali Pasha) were competing shoulder to shoulder for artillery. It is also interesting that men sent by Mustafa Pasha, Ali Pasha's neighbor to the north, were also in Corfu vying for a share of the supplies, especially as both pashas were nominally in the service of the sultan and presumably would not have to fight over weapons and materials if they were united in the goal of defending the frontier.

There is evidence, however, that when it suited him, Ali Pasha occasionally chose to participate in the more centralized system of fort construction and maintenance, whereby Istanbul maintained direct oversight on projects by sending construction supervisors (*binâ' emîni*) and keeping official building and repair (*tamirat*) registers.[115] This was the case at Nafpaktos, the only coastal fortress in Ali Pasha's territory that regularly appears in the *tamirat* registers now kept at the Ottoman archives.[116] In 1807, Ali Pasha's son Muhtar sent a report to his father from Nafpaktos stating that the fortress was in desperate need of repair. Muhtar believed that the regular workmen at his disposal would not be capable of executing the necessary renovations in a satisfactory manner, so he requested permission from his father to contact the Porte, which he referred to as "the state" (*ντεβλέτη*, *devleti*), and to ask for a *bina emini* to come and supervise the project.[117] Perhaps Muhtar Pasha felt comfortable reaching out to Istanbul in the case of Nafpaktos, as this site belonged to the canonical list of fortresses that the Porte had maintained for centuries in the defense of the empire. That the Antirrio *kastro* continued to be of interest to the Porte could be due to Ottomans' long memory of Lepanto. The site also guarded the entrance to the Gulf of Corinth, which the Ottomans were legitimately concerned could be breached by the French and would open an opportunity to invade the Aegean and, by extension, Istanbul itself. It seems, however, that even if an official was brought from Istanbul, the local governors were still expected to foot the bill. An 1801 petition to Istanbul requests that Ali Pasha be permitted to pay in installments the expenses of the *bina emini* sent to oversee repairs at the citadel and coastal fortress at Nafpaktos.[118] As for the rest of Ali Pasha's fortifications, the governor was left to his own devices.

Ali Pasha and his network of administrators therefore effectively managed the logistics of multiple large-scale construction projects that can perhaps best be understood as subimperial. In other words, these military works were executed outside any oversight or financial support from Istanbul. As has been seen, this more independent and localized style of architectural patronage at times became a source of friction with both the Porte and Ali Pasha's transimperial neighbors on the Ionian Islands. The governor was always testing the boundaries of decorum, which led to an uneasy relationship with Istanbul at best. Military architecture—and all the fraught negotiations surrounding it—is a particularly fruitful area in which to measure the precise nature of a particular actor's political stratagems. Ali Pasha's claim on the western coast of Epirus throws into question any portrayal of the governor as a dutiful defender of the Ottoman state.[119] If anything, these structures openly served Ali Pasha's self-aggrandizement and his ultimate mission to expand his territory and capture the seven Ionian Islands once and for all. One of the most important aspects of these fortifications, especially when it comes to the political conflict they provoked, is that they are not easy to explain away. Buildings are stubbornly material—striking evidence of a patron's ambitions and the situation as it unfolded on the ground.

MILITARY FORTIFICATIONS AS SPECTACLE

After Ali Pasha had gained full control of Preveza, visitors who entered the port were confronted by a large sailing vessel that was permanently moored in front of the town. Originally a gunboat that the governor had purchased from the British, the ship was outfitted with a set of eighteen cannon, their yawning mouths facing all who approached.[120] At first glance, this ship was no doubt impressive, even intimidating, a testament to Ali Pasha's ability to navigate and protect his maritime assets. Yet further inspection would reveal rigging that was half-decayed; none of this equipment was being maintained, and it had probably not been moved for years. Furthermore, the channel leading into the Preveza harbor was treacherously shallow, in some places only three to five meters deep.[121] In order to be moved from its position out into the wider sea, this ship would have had to have all its guns removed just in order to clear the strait—hardly a practical or convenient tactical maneuver.

Ali Pasha's corvette at Preveza functioned like theater scenery, a set piece that was visually convincing but could never ultimately deliver on the promise made by its appearance. The governor's coastal fortifications can be seen as functioning in a similar way. In their travel accounts, Western European visitors to the governor's realm—many of them specialists in war technology and military architecture—frequently found these structures lacking in effectiveness, citing their bad design and poor construction. These Europeans usually found fortresses not designed or maintained to optimal operational potential deeply frustrating. When Thomas Hughes toured the Fortress of Agios Georgios in Preveza, he recounted that Colonel Vaudoncourt was entrusted with this commission, "who complains bitterly of the pasha's avarice, which interrupted all his plans, until he was obliged to yield implicitly to the suggestions of a semi-barbarian, and build works for shew rather than resistance."[122]

I would like to turn this critique of building for show on its head and suggest that Ali Pasha was deeply cognizant of the performative power of military construction. Instead of simply accepting "resistance" as the single criterion by which successful military architecture is measured, what if building forts "for shew" was considered not an inherent flaw but a strategy in and of itself? In this chapter I have emphasized the importance of the sightlines of these fortifications, i.e., what the soldiers of a garrison could see and who in turn could see them. While the notion of a building designed to anticipate spectators is more commonly found in scholarship examining spaces of ceremony and ritual, such as palaces and religious architecture, the questions of audience and long-range visibility are crucial in understanding Ali Pasha's coastal fortifications and how they worked.[123] In the case of Butrint, Parga, and Preveza, these fortifications sat within one or two kilometers of properties that the governor had ambitions to acquire. From this perspective, the primary function of these installations was to intimidate the people living in the ex-Venetian territories on the mainland and the Ionian Islands, a form of psychological warfare intended to create feelings of anxiety among the inhabitants and their foreign administrators. As mentioned above, the governor relied on rumors, and even on public ceremonies marking the commencement of a fort's construction, to generate fear among his neighbors. In multiple cases, even the mere sight of Ali Pasha's workmen busily working on batteries and forts across the water was sufficient to provoke protest. In a way, it does not really matter how technologically advanced these structures were—what mattered was how they looked. One of the most interesting aspects of the second type of masonry style that appears in some of Ali Pasha's fortifications, described above, such as the Tekes Fort opposite Lefkada, is that the workers attempted to imitate the first type of masonry style by covering the curtain walls built of irregular fieldstones with a layer of plaster and tracing lines into the material while it was still wet, creating a trompe l'oeil effect that gave the illusion of regular courses of cut blocks (see fig. 47). From the deck of a ship sailing into the port of Lefkada, the Tekes Fort would have appeared convincingly on brand as one of Ali Pasha's fortifications, a silent sentinel reminding the vizier's neighbors of his omnipresent gaze. This was architecture as antagonistic spectacle.

For Ali Pasha, there was certainly a prestige factor in being able to boast of his access to the best specialized knowledge available in artillery and fort building. By the end of the eighteenth century, expertise in military engineering, especially in the tradition of Sébastien Le Prestre de Vauban (1633–1707), was highly prized throughout Europe and the Eastern Mediterranean.[124] Yet, as explained above, Ali Pasha already had his own firm conception of what a modern, Vaubanesque fortification should be, and, most significantly, what it should look like. In the back-and-forth with Vaudoncourt over the designs for the Agios Georgios Fortress in Preveza, the views of the vizier clashed with this hired consultant when Vaudoncourt's proposal—although technically sound—proved to be visually underwhelming. Again, upon seeing the designs, Ali Pasha disapproved of the fortress's being set so far back from the sea, and of its not having "square towers" (*tours quarrés*). At the time, the other major coastal fortifications under the governor's control like at Aktion and Porto Palermo were all defined by symmetrical, geometric layouts. When Ali Pasha first saw the irregular curves of the Agios Georgios Fortress on paper, therefore, this plan did not meet his expectations. It is interesting to note that the Pantocrator Fortress, built several years later just down the beach from Agios Georgios, follows the criteria that Ali Pasha originally demanded for Agios Georgios: a geometric (pentagonal) ground plan and a location directly on the beach. In the end, the governor found a way to get his dream fort built on the Preveza peninsula.

The construction of coastal fortresses, part of Ali Pasha's relentless pursuit of the Ionian Islands, reveals how architecture, especially military architecture, can work to expand geographic borders and thus potentially create new political realities. These fortifications also show the limits of imperial authority and undermine the assumption that the Porte was all-knowing when it came to the maintenance of the frontier. By design, the buildings were intended to convey multiple messages to a variety of audiences near and far: while the people of Lefkada were quite right to interpret Ali Pasha's construction of fortresses in Preveza as a hostile act, the vizier's agents in Istanbul reminded the Porte that it was his duty to defend the border. It was to the governor's distinct advantage to keep everyone guessing about his ultimate plans and motivations, and it seems paradoxical that something as concrete as stone and mortar could cause so much confusion. Ali Pasha's line of defensive works on the Ionian Sea served as icons of power, marking the liquid frontier, but the issue of exactly whose power these icons represented—that of the governor or of the sultan—ultimately remained fluid.

Building Local Support

PATRONAGE FOR MULTICONFESSIONAL COMMUNITIES

CHAPTER 3

Epirus, a geographic region that today is split in half by the national borders of Greece and Albania, was extremely diverse when it came under the administration of Ali Pasha in the late eighteenth century. As we can see from a map of the area produced just a few decades later, Muslims constituted a slight majority among the Albanian-speaking people to the north, while the Greek-speaking population further south maintained a stronger Orthodox Christian presence (fig. 50).[1] Yet, while the countryside was more homogenous in its religious makeup, all the major cities in Epirus maintained a more mixed population of Muslim, Christian, and Jewish neighborhoods. This map is an important document for several reasons. First, closer examination reveals that the central panel, representing the languages spoken in a particular area, does not overlap neatly with the inset map indicating religious confession—a visualization of the complex identities in the region under Ali Pasha's rule, when it was possible, for example, to be a Greek-speaking Muslim or an Albanian-speaking Christian. Second, the various delineations on the map do not correspond to present-day political borders. This was a time before emerging nationalist movements in the Balkans enforced the concept of a common ethnicity based on a single shared language and faith tradition. If we were to rely exclusively on the accounts of Western Europeans traveling in Ottoman lands, who tend to refer to Muslims as "Turks" and Christians as "Greeks," we would get the impression that this collapsing of nation and religion already applied in the days of Ali Pasha. Alternative sources like this map offer a clearer view of the characteristic syncretism of nineteenth-century Epirus, which was subsequently erased or silenced.[2]

In his role as provincial governor, Ali Pasha learned that in order to govern this territory effectively, he would need to be adept at accommodating the wide range of communities under his authority, from the urban class of Christian scribes and translators employed at his court to the Muslim mountain villagers who supplied troops for his frequent military incursions. In other words, rather than align himself exclusively with a particular group, Ali Pasha sought support from all sides. This strategy of cultivating a multiplicity of audiences is reflected in the vizier's direct patronage of an impressive spectrum of religious architecture throughout the region, from mosques to monasteries. In what follows, I reconstruct a "religioscape" of buildings that enjoyed the patronage of Ali Pasha and his family, whether through major structural repairs or pious endowments.[3] That this corpus of material includes Friday mosques, Sufi dervish lodges, and Orthodox churches is important

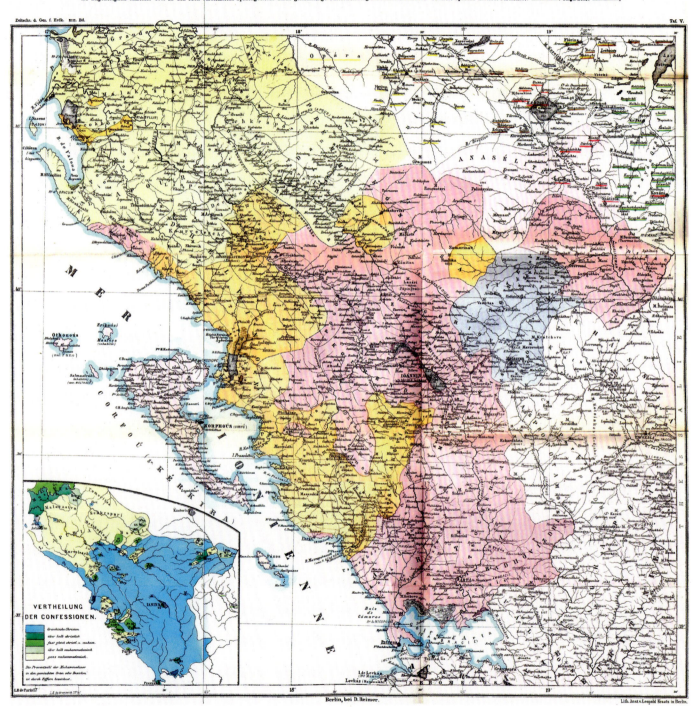

evidence of a revolutionary leadership style that appealed to the various confessional communities living under Ali Pasha's jurisdiction—another alternative archive that encourages a holistic approach to understanding Ottoman architecture writ large.

What of Ali Pasha's own religious views? It seems that the governor held beliefs that can be characterized as ambiguous, unorthodox, and flexible. He was raised as a Muslim and publicly identified as such, but many European travelers were quick to observe that Ali Pasha was not terribly fervent in his adherence to Sunni doctrine. William Martin Leake, after visiting the head shaykh (şeyh) of the dervish lodge constructed by the governor in Trikala, wrote:

> Though the [shaykh] did not very clearly explain his philosophy to me, he often used the word ἄνϑρωπος [anthropos, man] with some accompanying remark or significant gesture conveying a sentiment of the equality of mankind. The Vezír [Ali Pasha], although no practical encourager of liberty and equality, finds the religious doctrines of the Bektashlí [order] exactly suited to him. At the time that Christianity was out of favour in France, he was in the habit of ridiculing religion and the immortality of the soul with his French prisoners; and he lately remarked to me, speaking of Mahomet, καί εγώ είμαι προφήτης στα Ιωάννινα: and I too am a prophet at Ioánnina.[4]

About fifteen years later, the British consul in Ioannina, William Meyer, reported to his superiors that as Ali Pasha faced the looming threat of being removed from his position by the Porte, he was considering converting to Christianity, ostensibly to draw Greek revolutionaries to his cause: "If all measures of a more regular nature should fail, the baptism of a great personage in this once Christian country is talked of, together with that of many of his adherents. Mahomet never had to deal perhaps with a set of greater freethinkers."[5] About a year after sending this dispatch, the sultan's men having arrived at the gates of Ioannina, Meyer reported again that the governor was occupied with "affect[ing] punctilious observance of the ceremonies of his religion," probably a reference to the namâz, or prayer, performed five times a day at prescribed times. These public demonstrations of Islamic faith became imperative when copies of letters to the vizier from Russian and Greek agents addressing him by the newly christened name of "Constantine" were intercepted by the sultan's men and "designedly introduced into [Ali Pasha's] garrison," resulting in a scandal among the Muslim soldiers.[6]

These anecdotes highlight the balancing act that Ali Pasha performed when dealing with different confessional communities. Despite the diverse makeup of the population, he did not usher in a golden age of multiculturalism, at least not in today's sense; any show of favor to one group could potentially incite the anxiety of another. The governor's widespread support of the various religious institutions that formed the nuclei of these communities thus does not necessarily suggest an idyllic or harmonious coexistence among them. What this collection of buildings *does* suggest is the role of rumor and gossip in maintaining order during a time of political uncertainty. It is important to observe that while Ali Pasha's mosques and dervish lodges tended to be situated in the main urban centers under his control, the two known cases of churches funded directly by the governor and his family were located in

FIGURE 50 (*opposite*) An ethnographic map of Epirus organized according to language (*central map*) and religion (*inset*). In the central map, areas are indicated as predominantly Albanian-speaking (*light yellow*), Greek-speaking (*pink*), and a mixture of both (*dark yellow*). In the inset, while the mountains and plains of the countryside are labeled as either predominantly Orthodox Christian (*blue*) or Muslim (*yellow*), urban centers and their immediate hinterlands are represented as spots of green, indicating that these areas are split almost equally between Christians and Muslims. Map by H. Kiepert, 1878. The National Archives, London.

relatively remote places, unlikely to be visited by local Muslim elites or representatives from Istanbul. Much like the coastal fortifications discussed in the previous chapter, the distant locations of these churches offered the governor a degree of plausible deniability. Rumors are powerful precisely because they are unstable.

That Ali Pasha's Islamic and Christian foundations were not geographically near each other meant that the vizier could keep all major stakeholders guessing where his true loyalties lay. The governor thus demonstrated an exceptional ability to calibrate his actions according to the strengths, motivations, and aspirations of his subjects. Both the buildings themselves and the political capital they generated ultimately had very real material effects, such as military backing. A local folk ballad composed shortly after Ali Pasha's death marvels at how both Muslim and Christian notables from all over Epirus, including the vizier's longtime adversaries from Souli, banded together to send soldiers to Ioannina and assist the governor in thwarting the sultan's troops, who had overrun the country: "with one heart, they began to strike the [Ottoman] army fiercely from all directions."[7] In the revolt against the sultan, the people of the region easily set aside the issue of creed.[8]

Before the Tanzimat reforms of the mid-nineteenth century, religious foundations constituted the social core of the Ottoman Empire. Blurring today's distinction between sacred and secular, pious institutions not only provided space for people to gather and worship but also formed the basis of leadership for various communities and dispensed essential social services like education, legal arbitration, and care for the poor. An examination of the religious institutions that benefited from Ali Pasha's patronage challenges the trope of the tyrant who achieves results through sheer force of will, which is frequently rehearsed in the historical literature on the vizier. As I argue in chapter 4, while the threat of violent retribution and the governor's personal charisma certainly played a role in his administration, tracing how Ali Pasha invested in different kinds of religious architecture demonstrates that his success also depended on securing the financial, political, and military support of the various religious communities of the region.

FRIDAY MOSQUE COMPLEXES

Although Ali Pasha was not known for his piety, he sought to capitalize on the symbolic importance of constructing Friday mosque complexes within the Ottoman context in which he operated. In doing so, he followed a long-established practice of the Ottoman ruling elite, who, as architectural historian Howard Crane notes, built mosques to serve as "ever present reminders of the majesty and power of their imperial founders" and to bear witness to the "ideals and ideology by which Ottoman society and the Ottoman polity lived."[9] In the sixteenth century, under the reign of Süleyman I, imperial legitimacy was based first and foremost on strict adherence to Sunni-Hanafi doctrine, and this cultural climate encouraged courtiers to focus their patronage efforts on Friday mosques, in both Istanbul and the provinces.[10]

Looking more broadly at Ali Pasha's peers across the empire—i.e., the *ayan* class of provincial governors who rose to prominence at the end of the eighteenth century—commissioning congregational mosques in their respective capital cities became one of the most effective means of announcing their administrative capabilities. As mentioned in

FIGURE 51
Postcard showing the Mosque of Mehmed Ali Pasha on the Cairo Citadel, contrasted with Mamluk-era tombs and minarets in the foreground, early twentieth century. Courtesy of Special Collections, Fine Arts Library, Harvard University.

the introduction, in the case of the Çapanoğlu clan in central Anatolia, the construction of a Friday mosque in 1779 at the clan's ruling seat in Yozgat was part of a larger urban development project, transforming what had been a family village into a town of consequence practically overnight (see fig. 7).[11] In the subsequent decades, members of the Çapanoğlu retinue such as the *vekîlharc* (chief steward, majordomo) and *başçavuş* (local Janissary leader) continued this urbanization initiative by commissioning their own, smaller mosques in close proximity to the central dynastic foundation.[12] Another notable example of religious architecture among the provincial adminstrators can be seen at the Citadel of Cairo, with construction of the Friday mosque of Mehmed Ali Pasha initially begun in 1828 (fig. 51).[13] In stark visual contrast to the earlier Mamluk funerary complexes that had come to define Cairo's urban landscape, Mehmed Ali Pasha's mosque adopts an architectural vocabulary that recalls Ottoman Istanbul, especially in its cascading domes and pencil minarets. In this case, however, citing the sultan's architecture did not necessarily translate into political fealty. As the architectural historian Mohammad al-Asad observes, "Ironically, it was the governor who most aggressively sought Egypt's independence from Istanbul who also provided Cairo with its most Ottomanized structure."[14] In 1831, just as construction for his mosque got under way, Mehmed Ali Pasha directed his son to invade Syria, an action that launched an almost decade-long war with the Porte and concluded with his family's being granted autonomous rule over Egypt.

Against this backdrop, Ali Pasha laid claim to several Friday mosques in most of the major cities within his territory. Ali Pasha's son Veli

BUILDING LOCAL SUPPORT   105

Pasha likewise emerged as a patron of mosque complexes, creating a charitable foundation directly adjacent to his own palace in Ioannina, which contained not only a Friday mosque but also a *medrese* and a library, the only institution of its kind in the region.[15] In their construction of these prominent urban mosques, supported by pious foundations (*vakıf*) that funded accompanying charitable services, Ali Pasha and his son were to some extent fulfilling what was expected of any Ottoman administrator of their rank. In comparison with his predecessors and contemporaries, however, the vizier oversaw a rather large geographic region for a long period of time, more than thirty years. He was therefore able to channel his energy and wealth into not one but several Friday mosque complexes. Beyond these larger foundations, Ali Pasha was responsible for the construction of several smaller village mosques, often attached to dervish lodges, as I discuss below. In a few notable cases, the governor ordered the conversion of churches into mosques for the specific purpose of declaring his victory over communities that had once staged resistance to his direct authority, as can be seen during his war against the mountain enclave of Souli.[16] Ali Pasha's dedication to building Friday mosques was thus one of his clearest efforts to leave his mark throughout the territory under his jurisdiction.

Because Ioannina served as his primary seat of power, one would expect the governor to have prioritized the construction of a Friday mosque in the city—a clear declaration of his political ascendance. Ali Pasha did pursue such a project, but rather than build an entirely new foundation, he seems to have appropriated a preexisting monument: the Fethiye Mosque, a small but striking structure prominently located in the town's citadel (fig. 52). In Ali Pasha's time, visitors arriving in Ioannina along the main roads were greeted by the city's iconic silhouette of massive fortification walls rising from the lake, with twin promontories crowned by the domes and minarets of the Arslan Pasha Mosque to the north and the Fethiye to the south (see fig. 2). Although these two mosques resemble each other in terms of materials and layout, more than 150 years separate their construction. While the Arslan Pasha Mosque was commissioned in the early seventeenth century by the governor of the same name, many scholars attribute the Fethiye as it stands today to the patronage of Ali Pasha, claiming that he ordered the rebuilding of the mosque early in his career as part of the creation of his central palace complex (see fig. 14, no. 6).[17] Some epigraphic evidence presented below, however, suggests that the most recent iteration of the Fethiye Mosque was constructed just before Ali Pasha's rule and was then taken over by the vizier, to be incorporated in his palace in Ioannina's inner citadel. In any case, Ali Pasha would soon thereafter go on to emulate the Fethiye by situating new mosques of similar design in prominent urban locations throughout his territory. By creating a recognizable formal typology of religious architecture, the governor was engaging with an established tradition of local mosque construction and positioning himself as the rightful heir to the administrators who had come before him.

The Fethiye Mosque sits on a site that has undergone several transformations over the centuries. Ali Pasha's total occupation of the southwest promontory of the walled city in Ioannina was significant not only because, as discussed in chapter 1, he consolidated the roles of the administrative and military into a single geographic area, but also because of the longer history of this location during the Despotate and early Ottoman periods. In other

FIGURE 52
The Fethiye Mosque in the southeastern citadel of Ioannina. Photo by author.

words, Ali Pasha focused on reviving a zone in the city that had long been designated a locus of power, building upon the accretions of previous monuments and settlements. In the thirteenth century, after Ioannina had become independent from Byzantium as part of the new Despotate of Epirus in the wake of the Fourth Crusade, this citadel area served as the acropolis, where the wealthy notables built their houses and worshipped at the metropolitan church dedicated to the archangel Michael.[18] Yet the transition from metropolitan church to congregational mosque took place only several centuries after the Ottoman conquest of Ioannina. When the Ottomans first took the town in 1430, they granted certain freedoms to the local population, as the inhabitants had capitulated without resistance. These freedoms included the right to continue residing within the city walls and the guarantee that their houses of worship would not be converted into mosques. The Cathedral of the Archangel Michael, therefore, continued to serve the Christians of Ioannina, who, as sixteenth-century Ottoman tax registers attest, outnumbered the newly arrived Muslim inhabitants.[19] The first Muslim neighborhood (*maḥalle*) was in fact located extra muros in the market area. The mosque built there, said to have been founded by Sultan Bayezid II (d. 1512) at the end of the fifteenth century, became the center of religious life for the Muslim community in Ioannina.[20]

It was only around the end of the sixteenth century that the metropolitan cathedral was converted into a mosque, and the building was first dubbed the Fethiye, or "Mosque of the Conquest."[21] While many scholars cite this conversion as a direct consequence of a local bloody uprising in 1611 led by the bishop of Trikala, more recent studies have pushed back the moment of transition slightly earlier, based on a source that dates the mosque's foundation around 1596–97.[22]

At any rate, the push to wrest the citadel from the Christian population was the first sign of turbulent times. The revolt two decades later, in 1611, resulted in the sultan issuing a series of orders that withdrew the remaining special privileges for the Christians of Ioannina, and from that point forward only Muslims and Jews were permitted to live within the city walls.[23] This decision dramatically reconfigured the geographic dynamics of the city in a very short period of time. All Christian families left the citadel, and the Muslims, who had previously been concentrated in the market area beyond the walls, arrived to occupy the abandoned houses. It was also around this time, in 1618, that the Ottoman governor Arslan Pasha ordered that his own mosque complex be constructed in the northeastern promontory of the lake, on the former site of the monastery dedicated to John the Baptist.[24] Thus it was not until the beginning of the seventeenth century that Ioannina's famous profile of the two mosques crowning the city above the lake took shape.

When Ali Pasha arrived in Ioannina in 1788 to take up the position of governor, he inherited a situation in which the Ottoman ruling elites had already based their sites of authority—the palace and the Friday mosque—within the walled city for almost two hundred years. It seems that just before he arrived, however, the Fethiye had undergone a major metamorphosis in its architectural fabric. According to an account by Kosmas Balanos, the scion of one of the families leading the Greek Enlightenment movement in Ioannina, the building and decorations of the metropolitan church had largely been left intact when it was originally

FIGURE 53
Plaque with an inscription recording the late eighteenth-century renovation of the Fethiye Mosque in Ioannina. Photo by author.

converted into a mosque in the seventeenth century, the only major changes being the addition of a minaret and the necessary accoutrements (mihrab, minbar, etc.). This was how things stood until 1770, when the Ottoman authorities, for reasons unknown, decided to raze the structure to its foundations.[25] Again, most scholars posit that Ali Pasha rebuilt the mosque around 1795, when he was said to have been working on his palace complex in the citadel, leaving a twenty-five-year period when the site would presumably have been vacant.

An inscription on the exterior of the Fethiye Mosque, however, suggests otherwise. It appears on a stone plaque embedded in the northwest corner of the minaret base, above a rudimentary representation of an Ottoman mosque (fig. 53). Located between the pencil minarets of this mosque, the text reads "in the year 1 Muharram 1190 [H]," corresponding to February 21, 1776. This is probably the date when the mosque's restoration was commemorated, because it is an auspicious day (the first of the Muslim calendar year), and the inscription is accompanied by the image of the mosque and the seal of Solomon. If this inscription does give the date of the restoration, then the reconstruction of the mosque was initiated shortly after its destruction in 1770, and more than a decade before Ali Pasha's arrival in 1788. Additionally, the interior decoration of the Fethiye Mosque, which, as I explain below, was executed by a group of craftsmen who had refurbished a church in the same region in 1778, places the main structure of the mosque squarely within the 1776 reconstruction date. In sum, we know that a structure originally built in the medieval period as

FIGURE 54
Mausoleum at the Arslan Pasha Mosque in Ioannina. Photo by author.

a church stood on the Ioannina citadel until it was demolished in 1770, and that it was rebuilt shortly thereafter. When Ali Pasha arrived in the city, he opted to lay claim to the entire citadel area, including its mosque, and incorporated the building into his new palace complex. As explained in chapter 1, the palace was built all around the mosque, looking onto a central open courtyard space that formed a nexus of military, political, and religious power.

The Fethiye quickly became synonymous with Ali Pasha and his household. In Ottoman documents dated after the governor's rule, the mosque is often associated with the name of Ali Pasha, instead of its earlier designation, "Fethiye."[26] The most concrete expression of Ali Pasha's effort to affiliate himself with this mosque was the addition of an open-air mausoleum intended for the vizier and his family, situated adjacent to the front entrance of the building (see fig. 52 and fig. 14, no. 7). Accentuated by an elegantly wrought iron covering, a testament to the skill of Ioannina's famous metalworkers, this funerary monument seems to have been constructed in the first decade of the nineteenth century upon the death of Ali Pasha's Muslim wife, Ümmülgüsüm Hanım, the mother of his sons Veli and Muhtar Pasha.[27] The establishment of this family mausoleum follows a local precedent set by the Arslan Pasha Mosque on the northeast promontory of the citadel, which includes a separate stone *türbe* (mausoleum) for the founder located behind the qibla wall (fig. 54).[28] When Thomas Hughes visited Ioannina in 1813, he reported seeing the Fethiye Mosque and Ali Pasha's mausoleum as part of his tour of the palace after his audience with the governor: "We proceeded to the south-west corner of the castron where a large mosque, appropriated to the serai, stands upon the site of the most ancient church of Ioannina: near it is a large tomb surrounded by an iron railing, wherein repose the ashes of one of Ali Pasha's wives, the mother of Mouchtar Pasha, a woman whose character was universally respected and who is still spoken of in terms of the highest admiration."[29] In establishing in the Ioannina citadel the final resting place of his wife and the mother of his two eldest sons, Ali Pasha thus co-opted the preexisting Fethiye Mosque and recast it as a dynastic monument.

This early initiative to map the governor's legacy onto an older Ottoman monument in Ioannina was soon followed by the construction of several new mosques throughout the region. The Fethiye in Ioannina became the template for Ali Pasha's subsequent mosque-building activities, most notably in the cities of Tepelena and Preveza. Like the Fethiye, the central congregational mosque that Ali Pasha constructed

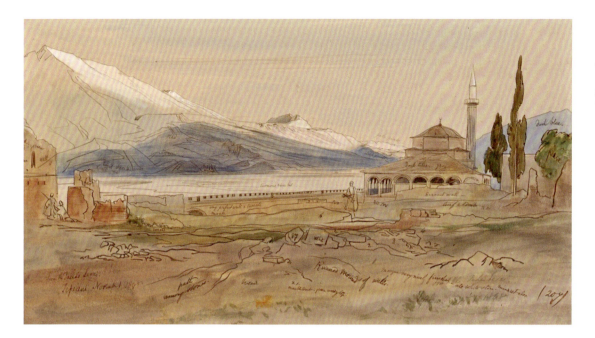

FIGURE 55
Edward Lear, *View of the Citadel of Tepelena* (from the northwest), 1848. Ink, pencil, and watercolor on paper, 26.2 × 47.1 cm. MS Typ 55.26, Houghton Library, Harvard University.

for the city of Tepelena was also located within the citadel.[30] The traveler John Hobhouse reported that he heard the call for prayer from the minaret "of the mosck attached to the palace."[31] Although we do not have a firm date for the construction of this building, there is a *terminus ante quem* of January 1805, when Leake visited the mosque complex, writing, "Adjoining to a mosque which he built near his palace some years since, is a garden, which was then laid out for him by a Frenchman. On the wall which bounds it toward the river three guns are mounted, and two small kiosks are built."[32] Leake's comments suggest that the mosque came slightly later than the palace grounds, placing its construction around 1803 or 1804, only a few years after Ali Pasha's development of his residential complex in the Ioannina citadel.

Ali Pasha's mosque in Tepelena no longer survives, but its general features can be surmised from a detailed drawing by the traveler Edward Lear (fig. 55). We can also conclude from this drawing that by the mid-nineteenth century, while Ali Pasha's palace had been largely reduced to a pile of rubble, the mosque was left intact in the aftermath of the pasha's demise.[33] The mosque itself consisted of a single dome sitting on an octagonal drum, transitioning to a square base. The structure was surrounded by an elevated colonnaded porch at least on the northwestern and northeastern sides, maintaining a vista toward the river and what had been the palace courtyard. Presumably, the main entrance would have been on the northwestern side, which is most prominent in the drawing, the interior mihrab placed at the opposite qibla wall facing southeast. A single minaret was originally tucked behind the porch. According to a note penciled by Lear directly onto his sketch, the entire structure was "very nicely finished—all white stone."

Looking across Ali Pasha's wide territory, the building in Tepelena greatly resembles in

BUILDING LOCAL SUPPORT 111

FIGURE 56
Early twentieth-century photograph of the Ali Pasha Mosque in Preveza. From Fotios Petsas, "Eidiseis ek tis 10is Archaiologikis Perifereias (Ipeirou)," *Archaiologiki Efimeris* 89–90 (1950–51): 32. Photo: Archaeological Society of Athens.

both scale and design another mosque built by the governor in the port of Preveza. In this case, the mosque was built within the walled settlement adjacent to the fort at Agios Andreas, where Ali Pasha initially took up residence in the city. Again, we do not have an exact date of construction, but it had to have been between 1806, when Ali Pasha finally took control of Preveza, and 1812, the earliest mention of the structure in both Ottoman and Western European documents.[34] Therefore, the Preveza mosque seems to postdate the one at Tepelena by a few years. Ali Pasha's mosque in Preveza also no longer survives, although it was still standing essentially intact until World War II, long enough for it to serve as the first site of the city's archaeological museum. According to a number of photographs included by Fotios Petsas in his 1950 article recounting the damage sustained by the building during the war, it is clear that the Preveza mosque employed virtually the same structural vocabulary as the mosque in Tepelena: a single dome on an octagonal drum (although in this case supported by four small external buttresses), a single minaret base positioned flush against the core structure to the right of the main entrance, and an arched colonnade that wraps around the building on all four sides (fig. 56).[35] Another photograph, of the interior of the mosque, indicates that above the main door was an arched structure supported by columns, a kind of loggia that can also be found in the Fethiye Mosque in Ioannina.

In both Tepelena and Preveza, Ali Pasha thus constructed mosques that share a remarkably similar design, despite the considerable distance between these two sites, about 150 kilometers as the crow flies. Keeping in mind the mobility of masonry specialists in the construction of the governor's military fortifications, it is probable that these monuments were erected by the same group of builders. Indeed, knowledge of how to construct the vaulting for the domes would have been restricted to only a select few in the region. Even though there is scant visual documentation for the mosques at Tepelena and Preveza, it is clear that—at least in terms of scale, materials, and basic structural elements—both follow a distinctively local type of mosque design emulated by the reconstructed Fethiye Mosque in Ioannina. And a comparison of the Fethiye and Arslan Pasha Mosques in the Ioannina citadel show that the central prayer halls of these two structures follow almost the exact same layout of a dome-on-square plan, with squinches transitioning to the dome and a gallery for women on the northwestern side (figs. 57 and 58).[36] This "local type" thus goes back at least to the seventeenth century.

In every large city in his territory, Ali Pasha endeavored to establish nodes of sovereignty

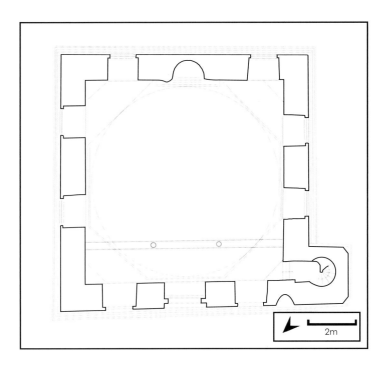
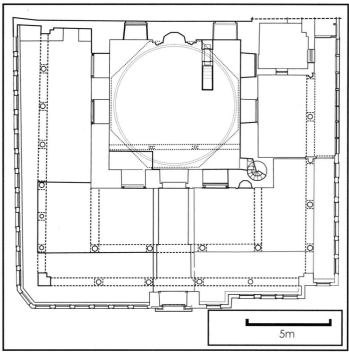

by building, or appropriating, mosque structures in a local style that was recognizable as "Epirote." We also know that he was supposed to have built a mosque for the district capital of Delvina, but unfortunately this building does not survive, and I have found no visual documentation that could assist in reconstructing its design.[37] Ali Pasha's decision to adhere to the well-established practice among Ottoman notables of mosque patronage, but deploying a more local style, serves as a barometer for his social and political relationship with the imperial center. Individuals who maintained closer ties with the court had both the incentive and the ability to use engineers or plans sent from the corps of royal architects in Istanbul. For example, during the construction of his family mosque in Safranbolu in 1794–98, the grand vizier İzzet Mehmet Pasha seems to have hired the stone carvers who were responsible for the decoration of the imperial Mosque of Beylerbeyi in Istanbul, constructed by Sultan Abdülhamid I in 1777–78, the connection made clear by a comparison of the two mihrabs (figs. 59 and 60). An older but more geographically proximate example is the Osman Shah Mosque in Trikala (fig. 61). Commissioned by the eponymous Osman, who was Sultan Süleyman's nephew and the longtime governor of the Trikala district, this sixteenth-century mosque was designed with plans sent by Mimar Sinan.[38] The Osman Shah Mosque fits into a wider corpus of Sinan's work that stretches across the empire, of the same genealogy as, say, the Selimiye Mosque in Konya.[39] Thus, unlike other governors or viziers who enjoyed closer connections with the imperial center, and thus access to the building knowledge of the corps of royal architects, Ali Pasha opted to favor groups of local Epirote architects who carried

FIGURE 57
The Fethiye Mosque in Ioannina. Plan by Lisa T. D. Backhouse. Adapted from Giorgos Smiris, "Ta mousoulmanika temeni ton Ioanninon kai i poleodomia tis Othmanikis polis," *Ipeirotika Chronika* 34 (2000): 89.

FIGURE 58
The Arslan Pasha Mosque in Ioannina. Plan by Lisa T. D. Backhouse. Adapted from Giannis Kanetakis, *To Kastro: Simvoli stin poleodomiki istoria ton Ioanninon* (Athens: Techniko Epimelitirio Elladas, 1994), 107.

BUILDING LOCAL SUPPORT   113

FIGURE 59
Mihrab of the İzzet Pasha Mosque in Safranbolu, Turkey. Photo by author.

FIGURE 60
Mihrab of the Beylerbeyi Mosque in Istanbul. Photo: Ünver Rüstem.

FIGURE 61
The Osman Shah Mosque in Trikala. Photo by author.

on in a style of mosque architecture that had been prevalent in the region for at least two centuries.

This was the case not only for the structural morphology of these mosques—all being of around the same size and consisting of a dome-on-square plan and wraparound arcaded porch—but also in terms of the placement of the buildings within the surrounding environment. Ali Pasha's mosques were sited in prominent locations, where the dome and minaret could be seen from miles away as a visitor approached the respective city. In this way, the governor mobilized the Fethiye into his own identifiable brand and claimed a new city as his own with his signature building style.

Veli Pasha followed in his father's footsteps in the construction of his own mosque complex, which was attached to his palace at the foot of the Litharitsa hill in Ioannina. Luckily, this mosque still stands today, although it is in need of restoration (fig. 62). A mid-nineteenth-century sketch of the mosque suggests that the building did not have an arched colonnade, like the mosques of Ali Pasha, but rather a lighter, double-level wooden vestibule wrapped around a three-dome stone porch serving as the main entrance (fig. 63). The wooden vestibule is long gone, and the masonry of the stone porch seems to have been remodified, probably part of a restoration from the late nineteenth or early twentieth century.[40] The structure can be first dated around 1804, the year a certificate of pious endowment was issued to the patron, around the same time that his father's mosque in Tepelena was being constructed.[41] Although Veli Pasha's mosque deviates slightly from the formal model seen in his father's mosque structures, it is still in line with the practice of establishing an urban mosque near or adjacent to a residential complex. With his own administrative appointments, Veli was clearly being prepared as the heir apparent to his father's vast territory and properties. It was only logical that he would leave his own mark and invest in a mosque complex for the city of Ioannina.

FIGURE 62
The Veli Pasha Mosque in Ioannina. Photo by author.

Ali Pasha's commissioning of mosques was not necessarily part of a personal conviction to assert the dominance of Islam in the region. The vizier was a pragmatic ruler and drew upon a recognizable language of power and good governance already established by such predecessors as Arslan Pasha. Still, Ali Pasha's construction of his mosque in Preveza, only a year or two after the fall of the Septinsular Republic, was certainly intended to send a clear message to the entirely Christian population that had for so long resisted the governor's sovereignty. William Leake notes a local tradition among the people of Preveza that directly blames the construction of Ali Pasha's mosque on the loss of a miraculous icon of Agios Charalambos during

FIGURE 63
Edward Lear, detail of *View of Ioannina*, 1849. Ink, pencil, and watercolor on paper, 26.6 × 48.8 cm. MS Typ 55.26, Houghton Library, Harvard University.

the 1798 siege of the city.[42] Meanwhile, an Ottoman document credits Ali Pasha with bringing the "people of Islam" (*ehl-i Islâm*) to Preveza and building them a mosque after defeating the Russians in the war of 1806–7.[43]

The construction of mosques through the establishment of pious endowments was also a way to provide basic services to the Muslim communities that congregated predominantly in the region's urban centers. Attached to the endowment of Veli Pasha's mosque were a *medrese* and a library.[44] The arches of the *medrese* can be seen clearly in the Lear drawing, and the building still survives, standing across from the main entrance of the mosque. Ali Pasha's mosque in Tepelena also had a *medrese* and *mekteb* (schoolhouse) associated with it, although it is not clear whether they were in the same proximity to the mosque building itself.[45] The mosque in Preveza was built on top of a spring and included a public fountain, which is the only element of the complex that can still be seen today. Thus an essential part of the rhetoric of power and sovereignty embodied in these mosques and their associated institutions was a promise of the governor's generosity and beneficence in caring for the needs of the Muslims residing in his various court cities.

SUFI TIES: CONSTRUCTING TEKKES

In addition to developing several congregational mosque complexes in all the cities within his territory, the governor also proved to be a prolific builder of dervish lodges (tekke) throughout Epirus and Thessaly. While the endowment of urban mosques and related charitable religious foundations was a common patronage activity among most provincial power holders in this period, there is not much concrete evidence that this *ayan* class constructed tekkes as a widespread phenomenon.[46] Ali Pasha's concerted effort to promote Sufi shaykhs and their local dervish communities thus seems to set him apart from his peers.

TABLE 1
Tekkes Sponsored by Ali Pasha and His Sons

Patron	Sufi Order	Location
Ali Pasha	Halveti-Sünbüli	Ioannina, south of city (Greece)
Muhtar Pasha	Halveti-Sünbüli	Ioannina, north of city (Greece)
Ali Pasha	Bektashi/Sa'di	Trikala, west of city (Greece)
Ali Pasha	Halveti	Preveza (Greece)
Ali Pasha	[unknown]	Hormova (Albania)
Ali Pasha	Sa'di	Tepelena (Albania)
Muhtar Pasha	Halveti	Gjirokaster (Albania)
Ali and Muhtar Pasha	[unknown]	Karbon (Albania)
Ali Pasha	Bektashi	Elbasan (Albania)
Ali Pasha	[unknown]	Ohrid (North Macedonia)

Looking primarily at Ottoman archival sources, it is possible to identify at least ten tekkes that enjoyed the direct patronage of either Ali Pasha or one of his sons, a significant number by any reckoning (table 1).[47] An examination of these various tekkes not only raises broader questions about the role of the dervish lodge within Ottoman cities but also specifically highlights Ali Pasha's attempts to secure the political support of the local Muslim population by building relationships with these Sufi orders.

In several cases, the governor sponsored a significant repair campaign or total reconstruction of an older lodge, rejuvenating institutions that had been languishing or were defunct. Thus Ali Pasha was not so much creating a new tradition of architectural patronage in the region as he was expanding upon an already established trend of local administrators' funding dervish communities. For an example, one need look no further than Ioannina, where a tekke belonging to the Nakshibendi order of dervishes was situated directly adjacent to the seventeenth-century Mosque of Arslan Pasha in the northern citadel.[48] In the Ottoman context, tekkes contributed to the social and political life of the empire even in the earliest periods, but it was only in the mid-fifteenth century that they became common features of the Ottoman landscape, in line with the flourishing of various *ṭarîḳât*, or mystical orders, such as the Bektashi or the Halveti.[49] Usually described in English as a dervish lodge, a tekke functioned primarily as a place for instruction in one of these Sufi orders, under the direction of a head dervish, the shaykh.[50] These lodges were also often associated with the grave of a notable holy person, some locations also serving as a shrine and pilgrimage site. Tekkes could also act as gathering spaces for the surrounding neighborhood or town, with male representatives from among the populace also belonging to the fraternity. Located both in cities and along caravan routes, tekkes were not only spiritual and community centers but also provided important social services, many operating as trading posts, soup kitchens for the poor, and roadside way stations. By the early nineteenth century, being the head of a tekke was considered to be a government position, and shaykhs were appointed by the state. In many cases, these appointment records are the only proof of Ali Pasha's patronage of a particular lodge.

While there is still a good amount of physical evidence that testifies to Ali Pasha's role as a great builder of fortresses and palaces, the material record remains overwhelmingly silent regarding his construction of tekkes. Virtually none of the dervish complexes that can be attributed to Ali Pasha and his family have survived, the one notable exception being the lodge located in the village of Hormova, discussed below. It is not surprising that of all of

Ali Pasha's building endeavors, his tekkes have fared the worst in terms of the survival of the building fabric. While congregational mosques are sturdy, monumental structures built of stone (and, as noted above, even those had a mixed survival rate), Ali Pasha's tekkes can be described more as vernacular architecture, resembling the local domestic edifices found in this region of the Balkans: low, two-story buildings with the ground floor built of rubble masonry and the second floor of lighter wood and plaster. Additionally, while a mosque can usually last for multiple generations, because any Muslim community requires a religious space in which to congregate, a tekke is more subject to the political or economic fate of individual shaykhs. These vernacular, domestic-like constructions can quickly become dilapidated without constant attention and repair. For a building to stand the test of time, it must remain relevant.

It is not just the tekkes sponsored by Ali Pasha that have vanished, and various political factors have contributed to the virtual disappearance of the tekke as a building type in this region. In the early twentieth century, the population exchange between Greece and Turkey led to the mass exodus of Muslim communities living in Greek territory, and the tekkes in northern Greece were abruptly abandoned in the 1920s.[51] Similarly, the rise of communism in Albania eventually led to the closing of all religious institutions—including tekkes— in the 1960s. Thus, by the middle of the twentieth century, these structures found on either side of the Greek-Albanian border had begun to deteriorate rapidly. For example, after the Treaty of Lausanne, the Durbalı Sultan Tekke, located outside the town of Farsala in Greece, was occupied by only a single dervish until his death in 1972.[52] While I found the cemetery and *türbe* there well tended (and, fascinatingly, bearing signs of both Sufi and Orthodox Christian worship), the adjacent walled living complex had fallen into complete ruin.

With so little of the physical remains of Ali Pasha's tekkes left, trying to reconstruct a clear picture of this aspect of the governor's patronage activity proves a challenging task. To track Ali Pasha's tekkes, I have relied primarily on *vakıf* records from the State Ottoman Archives in Istanbul and the archive of the Directorate General of Pious Foundations in Ankara.[53] In the now classic volume *Christianity and Islam Under the Sultans*, Frederick Hasluck associates Ali Pasha with several Bektashi tekkes, his assertions based mostly on traveler accounts and field interviews that he and his wife Margaret Hasluck conducted with dervishes in both Greece and Albania in the early twentieth century.[54] While it is fascinating for the study of twentieth-century nationalism that Ali Pasha's specific ties to the Bektashi order have emerged as a persistent idea in Albania, the question remains to what extent this oral tradition reflects the political and social landscape as it was in Ali Pasha's own day.[55] As can be seen from table 1, it seems that the governor and his family were in fact open to supporting dervishes representing multiple *tarikat*.

With so many buildings constructed by Ali Pasha in various stages of disrepair, information from the written record as a guide for conducting field surveys can be useful in reconstructing entire landscapes that have been lost. Ali Pasha's tekke and mosque complex in Hormova is an instructive example. I first became aware of this complex's existence thanks to a small note in an Ottoman document in Istanbul confirming the appointment of an imam to a mosque built by Ali Pasha in a place named "Ḥûrumva."[56] No such foundation had been mentioned in the secondary literature, and I conjectured that the register referred to Hormova, a small mountain village located between Tepelena and Gjirokaster. Several months later, I navigated the steep and windy road into the village square. Residents pointed me to a small tekke complex shaded by a large plane tree. The lodge consists of a community center suitable for hosting gatherings, with a large porch and fountain, a stone mosque in ruins, and a mausoleum. All the posted signage identifies the site as the final resting place of the local shaykh, Ali of Hormova (1902–1984), and makes no mention of Ali Pasha. Yet the accompanying mausoleum, which does indeed house the remains of Shaykh Ali of Hormova, also contains the grave of the imam who had been named in the Istanbul register, confirming that this complex was originally established by Ali Pasha. Thus, by evaluating the minutiae of bureaucratic state documents alongside the material record, the different historical layers of a built environment may be recovered.

While Ali Pasha's mainstream Sunni foundations, i.e., Friday mosque complexes, were typically found in city centers, most of his tekkes were situated in what could be described as extra-urban locations, outside the heart of a town but not so remote as to be practically inaccessible—as opposed, say, to the Orthodox monastic communities in Meteora or Mount Athos. Many lodges were located at the city gates, or on the side of the main road leading into a town. Even if a tekke no longer survives, archival records usually indicate the town or village in which it was located. Thus general observations can be made about the geographic distribution of these institutions throughout the territories under the administrative jurisdiction of Ali Pasha and his sons. Table 1 presents the approximate locations of the tekkes established by Ali Pasha, indicating that the governor and his family sponsored a lodge in every major town within his control: Ioannina, Preveza, Trikala, and Tepelena. Interestingly, there are two examples of Ali Pasha constructing a tekke in an area outside his immediate political reach (where neither he nor any of his family members served as the governor, or *mutasarrıf*), in the towns of Elbasan and Ohrid, both the seats of their respective provincial districts. In a handful of cases, tekkes were established in smaller, more remote locations, most notably in mountain villages near Tepelena.

In the governor's capital at Ioannina, the British traveler Thomas Hughes reported that the town had three tekkes in 1813, one of them located on the southern outskirts of the city.[57] The French consul François Pouqueville mentioned in his travel account that outside Ioannina was a *han* at "Pogoniani," as well as a tekke of dervishes.[58] The map of Ioannina produced by the French cartographer Jean-Denis Barbié du Bocage in 1820, which ultimately follows Pouqueville's description, shows this same tekke next to the *han*, off the side of the main southern road to Arta and Preveza (see fig. 13, no. 7). It seems that this lodge survived at least until the turn of the nineteenth century, as an 1899 Ottoman panorama of Ioannina offers a glimpse of the building (fig. 64). In this view, which was produced by placing a camera on a high hill west of the city, we see the southern quarter of Ioannina and the plains beyond. A small complex is located directly on the Preveza road that trails off into the distance, labeled a "Sünbüli dergâh." This tekke is probably the lodge commissioned by Ali Pasha for a Halveti order of dervishes in Ioannina (the Halvetis are a wider branch of Sufism that includes the Sünbüli order).[59] A document

FIGURE 64
A section of an Ottoman panoramic view of Ioannina looking south, 1899. BOA, Istanbul, FTG, photograph 5, from Yıldız Album YEE d. 404.

from the Ottoman archives dated about two years after the 1899 panorama mentions that Ali Pasha's Halveti tekke in Ioannina had fallen on hard times and required restoration, along with an injection of funds from the pious foundation treasury (*Hazine-i Evkâf*) in order to provide sufficient resources for the care of the poor who were coming to the lodge. The same document also describes this tekke as having undergone a "renewal effort" (*iḥyâ kerdesi*) on behalf of Ali Pasha, suggesting that some kind of lodge had already been on the site before the early nineteenth century and that Ali Pasha restored it.[60]

The other tekke in Ioannina built in the time of Ali Pasha was located on the opposite side of the city, at its northern gates. The traveler Henry Holland noted "a convent of Dervishes, shaded by trees," in the northern suburb of Ioannina, outside the walled city and situated along the lake.[61] On the 1820 Barbié du Bocage map, this tekke appears due east of Ali Pasha's large garden palace complex and located off the main road leading north out of the city (see fig. 13, no. 6). The French cartographer was unsure about the order of dervishes who resided there, labeling the building on the map a "Teké du Bektachi ou Heurlevis." Ottoman documents make clear that this tekke was a dervish lodge commissioned by Muhtar Pasha, one of Ali Pasha's sons, first endowed in 1806.[62] This tekke also appears in the 1899 Ottoman panorama, in which the building complex is labeled "Sünbüli dergâh," thus linking this tekke with the Halveti order.[63]

In addition to Ioannina, Ali Pasha also supported a dervish community in Trikala, the governor's largest stronghold east of the Pindus Mountains, in the plain of Thessaly.[64] There is a good deal more information about the Trikala tekke than there is about the ones found in Ioannina. First, in 1804–5, William Leake had the opportunity to visit the site, writing:

> Tríkkala has lately been adorned by the Pashá with a new Tekiéh, or college of Bektashlí dervíses, on the site of a former one. He has not only removed several old buildings to give more space and air to this college, but has endowed it with property in khans, shops, and houses, and has added some fields on the banks of the *Lethaeus*. There are now about fifteen of these Mahometan monks in the house with a Sheikh or Chief,[65] who is married to an Ioannite woman, and as well lodged and dressed as many a Pashá. Besides his own apartments, there are very comfortable lodgings for the dervíses, and every convenience for the reception of strangers.[66]

Because Leake emphasized the openness of the complex and noted that to reach the tekke a visitor had to cross a bridge over the river, we can assume that this tekke, revived by Ali Pasha, was located somewhere on the western bank of the Lithaios River, facing the town's citadel and Ottoman city center on the opposite bank. Although Leake calls this a Bektashi tekke, Ottoman documents refer to Ali Pasha's lodge in Trikala as belonging to the Sa'di order, meaning either that Leake was mistaken on this point, or, less likely, that there was a second Ali Pasha tekke built in Trikala.[67]

While Ali Pasha constructed tekkes in all the major cities in the southern part of his territory (i.e., Ioannina, Trikala, and Preveza),[68] he focused his support for dervish communities in the northern mountains of Albania, especially in and around his hometown of Tepelena. Within the city itself, for example, the governor sponsored a Sa'di tekke. Although the

FIGURE 65
Photograph of the *semahane*, mausoleum, and living quarters of the Kurt Ahmet Pasha Tekke in Berat, 1960. Archive of the Institute of Cultural Monuments of Albania, Tirana.

endowment record for this institution survives, it is unknown where exactly in Tepelena the lodge was situated.[69] Dervishes held sway and maintained a high degree of visibility in the network of mountain villages surrounding Tepelena, and the tekke in Hormova fits into this broader constellation of Ali Pasha's patronage of Sufi orders in the area. Western European travelers also frequently mention a tekke that was located on the mountain of Trebushin in the village of Beçisht, traditionally held to be the place where Ali Pasha grew up and sitting in clear view of Tepelena, which lies at the meeting point of two important mountain passes along the banks of the Vjosa River (see fig. 5).[70] Ali Pasha seems to have placed dervish lodges in Muslim villages where he could curry favor with the wider population by appointing shaykhs who were loyal to him. This was the case in Karbunara, a village in what is today the Fier district of Albania.[71] By the time Henry Holland visited this place in 1812–13, the village had a completely Muslim population, and he "found the principal person here to be a Dervish, who is said to have great influence in the district; and whose manners were extremely authoritative toward the people."[72]

In his patronage of dervish lodges, Ali Pasha followed a precedent set by his former employer turned political rival, Kurt Ahmed Pasha. In the last decades of the eighteenth century, Kurt Ahmed Pasha served as the *mutasarrıf* of the Avlonya district, with his capital in Berat.[73] During his tenure as governor, Kurt Ahmed Pasha oversaw several construction projects in the town, including the great stone bridge spanning the Osum River and repairs to the fortification walls of the citadel.[74] Most pertinently, in 1781–2 Kurt Ahmed rebuilt a Halvetiye tekke complex on the eastern side of Berat, which, according to Evliya Çelebi, was originally commissioned by Sultan Bayezid II, a known proponent of the order.[75] The present complex, which is still in good condition today, includes the *semâhâne* (meeting hall) and *türbe* of Kurt Ahmed Pasha, as well as a humbler structure containing the cells for the dervishes (fig. 65). The *semahane* and *türbe* are solidly built in limestone, the interior of the reception hall painted in the baroque style popular during the period. Ali Pasha probably would have seen this tekke—in either its original or rebuilt state—as a young man. In 1776, when Ali was making his name in the region, Kurt Ahmed Pasha enlisted his help in an internecine war against Mehmed Pasha Buşatlı, *mutassarıf* of Shkodra.[76] At some point thereafter, however, Ali had a falling out with his patron, and the two remained locked in an ongoing rivalry until the latter's death in 1786. Despite this feud, Ali Pasha seems to have learned some lessons about how to rule a territory from Kurt Ahmed

Pasha, including the importance of cultivating a relationship with local dervish fraternities. In any case, the tekke at Berat is significant because it indicates that Ali Pasha was not alone among local provincial power holders in his patronage of Sufi orders. Kurt Ahmed Pasha was so invested in this dervish community that he had his *türbe* incorporated into the new *semahane* complex. Also, because tekke architecture so rarely survives, the *semahane* and cells of the complex in Berat provide some idea of how the now-lost tekke complexes in Trikala and Tepelena may have looked.

European accounts frequently characterize dervishes in unfavorable terms, drawing on a repertoire of familiar stereotypes—roguish, untrustworthy, and strongly antagonistic toward the Orthodox Christian population.[77] These travelers seemed to have found the mendicant lifestyle and various rituals of these individuals unfamiliar and off-putting. What remains invisible in these narratives, however, is the significant function that dervishes and their lodges played in the social life of the region. Again, tekkes served as community centers for local Muslim communities and were frequented by both men and women who sought the advice of the shaykh.[78] As the list of tekkes in table 1 shows, patronage of dervish communities was especially a priority for Ali Pasha's son Muhtar, who maintained the Halveti tekke in northern Ioannina as well as the one in Gjirokaster, and, with his father, helped establish the lodge in Karbunara.[79] While his brother Veli concerned himself more with congregational mosques, Muhtar seemed to cultivate a strong relationship with the dervishes. This may have been in part because Muhtar was the more martially inclined of the two brothers, keeping company with soldiers and always out on a hunting or riding excursion.[80] Historically, Sufi orders (especially the Bektashi) maintained close ties with the Janissary ranks throughout the empire, being commonly associated with these security forces.[81]

A review of the documents from Ali Pasha's chancery makes it clear that dervishes held a place of importance in the governor's retinue. In an 1801 register listing the amount of bread required to feed the vizier's court in Ioannina for three days, numerous shaykhs and dervishes are listed by name, receiving anywhere from three to twelve loaves depending on their rank and influence.[82] Included in this list is also enough bread (fifty-four loaves) to feed the entire "tekke of Shaykh Salih," which may refer to one of the Halveti tekkes maintained by Ali and Muhtar Pasha in Ioannina. Several other documents in the chancery chart Ali Pasha's and his son Muhtar's dealings with dervish leaders throughout their territory, solidifying oaths of fealty and ensuring the upkeep of village tekkes.[83]

Many different modes of language are used to describe the members and leaders of tekkes throughout both Ottoman documents and Ali Pasha's chancery records. The Ottoman archival record, which consists mostly of pious endowment and appointment registers, usually refers to a tekke by its particular Sufi order. Meanwhile, the Greek documents from Ali Pasha's archive almost never indicate the order of a lodge, but rather describe a tekke according to the original founder or the current head of the community. As mentioned above, historians have spent a good deal of time trying to determine to which order Ali Pasha ultimately held allegiance. The effort to add nuance to the picture of the governor's patronage patterns is prompted by Albanian nationalist claims on Ali

FIGURE 66
Muntaz Dhrami, *Ali Pashe Tepelena, 1740–1822*, 2002. Tepelena. Photo by author.

Pasha as a Bektashi, claims so far-reaching that the modern statue of the pasha in Tepelena has the Bektashi ten-point star hanging around his neck (fig. 66).[84] Yet this question of Ali Pasha's (and his family's) "true" loyalty to a particular branch of Sufism misses the point that the governor did not restrict his sponsorship to a single community but supported a number of different orders, predominantly the Bektashi, Halveti, and Sa'di traditions. As a survey of Ali Pasha's tekkes reveals, the vizier spread his wealth and favors around to different lodges throughout the region whenever he discerned an opportunity to form an alliance with a specific shaykh or village. The governor was a free agent when it came to matters of religion, and that is putting it mildly, especially when one turns to his engagement with the Christian communities in his realm.

THE CHURCH THE PASHA BUILT

Ali Pasha's patronage of both mosques and tekkes might be construed as part of a plan to further Islamize the region. Yet the governor's personal construction of a Christian monastery, and his tacit approval of building and rebuilding churches throughout his territories, complicates this question. Many historians have emphasized Ali Pasha's exceptional tolerance of, and willingness to negotiate with, the Christians living in the region under his control.[85] In a dispatch to London in 1804, the British consul in Ioannina noted that the Christians in Epirus and Thessaly were in a more favorable position than they were in communities in adjacent regions, "owing perhaps to the indulgence that Ali Pasha, who knows the levity and vanity of their character, freely allows them of gratifying both, in the building of spacious houses, and wearing fine apparel, advantages which in the estimation of modern Greeks, are a very liberal return for their contributions in money."[86] Leaving aside Western European biases about the "vanity" of contemporary Ottoman Christians, the consul's remarks are useful in understanding how Ali Pasha maintained a transactional relationship with the Christian communities under his jurisdiction, allowing them to forego many of the sartorial and architectural restrictions placed on non-Muslims in the empire.[87] These sorts of concessions seem to have been met with both financial and military support from local Christian leaders.[88]

While some might romanticize Ali Pasha's amicable relations with the Christian communities of Epirus as being due to influence from his young Christian wife, Vasiliki (1789–1834), the governor in fact maintained such policies from the earliest days of his rise to power in the 1790s, well before he and Vasiliki married in 1816. If anything, the reverse could be argued: that a Muslim governor married to a Christian woman who continued to maintain and practice her faith—a highly unusual situation within the context of the Ottoman Empire—was the result of the vizier's long-standing practice of openness to other faith traditions. It is perhaps better, therefore, to understand Ali Pasha's stance toward the local Christian communities as a sensible partnership. After all, with the high concentration of Christians living in this region, and the considerable influence that religious leaders such as the local metropolitans had over these communities, it would have been nearly impossible for Ali Pasha to maintain his position without the backing of the Christian inhabitants.

A virtually unexplored aspect of Ali Pasha's relations with local Christian communities is his position regarding the restoration and construction of churches. The accepted wisdom on the subject is that before the modernization reforms of the mid-nineteenth century, non-Muslim groups throughout the Ottoman Empire faced strict regulations regarding their religious architecture.[89] These groups thus pursued long petition processes to secure the necessary permissions to reconstruct or repair any church and its accompanying properties. One case study that yields a more nuanced understanding of how these broader dynamics played out is that of an Orthodox church dedicated to the martyr-saint Kosmas Aitolos, located in present-day Albania. From an architectural perspective, this church is an important example of the distinctive construction style made famous throughout the Balkans in the eighteenth and nineteenth centuries. Yet the aspect of this building that makes it truly extraordinary is its patron, Ali Pasha. To the best of my knowledge, this church is the only example of a Christian monument commissioned by a Muslim administrator in the history of the Ottoman Empire—and, for that matter, one of the few instances in the wider Islamic world.[90]

Today, the complex of Kosmas Aitolos occupies a quiet spot along the winding Seman River (fig. 67). Surrounded by a curtain of cypresses and a maze of cultivated fields, the monastery is approached from the north by a wide dirt road, which is often humming with the sound of the local farmers' tractors and pickup trucks. The site is approximately ten kilometers north of the modern large town of Fier in southern Albania, about a forty-five-minute drive from the main highway. Although this church complex is situated between two important historical sites—the ancient ruins of Apollonia and the Ardenica Monastery—the place is rather isolated and difficult to reach for most tourists. Like most monasteries in Albania, the site no longer serves an active community and is only used on special feast days and funerals. The only person a visitor is likely to meet at the monastery is the caretaker, who looks after the cemetery on the northern side of the complex, used primarily by those who live in the nearby village of Rreth-Libofshë.

The remote location of the monastery on the river directly relates to the life and martyrdom of Kosmas Aitolos in the late eighteenth century. The most authoritative account of the life of the saint is a biography first published in 1814 by Sapfeiros Christodoulidis, a disciple of Kosmas and himself an instructor at Christian schools in Ioannina during the period of Ali Pasha's rule.[91] As Ioannina served as the governor's capital city, it is important to note that the myth of the martyr saint was formulated within the context of Ali Pasha's court. It is probably not a coincidence that this biography was published the same year that the governor constructed the church in question. According to Christodoulidis's account, Kosmas was born in Aetolia (near the Gulf of Corinth) in 1714. A precocious youth, Kosmas studied with great religious scholars and eventually found himself residing in the monasteries of Mount Athos. Called to serve as an apostolic preacher to the common people, Kosmas left his cloistered life in the 1760s and traveled to Istanbul to obtain the patriarch's blessing for his new role as an itinerant preacher. Kosmas then proceeded to traverse what is now northern Greece and the Ionian Islands and southern Albania. Christodoulidis writes, "here he preached to the Christians, walking and going through those barbaric provinces, where piety and Christian life were in danger of disappearing completely." Kosmas won the hearts and minds of many through his fervent teaching, including Kurt Ahmed Pasha, who was already the governor of Berat at that point and who is said to have been impressed when he granted Kosmas an audience and had a special collapsible wooden throne or platform made for the preacher, "in order that he might go up on it and teach the people from an elevated place."[92]

Despite these warm sentiments, Kosmas was ultimately martyred at the hands of the same Ottoman authorities in 1779. It is not entirely clear why relations soured between Kosmas and Kurt Ahmed Pasha. Christodoulidis blames members of the Jewish community of Ioannina, who he says went to Kurt Ahmed Pasha and accused the preacher of trying to lure Christian subjects to Russia. It is perhaps more likely that the falling out was related to the uprising that broke out in the Peloponnese a few years earlier. In any case, it seems that the governor of Berat did ultimately issue a warrant for Kosmas's arrest. At the time, the preacher was traveling in the region of Fier, near where the later church was established. He learned that Kurt Ahmed Pasha's mullah lived nearby and appealed to him for permission to preach in that region. The mullah, who had received the governor's orders to execute Kosmas, detained the preacher. Kosmas, upon learning that the mullah intended to put him to death, was reportedly delighted that he would meet his end through martyrdom and eagerly awaited the appointed hour. The next day, the mullah's men took Kosmas to the riverbank and showed him the firman from Kurt Ahmed Pasha that mandated his death. The preacher knelt and willingly accepted his fate. After killing Kosmas, the men were said to have cast his body into the river with a large stone tied around his neck. Upon learning about the incident three days later, the priest Markos, head of

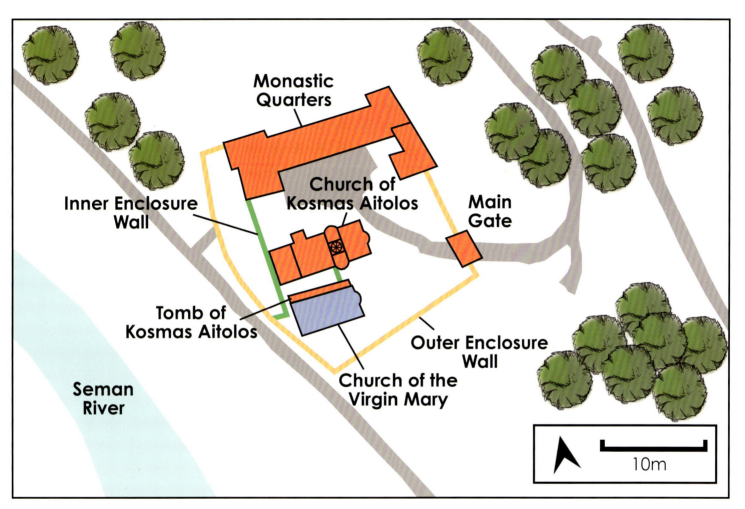

FIGURE 67
The Monastery of Kosmas Aitolos.
Plan by Matthew J. Jacobson.

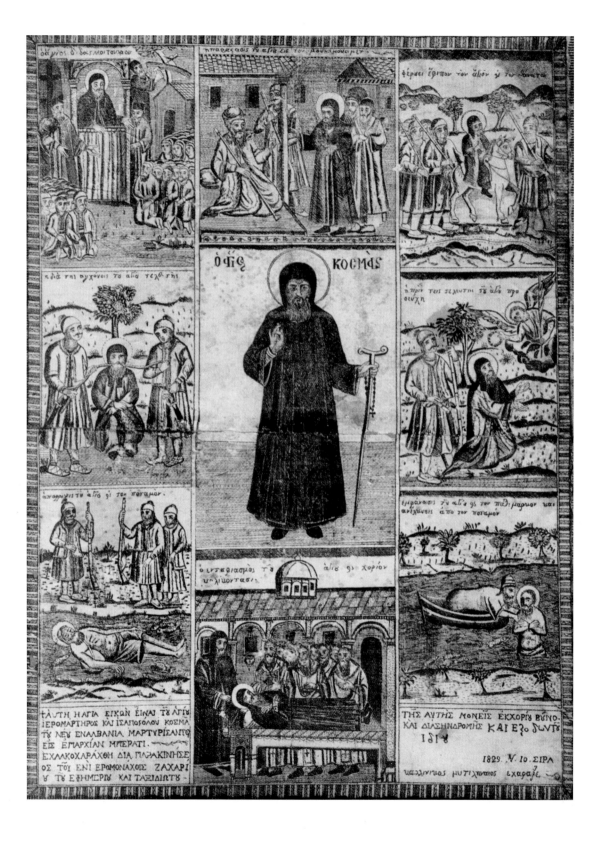

FIGURE 68
A printed icon showing events from the life of Kosmas Aitolos, 1829. From Michalis Pantoulas, *Kosmas Aitolos: Ta eikonografika (1779–1961)* (Ioannina: Michalis Pantoulas, 2015), 195.

a nearby monastery dedicated to the Theotokos, went to the river and retrieved the body, which he buried properly behind the main sanctuary of the church.[93]

Kosmas's fame as a martyr and holy figure spread astonishingly quickly after his death in 1779. As mentioned above, his life was published only a few decades later, in 1814. A popular icon of the saint painted in 1829 indicates how these stories about Kosmas began to circulate among the Christians of the region (fig. 68). This image relates the key moments of the life and death of the preacher, including his meeting with Kurt Ahmed Pasha (top center panel), the special throne the governor had built for Kosmas (top left), the execution of the preacher at the river (middle left) and the retrieval of the body (bottom right) and burial at the monastery (bottom center).

The life of Kosmas as presented by Christodoulidis and in this icon can be used to lay out the various building phases of what is now the Monastery of Kosmas Aitolos (see fig. 67).[94] The complex today has two churches, adjacent to each other—the Church of Kosmas Aitolos and another ruined church to the south. The tomb of the saint is in a small chamber located between the two sanctuaries, structurally joined to the ruined church but accessible only from a small entrance to the north.[95] The ruined church to the south must be the sanctuary of the Monastery of the Theotokos that Christodoulidis describes, where Kosmas found his final resting place. Although only part of the apse and northern wall of the church remain, an inscription survives on the exterior façade, which informs us the sanctuary was renovated in 1782 (fig. 69).[96] Therefore, following Christodoulidis and the existing material evidence, we can conclude that, at the time of Kosmas's martyrdom and burial in 1779, there was already a monastic church dedicated to the Theotokos on the site. Then, only a year or two later, this church somehow suffered significant damage (earthquake and fire are the most likely culprits) and was reconstructed in 1782. This is the church to the south that can be seen today. Shortly thereafter, the second church dedicated to Saint Kosmas was built, commissioned by Ali Pasha himself.

At the end of his biography of the saint, Christodoulidis describes the circumstances surrounding the erection of this second church. He mentions that Kosmas had in fact met Ali Pasha when he was still a young man and in the service of Kurt Ahmed Pasha. Kosmas was prone to making prophetic proclamations, and he told the young Ali that "the district that he governed would grow a great deal" and that he would "conquer many cities and all of Albania."[97] Supposedly having remembered this encounter and the words of the martyred preacher, Ali Pasha contacted the metropolitan of Berat decades later to arrange the construction of a church dedicated to Kosmas.

The story of Ali Pasha's role in the foundation of this second church of the monastery continues on the walls of the building itself. There are two Greek inscriptions on the exterior of the sanctuary dedicated to Kosmas Aitolos, the first located on the external wall of the eastern apse (fig. 70). This inscription is easy to miss because it is badly eroded and difficult to read, but the text is crucial because it names Ali Pasha himself as the patron of the building: "This holy and sacred church was raised from the foundations by the order and exhortation of his highness Vizier Ali Pasha from Tepelena."[98] There are several important points to note about this inscription. First, the text unequivocally names Ali Pasha as the patron of the church. Within the wider context of

FIGURE 69
The ruined apse of the Church of the Theotokos, located within the Monastery of Kosmas Aitolos. Photo by author.

ecclesiastical inscriptions, it was not necessarily unusual for the name of the Ottoman sultan or regional administrator to appear in a foundation text. For example, in an inscription at a church dedicated to the Theotokos in Roupsia, a Greek village just south of the Albanian border today, Ali Pasha is acknowledged in his role as governor, but he is not named as the patron. Additionally, the phrase "from the foundations" (εκ βαθρών) implies that this building was an entirely new construction and not a simple repair. Finally, it is important to observe that this inscription refers to Ali Pasha both by his Ottoman administrative title ("Vizier") and by his place of origin, the nearby district of Tepelena, details that emphasize both political and local claims to authority.

From a visual standpoint, it seems that the masons who carved this inscription were emulating the design scheme of the adjacent Theotokos church, rebuilt approximately thirty-five years earlier, as the plaque containing the inscription resembles what appears to be a spoliated ancient ceiling coffer embedded in the apse of the ruined church (compare figs. 69 and 70). This coffer, like all the spoliated material in this complex, no doubt came from the nearby ancient site of Apollonia. In this way, the inscription declaring Ali Pasha's patronage of the monastery creates a visual line of continuity between the vizier's church and the earlier foundation, literally embedding Ali Pasha's name in the stones of the church. And with both apses featuring similar decorative characteristics, such as voussoirs in alternating colors and faux columns carved into the stone, it is quite possible that Ali Pasha's church was constructed by a subsequent generation of the same group of craftsmen.

A second inscription, found above the main entrance on the northern façade, provides even more information about the circumstances of the building's construction (fig. 71). Most significantly, this second inscription gives the date of the foundation as May 1814, this date appearing on a simple plaque also bearing a cross carved in relief. Below this plaque are two cartouches with Greek text, the first reading, "This church of Agios Kosmas was built during [the tenure] of his holiness Iosaf the Metropolitan of Belgrad (Berat) and his all-holiness Abbot Theoklitos, and [during the service of the] administrators Nikolaos Dimitriou and Hatzi Giankos as well as the chancellor Parthenios, through the labors and toil of all the faithful Christians, both clergy and lay."[99] The rest of the text in the lower cartouche reads, "The chamber of Agios Kosmas was [built] under the inspection of Captain Nikolaos, from the village of

FIGURE 70
Detail of the foundation inscription embedded in the exterior wall of the apse at the Church of Kosmas Aitolos. Photo by author.

Fourka in the parish of Agios Vellas."¹⁰⁰ The term "chamber" (δώμα, doma) of Kosmas may be a reference to the saint's tomb next to the church.

These inscriptions clarify the circumstances of the building's patronage and construction, with Ali Pasha identified as the primary benefactor of the foundation, acting in cooperation with the local religious leaders, such as the metropolitan and the abbot of the monastery, and lay notables from the village. This picture of the commissioning process is even further clarified by several orders issued by Ali Pasha regarding the church, which have been preserved and reproduced in their entirety in the nineteenth-century memoir of Anthimos Alexoudis, successor to Iosaf as the metropolitan of Berat.¹⁰¹ These memoranda offer a rare glimpse into the archival record that accompanied the construction of these monuments.

The first order, dated September 12, 1813, addresses the Christians of Berat, specifically the people of Myzeqe and Grabova, two villages located in the vicinity of the church.¹⁰² In this memorandum, Ali Pasha notifies these communities that he has appointed a representative to construct the monastery of Father Kosmas and commands them to offer whatever financial assistance the metropolitan asks of them, stating that he himself has also given money to the cause ("εβοήθησα και εγώ [με] άσπρα"). With characteristic flair, Ali Pasha continues with a warning: "anyone who does not assist me in my request will be in my debt and will later be required to pay double the amount." According to this document, Ali Pasha initiated this building project, providing some of his own funds for the church, but he also expected the local Christian communities to

BUILDING LOCAL SUPPORT   131

FIGURE 71
The northern entrance to the Church of Kosmas Aitolos. Photo by author.

assist in meeting the costs. Notably, Ali Pasha mentions the metropolitan, Iosaf, as a mediator with these communities, relying on the bishop's influence to collect the requisite monies. This arrangement is hardly uncommon in this time period; we know from documents in Ali Pasha's chancery that local notables were often expected to contribute to the costs of construction and maintenance of buildings in their region, as we saw in the previous chapter in the case of military fortifications.

The other memorandum of note comes exactly a year later, in September 1814.[103] In this letter, Ali Pasha writes directly to the metropolitan of Berat along with two individuals, Hatzi Giagkos and Koli Mitros, the same men named as lay notables in the inscription located above the main entrance of the church.[104] The construction of the complex must have been nearly complete at this point, as Ali Pasha relates that he has been receiving their regular communications about the building activities and has also heard from the abbot, probably the Theoklitos also mentioned in the inscription. Incredibly, the governor confides that he is "greatly amused" (το έκαμα χάζι πολύ) that they have been able to obtain a *muḵāṭaʿa* (μουκαέτιδες, *moukaetides*), or building permission, from the kadi (Islamic jurist) of Berat in the name of Father Kosmas. This candid remark indicates that Ali Pasha was familiar with Kosmas's biography, in that the preacher was said to have been executed by the Ottoman administrators of Berat for inciting sedition. Ali Pasha's comment suggests, therefore, that this construction project may be seen, at least in part, as a rather elaborate practical joke on the Muslim administrative officials in the nearby district capital, and perhaps on the wider political apparatus that conferred authority on these individuals, i.e., the sultan's government in Istanbul.

In the letter, Ali Pasha relates that he will be sending to the monastery a "master builder" (πρωτομάστορας, *protomastoras*), unfortunately unnamed, so that they can put the finishing touches on the complex, either enlarging or replacing the monastic quarters and building a new enclosure wall. He concludes by expressing how he is very much looking forward to visiting soon and finding everything ready, an allusion, perhaps, to plans for the official dedication ceremony of the complex. Unfortunately, we can only speculate about such an event, when everyone would have come to see the church the pasha built. The circumstances surrounding the construction of the Church of Kosmas Aitolos reveal a complex constellation of local actors—both Christian and Muslim—all working to realize a monument that was highly charged in meaning, the final resting place of a Christian monk whose name at that point was synonymous with thwarting imperial control.

This collective act of patronage directs our attention to another instance in which Ali Pasha and his family commissioned a church in the territory under their control. In a village approximately ten kilometers north of Trikala there is a church dedicated to Agios Nikolaos that was constructed in 1818 under the patronage of Ali Pasha's Christian wife, Vasiliki.[105] The church is in very good condition, and the masonry techniques in the arcades and walls of the main structure appear to date to the early nineteenth century. There is evidence of various restoration efforts, such as roof retiling and the insertion of three double-arched brick windows in the upper registers of the side arms and narthex of the church.[106] A tall bell tower was constructed adjacent to the main sanctuary, bearing a date of 1883 on its southern façade. The foundation inscription of this church, located above the southern entrance

FIGURE 72
Foundation inscription of the Church of Agios Nikolaos in Vasiliki, a village north of Trikala. Photo by author.

to the naos, states, "The holy church of Agios Nikolaos was rebuilt from the foundations with the financial support of the local inhabitants and assistance by Vasiliki, wife of the voyvoda, and her brothers" (fig. 72).[107]

While the memory of Ali Pasha's patronage of the Church of Agios Kosmas has faded in the secondary literature and at the site itself, the role that Vasiliki played in the construction of the Church of Agios Nikolaos is prominently celebrated those who live in the village today. A modern bust of the patron adorns the courtyard of the church and bears an inscription that describes Vasiliki as "a great benefactress of the place and commissioner of this church."[108] When brought together, the portrait of church patronage by a Muslim husband and Christian wife across a considerable geographic expanse—one church in modern-day Albania, the other in Greece—revises our current view of church building and restoration in the Ottoman Empire.

TOWARD A MULTICONFESSIONAL HISTORY OF OTTOMAN ARCHITECTURE

It is critically important that we compare the architectural projects of various confessional groups living side by side because there has to date been such a stark separation in the examination of Muslim and Christian monuments within the wider historiography on Ottoman architecture. It is rare to see scholarly studies on the built environment that consider both mosques and churches, even if they are situated within the same geographic region and chronological frame, as is often the case for the Balkans. This phenomenon is partly due to an epistemological framework that places the art and architecture of the Ottoman Empire under the broader category of Islamic art.[109] Although it is an accepted fact that minority communities of non-Muslims, especially Christians and Jews, have always played an integral role in the material and cultural production of the Islamic world, from Spain to Southeast Asia, the religious constructions of these communities have never found an easy place in the field of Islamic architecture.[110] The example of mosques, tekkes, and churches built by a single patron, although a highly unusual case, suggests that we might benefit from a multiconfessional approach to architectural landscapes that have been shaped under Muslim rulers. This multiconfessional perspective offers an architectural history more attentive to the experiences of and exchanges among the diverse communities who lived in these spaces.

It is fair to say that Ottoman architectural historians have been principally preoccupied with the mosque complex as the premier building type of the empire. This historiographic reality is proportionate to the fact that the Ottoman state itself devoted a great deal of labor and funding to the construction of these complexes. Especially after the capital was moved to Istanbul in the mid-fifteenth century, the sultans set their engineers to work in developing various iterations of the multitiered dome and minaret combination for their imperial mosques, these structures emerging in the process as the most distinctively "Ottoman" of Ottoman buildings.[111] In his autobiography, the famous sixteenth-century architect Sinan notably puts mosques first, ahead of other building types such as *medreses* and hammams, in the long list of structures attributed to his tenure as the head of the corps of royal architects.[112] Yet there is much to gain from a view of the multiconfessional nature of the sultan's subjects. As discussed in the introduction, historians have begun to approach the long eighteenth century as a time when the Ottoman state was more a system of negotiating and sharing power with local notables than a one-way process of issuing top-down edicts.[113] Many of these notables represented non-Muslim communities, and an investigation of the construction, use, and repair of their houses of worship, which were the most important physical spaces representing any *zimmi* (non-Muslim) community, could play a crucial role in understanding how these groups navigated within the imperial order.[114] As one scholar put it, "Why can't we talk about Ottoman churches?"[115]

The relative dearth of discussion about the religious architecture of non-Muslim communities in the Ottoman Empire may also be attributed to the official state policy (informed by the Hanefite school of Islamic jurisprudence) that churches and synagogues were not supposed to be built *ex novo*.[116] This was the case until the 1839 Tanzimat Charter and the 1856 edict establishing equality among all imperial subjects.[117] The building activity of non-Muslims, at least in theory, was thus limited to maintenance repairs of existing structures.[118] In the case of serious damage due to, say, fire or earthquake, non-Muslims could reconstruct a house of worship, but only if the new building followed the footprint of the previous site. Practice did not always follow principle, however, and even the briefest survey reveals that these policies were not universally applied. The restrictions placed on the construction of non-Muslim buildings were subject to the discretion of local authorities and could be rigorously enforced or ignored altogether.[119] And non-Muslim leaders developed strategies for sidestepping these regulations, like using language in official documentation that suggested the rebuilding of a church on the site of an old one, even if that was evidently not the case.[120] For instance, in the foundation inscription for the church of Father Kosmas, the verb used in the phrase I have translated as "raised from the foundations" (ανηγέρθη, anigerthi) indicates that the sanctuary had been rebuilt, yet the corresponding archival evidence makes clear that this was an entirely new construction. Thus a good deal of building activity was in fact undertaken by non-Muslim communities even before the modernization reforms, and this point is highlighted in the publication of scholarly works such as *Ekklisies stin Ellada meta tin Alosi: Churches in Greece, 1453–1850*.[121] A product of the National Polytechnic University of Greece, this work covers more than 150 monuments in seven volumes, and it explores only the geographic area now within the borders of modern Greece. Looking at this corpus alone, it is evident that the Ottoman lands witnessed a flourishing of church construction.

An examination of different kinds of confessional architecture side by side demonstrates that the repair or construction of Orthodox Christian structures fell to the local architects and craftsmen who were likewise engaged in other building projects, such as domestic architecture, fortresses, and even mosques. In the case of Ali Pasha and his domain, it appears that the same groups of local craftsmen worked on both mosques and churches. For example, the Fethiye Mosque in Ioannina, which seems to have been largely rebuilt during the late eighteenth century, features a lively interior decoration program in a baroque style (fig. 73). Formal analysis of these decorations suggests that the same group of craftsmen who produced them were also employed at the Church of Shen Meri (St. Mary) in Labova e Kryqit, a small village located in the Drino River Valley now in southern Albania. The core of the structure dates to the thirteenth century, when the area was politically independent from Constantinople under the Despots of Epirus. Yet the interior of the sanctuary was decorated in a style similar to that of the mosque in Ioannina, part of a 1776–78 renovation of the church that also involved the reconstruction of the apses and an exonarthex on the western side (fig. 74).[122] A close comparison of some design elements found at both the Fethiye Mosque and Shen Meri show that the craftsmen at both sites created elaborate curving strapwork designs in a light pastel blue on a white ground, interspersed with bunches of flowers and fruit (figs. 75 and 76). Although we do not currently have any information about the identity of these specific craftsmen, it is possible to conjecture that it was not unusual for artisans in this region to work on both Islamic and Christian monuments at the same time.[123] The functions of these buildings, as well as legal restrictions, still determined key differences in their overall structural composition—for example, mosques had domes and minarets, while churches were restricted to pitched roofs or barrel vaults. But we can still observe a unified regional aesthetic or visual culture that was shared among multiple confessional groups.

Examining both Islamic and Christian monuments together also yields a clearer understanding of how different religious spaces may have related to one another within the urban context of the major centers under Ali Pasha's control. In the absence of reliable census records, these buildings provide a useful approximation of where various religious

FIGURE 73
Interior of the Fethiye Mosque in Ioannina. Photo by author.

FIGURE 74
The Church of Shen Meri in the village of Labova e Kryqit, thought to have been originally constructed in the thirteenth century, with a porticoed exonarthex added in the late eighteenth century. Photo by author.

FIGURE 75
Detail of wall decorations in the southeast arcade in the interior of the Church of Shen Meri in Labova e Kryqit. Photo by author.

communities were based. The 1820 map of Ioannina in the Bibliothèque national provides a general idea of the town's makeup in that time period (see fig. 13). The cartographer has indicated all of the major religious monuments of the town, and it can be presumed that most of these foundations represented the nucleus of a particular neighborhood and faith community. By this time, only Muslims and Jews were permitted to reside within the old city walls (the *kastro*), and as a result there are no churches in this quarter, only the two mosques sitting on the two crests of the peninsula (fig. 13, nos. 22 and 23) and a synagogue in the northwest quarter (no. 30). Beyond the walled city, neighborhoods appear to have been fairly mixed with respect to religion, with many churches situated near mosques. This is the case with an unnamed mosque (no. 19) and Agia Ekaterini (no. 9), and also the mosque founded by Ali Pasha's son Veli Pasha (no. 25) and the Agia Marina church complex (no. 12). As discussed above, the two tekkes of the town, established by Ali Pasha and his son Muhtar Pasha, are located on the outskirts of Ioannina, just off the main roads leading north and south (nos. 6 and 7). Similarly, the Church of Agios Nikolaos Kopanon (no. 8) stands sentinel at the northern gate of the city, directly across from the customs control (*douane*). A cluster of mosques in the southern part of the city just beyond the bazaar area indicates a concentration of Muslim inhabitants there, while the island in Lake Pamvotis seems to have been occupied exclusively by Christians residing in the village and numerous monasteries.[124] Of all the structures indicated on the Barbié du Bocage map, we know that both of the tekkes, some of the mosques, and a number of the churches were either constructed anew or rebuilt in Ali Pasha's time. Mapping the variety

FIGURE 76
Detail of the decorations painted on the central dome of the Fethiye Mosque in Ioannina. Photo by author.

of religious structures in Ioannina thus allows for a view of the shifting dynamics of space among the Muslim and Christian communities living in the town during the Ottoman period.

Despite the evidence of stylistic tastes that transcend confession and the complex spatial relationships between Muslim and Christian architecture in the Balkans, there is still a lack of dialogue between two academic communities working on either "Ottoman/Islamic" or "post-Byzantine/Christian" architecture. The scholars in these two groups rarely acknowledge that the buildings under examination coexisted in the same regions at the same time and may have been built and maintained by the same groups of craftsmen. This situation can be explained partly by the political contingencies of the modern nation-state. Within the academic tradition of Greece, for example, archaeological and cultural material dating from the Ottoman era is typically divided between two categories, "post-Byzantine" (Μεταβυζαντινός) and "Ottoman" (Οθωμανικός). The term "post-Byzantine" is almost always restricted to the art and culture of the Christian communities living in Ottoman lands: church and monastic architecture, icons, liturgical garments and implements, religious manuscripts, and the like.[125] Meanwhile, the term "Ottoman," specifically in the context of architectural studies in Greece, is usually a catch-all to describe all other (non-Christian) buildings, both Islamic and secular sites.[126] Works on Ottoman architecture in what today is Albania also exclude Christian material from the same period, and "Ottoman" is implicitly defined as the realm of the Muslim population.[127] This silo effect in the academic literature makes it difficult, if not impossible, to account for how syncretic the region was at the time. Yet architecture stands as a fruitful area in which to examine the exchanges, conflicts, and negotiations among different confessional groups living together.

The religious monuments commissioned by Ali Pasha raise a host of questions about the political and social history of Ottoman Epirus and about the ontologies deployed to categorize architecture in the Balkans in this prenationalist period. For example, should we call the church of Father Kosmas an Ottoman building? An Islamic building? A post-Byzantine building? While the particular act of patronage behind this church emerged from the political culture of accommodation and pragmatic flexibility that typified Ali Pasha's approach to governance in Epirus, it also forces us to reevaluate the broader spatial and visual culture of the Mediterranean world during the Ottoman period. A methodology of comparing Islamic and Christian structures constructed in the same region at the same time is an initial step toward a new framework for examining the built environment from this period, in which we must shed our assumptions about the divisions among different religious groups. This framework allows us to see individual buildings within a wider multiconfessional landscape, a cultural field of intersecting communities that could produce—seemingly against all odds—mosques, dervish lodges, and churches, all under the oversight of a single patron.

Poetic Justice

EXPERIMENTS IN ARCHITECTURAL EPIGRAPHY

CHAPTER 4

A visitor to the history museum in Tepelena, Albania—Ali Pasha's hometown—is bound to stumble across a fascinating memento from the era of the governor's rule. In the center of the main exhibition space is a thick stone slab approximately seventy-five centimeters in length (fig. 77). Now lying flat on a short pedestal and broken into five separate pieces, the panel was once located above the eastern gate to the Tepelena citadel, one of the main entrances to the walled city.[1] The slab depicts a Friday mosque, its dome and minarets in profile. This image may very well have offered a preview of the mosque that Ali Pasha had constructed within the citadel, which was located just beyond the eastern gate and would have greeted visitors immediately after they passed under the plaque and through the bent entrance (see fig. 55).[2] At the top of the panel, the finial of the building's dome creates a vertical axis that divides a bilingual inscription, with Greek text on the left and Ottoman Turkish on the right. Although both sections are badly damaged, the Greek side is more legible, and the governor's name and title "Vizier Ali Pasha" (ΒΕΖΙΡ ΑΛΙ ΠΑΣΑ) are fully intact just above the dome. At far left, there seems to be the name of another man, perhaps an İbrahim Ağa, who may have been Ali Pasha's headman in the city.[3] Unfortunately, the right side, in Ottoman Turkish, has almost entirely worn away, but what looks like Ali Pasha's name in Arabic script partially survives on the top line. To the far right could also be a Hijri date of 1235, corresponding to the year 1819, which is clearly visible at the bottom of the plaque.[4] This panel thus commemorates either the date of completion or a subsequent repair of the outer wall system of Tepelena on behalf of Ali Pasha.

No one element of this foundation inscription is unusual in itself. Ottoman Turkish was the language of the state and the de facto language in official public inscriptions, especially those commissioned on behalf of the sultan. Meanwhile, along with Albanian, Greek was the predominant language spoken in the region of Epirus among Christians and Muslims alike. As suggested in the previous chapter, the centuries preceding Ali Pasha's rule were marked by a robust tradition of Greek architectural inscriptions, primarily in the context of ecclesiastical spaces. Finally, depictions of mosques had become increasingly common in Ottoman visual culture, from landscape paintings in elite Muslim households to carvings on the walls of mosques themselves.[5] What makes the panel in Tepelena noteworthy is the combination of all these elements in a single image. Bilingual inscriptions were rare in the Ottoman period, most examples coming only after the Tanzimat reforms of the late nineteenth and early twentieth centuries.[6] Even more striking

is the pairing of Greek text with the depiction of a mosque, as Greek inscriptions are almost exclusively associated with Orthodox Christian settings in Ottoman lands.

This inscription thus unsettles many of the most common assumptions about the linguistic landscape of the Ottoman Empire.[7] And while significant in its own right, it is just the tip of the iceberg: the commissioner of the epigraphic panel, Ali Pasha, mobilized a wider program of unconventional inscriptions in architectural spaces throughout his territory to promote himself as a legitimate and just ruler. This chapter explores his efforts to stage his public persona by way of three case studies of poetic inscriptions created to adorn a range of buildings, from the city walls of Ioannina to a macabre memorial marking the destruction of a town accused of insurrection. All three inscriptions employ a metrical text in demotic Greek, rare examples of this style of poetry being used for public display outside a strictly Christian context. By placing inscriptions above the thresholds of various monuments, already a well-established practice in Ottoman lands, Ali Pasha worked within certain preexisting "epigraphic habits" of imperial architecture, but he was also experimental in his approach to finding new configurations for coexisting yet disparate visual and textual traditions.[8]

PUBLIC TEXTS IN THE OTTOMAN WORLD

Inscriptions on architecture are nothing new. People have been writing on buildings for millennia, and to some extent all public texts convey an ideology and promote a certain worldview. In the case of Ali Pasha in Epirus, epigraphy can serve as a useful barometer for tracking the shifting political and cultural discourse between imperial center and periphery. Investigating how particular epigraphic habits are developed, upheld, modified, or completely disregarded in Ottoman lands helps us better understand what it was to be Ottoman, the answer being in a constant state of flux and a matter of negotiation.

As a point of comparison from another famous empire, scholars of ancient Rome have spilled much ink exploring the role of epigraphy in the definition of local identity vis-à-vis the central state.[9] One of the most important examples in this regard is the *Res Gestae Divi Augusti* (*The Deeds of the Divine Augustus*), a monumental inscription recording the accomplishments of the first Roman emperor. While one copy of the text was placed in the imperial center of Rome at the Mausoleum of Augustus, the only surviving examples can be found in what was then the province of Galatia, located in today's Turkey. The best-known version is located at the Citadel of Ankara, where the original Latin text and a Greek translation are inscribed on the exterior of the Temple of Augustus and Rome (fig. 78). The Greek version, however, is not a word-for-word translation and appears to have been generated in the provinces and adapted for the local Greek-speaking audience. The historian Alison Cooley has argued that this bilingual inscription could have been commissioned by the provincial governor of Galatia, and not at the impetus of the central authority in Rome, as has been generally assumed.[10] Cooley's new analysis brings the case study of Ali Pasha in Epirus into sharp focus. While the bilingual inscription of the *Res Gestae* in Ankara can be interpreted as a point of mediation between Rome and the provinces, the evidence pointing to the agency of local administrators in this process, there is no denying that the text itself is a blatant piece of political propaganda on behalf of the imperial center. Meanwhile, the inscriptions

FIGURE 77 (*opposite*) Bilingual inscription in Greek and Ottoman Turkish once located above the eastern entrance of the Tepelena citadel, 1819. Tepelena History Museum.

FIGURE 78
Remains of the Temple of Augustus and Rome in Ankara. The entirety of the *Res Gestae* in Latin and Greek translation can be found inscribed on this exterior wall of the sanctuary. Photo by author.

commissioned by Ali Pasha also serve as acts of political self-fashioning on behalf of a provincial ruler, but with little to no apparent engagement with epigraphic practices emanating from Istanbul.

As early as the first decades of Ottoman rule, architectural inscriptions played an important role in state formation.[11] Most studies of epigraphy from the Ottoman period divide such texts into three main categories: commemorative inscriptions, pious inscriptions found in Islamic religious settings such as a mosque or *medrese*, and epitaphs.[12] This literature tends to focus on imperial patronage and Muslim contexts, while the multiconfessional—and thus multilingual—nature of life in the empire remains relatively underexamined, with information about architectural epigraphy from, say, Greek Orthodox, Armenian, and Jewish communities confined to more specialized publications.[13] As already demonstrated by the inscription from Tepelena, these epigraphic traditions not only existed parallel to one another but also at times converged.

Because this chapter investigates a series of commemorative texts commissioned by an Ottoman administrator, a few comments about state-sponsored epigraphy are in order. While sultans tended to commission foundation inscriptions written in Arabic in the first centuries of Ottoman rule, continuing the practice of their predecessors in Anatolia, the Seljuks of Rum, by the sixteenth century Ottoman Turkish had become the conventional language for dedicatory texts.[14] By the early nineteenth century, when Ali Pasha came to power, foundation inscriptions for architectural monuments like sultanic mosques and fountains followed a predictable set of basic standards. These aesthetic principles can be observed in a representative example from the Selimiye Mosque in the Üsküdar district of Istanbul, constructed by Sultan Selim III in 1804–5 (fig. 79).[15] The Ottoman Turkish text commemorating the construction of the building is carved in relief on a stone panel, organized into cartouches with dividing lines and gilded against a dark painted ground to make it more legible from a distance. This panel is also surmounted by a *ṭuğra*, a stylized calligraphic form of the sultan's name and titles that serves as the ruler's official monogram.[16] While the *tuğra* had long been used in manuscripts, especially for imperial decrees, its

FIGURE 79
Foundation inscription of the Selimiye Mosque in the Üsküdar neighborhood of Istanbul, 1804–5. From H. Aynur, K. Hayashi, and H. Karateke, eds., Database of Ottoman Inscriptions, http://www.ottomaninscriptions.com, Card ID: K1718, accessed August 12, 2023.

regular appearance in architectural epigraphy only began in the early eighteenth century under the reign of Sultan Ahmed III (r. 1703–30).[17]

In the provinces, Ali Pasha's precursors and peers were commissioning their own foundations and setting up inscriptions that more or less followed similar conventions. Take, for instance, the foundation inscription of the central congregational mosque in Yozgat, which was first established in 1779 by members of the Çapanoğlu family, Ali Pasha's *ayan* contemporaries (fig. 80, and see fig. 7). The text of the foundation inscription is in Ottoman Turkish and celebrates the head of the district, Çapanoğlu Mustafa Bey, for raising the "lofty dome" of the mosque; the panel is crowned by an immense *tuğra* of Sultan Abdülhamid I, the ruling sultan at the time.[18] As a family of notables who maintained fairly close and congenial relations with the Porte, the Çapanoğlus likewise opted for a foundation inscription that rehearsed a visual and textual vocabulary in line with what was being produced in Istanbul. A few decades later, in 1812, another provincial administrator named Muhammad Ağa Abu Nabbut established his own mosque complex in the city of Jaffa, today part of the wider municipality of Tel Aviv. The cross-vaulted arcades and cylindrical buttresses found in these structures adhere to more local architectural idioms, and the foundation inscription above the southwestern entrance to the prayer hall is in Arabic,

POETIC JUSTICE   145

FIGURE 80
Foundation inscription of the Çapanoğlu Mosque in Yozgat, 1779. Photo by author.

the predominantly spoken language in the region.[19] Yet the patron Abu Nabbut had also included the *tuğra* of Sultan Mahmud II in this epigraphic program, indicating official imperial support for the project.

If architectural epigraphy serves as a gauge for a provincial ruler's negotiated relationship with the imperial center, Ali Pasha's approach falls at the opposite end of the spectrum from that of the Çapanoğlu family in Yozgat, with Abu Nabbut in Jaffa somewhere in the middle. This is a simplification, but it is important to emphasize just how divergent Ali Pasha's inscriptions were at a time when the iconography of the sultan evidently possessed a certain cachet throughout Ottoman lands, from central Anatolia to the shores of Syria-Palestine. The following case studies rely on other markers of legitimacy, introducing a new script for

Ottoman administration and perhaps even paving the way for a new ruling order.

ENGAGEMENTS WITH ANTIQUITY

As part of the ongoing campaign to present himself as an effective leader, Ali Pasha sought to forge connections between himself and the heroes of the ancient world. I have explored elsewhere how the governor and his son Veli Pasha were engaged in a wide range of antiquarian pursuits, from archaeological excavations at Mycenae to the construction of a villa that commemorated Ali Pasha's victory over Napoleon's troops at the Battle of Nikopolis in 1798.[20] The villa is significant in that it seems to have been positioned in precisely the place where the Roman emperor Augustus had built his own memorial to his triumph over Anthony and Cleopatra at the Battle of Actium almost

FIGURE 81
Greek inscription commemorating Ali Pasha's renovation of the city walls in Ioannina, 1815, today held by the city's Byzantine Museum. Ministry of Culture / Ephorate of Antiquities of Ioannina / Fethiye Mosque–Archaeological Site of the Acropolis of the Its Kale Castle of Ioannina, no. 4858/2021.

two millennia earlier. Yet the most explicit effort to brand Ali Pasha as the scion of heroes past is a surviving architectural inscription written in Greek that frames the governor as the "new Pyrrhus" (fig. 81). A Hellenistic-era general, Pyrrhus (318–272 BCE) served as the leader of the so-called Epirote League, a coalition of the main city-states in the region.[21] This king of Epirus frequently challenged and prevailed over the early leaders of Rome, but at the considerable cost of his own men, which is why we owe to him the term "Pyrrhic victory." The association between Ali Pasha and Pyrrhus, which reflects a view of history that transcends the immediate political realities of the Ottoman Empire, was explored not only in public inscriptions but also in poetic works, indicating a broader local discourse on antiquity.

The Greek inscription in which Ali Pasha invokes the name of this ancient ruler once appeared in a niche on the right side of the southeastern entrance to the walled city of Ioannina (fig. 82, and see what is labeled Gate B in fig. 83).[22] This marble plaque is today on display at the city's Byzantine Museum. It commemorates the completion of Ali Pasha's

POETIC JUSTICE

FIGURE 82
Entrance to the Ioannina citadel on the southeastern side of the city walls. Photo by author.

FIGURE 83 (opposite)
The main entrance portals to the city walls (red) and southeastern citadel (yellow) of Ioannina. Map by Matthew J. Jacobson.

renovation and reconstruction of Ioannina's walls in 1815, which, as discussed in previous chapters, was a major infrastructure project that employed more than a thousand laborers and masons. Because archival and archaeological evidence suggests that the rebuilding of the wall system took place in phases over several years, the date found on the inscription can be considered a *terminus ante quem*.

The text itself, which has been carefully executed by a skilled stoneworker, consists of twenty lines of metrical verse, organized into ten rhyming couplets, with the second line of each couplet distinguished by an indentation on the left.[23] Although the top left corner of the inscription has been lost, obscuring our ability to comprehend the meaning of the first six lines in its entirety, it is clear that this text not only records Ali Pasha's building efforts but also situates his actions within an imagined longer history of the city. The fragmentary lines that remain indicate that the inscription begins with the initial construction of Ioannina in ancient times and then goes on to highlight the ineptitude of later rulers, when the fortification walls inevitably required maintenance and repair.

(7) In order to renew and rise up
(8) . . . to recover the walls again
(9) As the former bishops pled
(10) And always asked for renovation
(11) And though when many centuries passed
(12) And with them many rulers and sovereigns
(13) No one could take up the responsibility
(14) And prove to be a benefactor to this country
(15) And despite all the many years that passed
(16) Failed to lay down a single stone

Having thus justified the urgent need to update the city walls, the text continues:

(17) Until the most powerful Ali Pasha the vizier of Epirus
(18) The renowned descendant of Pyrrhus the marvelous
(19) As another wondrous flame he brings this [city] back to life
(20) And restores it as beautiful as ever
(21) 1815[24]

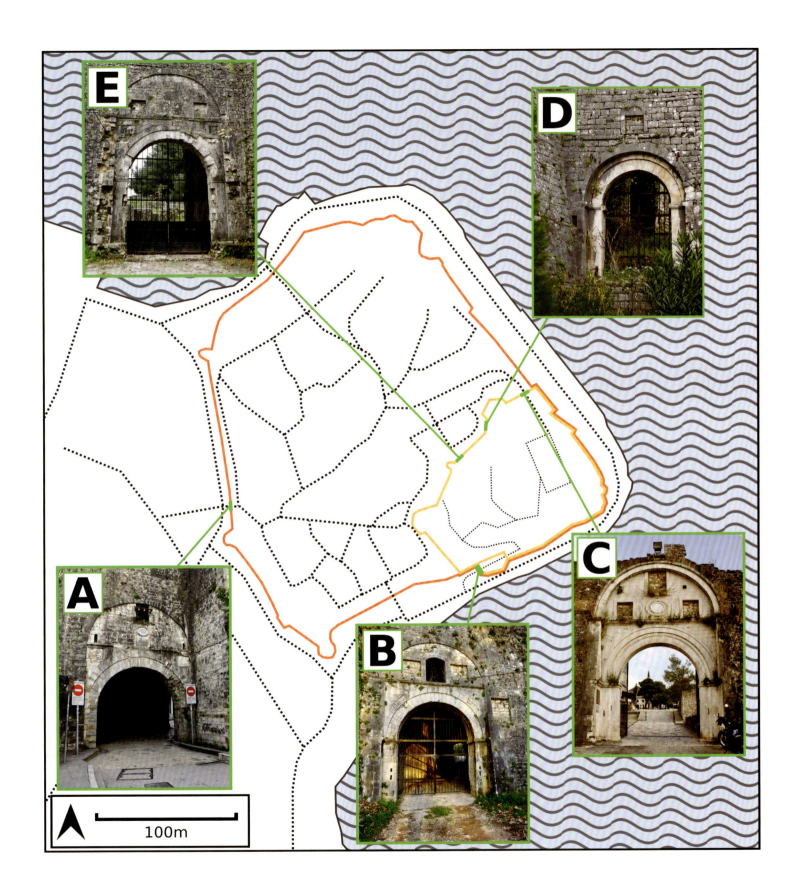

In this inscription, the main criterion of successful stewardship is measured by a ruler's capacity to build—in this case, to maintain the fabric of the town walls. As discussed in chapter 2, the majority of Ioannina's outer walls as we see them today were reconstructed in the early nineteenth century by Ali Pasha. When looking at the masonry on the interior of these curtain walls, it is possible to observe that, at least in some sections, Ali Pasha's engineers did not entirely replace whatever remained of the previous Byzantine fortifications, either leaving some portions exposed or jacketing them with a new skin of cut limestone blocks, updating the fortress design with polygonal bastions and an enceinte.[25] Thus, just as the inscription reflects upon the long lifespan of Ioannina's walls, these engineers were likewise engaged in actively "reading" the historical layers of the masonry. For a long time, scholars assumed that the city dated only to the Byzantine period, but recent archaeological excavations reveal that the walls of Ioannina were apparently first built in the Hellenistic period, upon whose giant ashlar stones the Byzantine fortification system was elaborated over the centuries.[26] While it is impossible to say whether Ali Pasha's masons came across these more ancient foundation blocks, which are submerged several meters below the modern street level, one should note that the governor's efforts to connect himself to a famed Hellenistic king in verse is mirrored in the stratigraphy of the walls themselves.

This inscription proposes a teleological view of the succession of civilizations and rulers who have governed the region, and Ali Pasha is presented as the necessary antidote to centuries of neglect and decline. The assertion that Ali Pasha—an Ottoman administrator who was confessionally Muslim—is the best thing that has happened to Epirus since antiquity undermines the notion that Ottoman authorities were oppressing the enslaved Hellas, an argument being made around the same time by Greek revolutionaries and philhellenes.[27] While the notion of the *Tourkokratia* (Turkish dominion)—a conventional Greek term used by modern historians for Ottoman rule—frames state functionaries as an external occupying force, the inscription in Ioannina positions Ali Pasha as the ultimate insider. He is styled as the "vizier of Epirus" (line 17), a conflation of different political configurations in that "vizier" is a distinctively Ottoman title, while Epirus is the historical name for the region from antiquity to the medieval period. At least from the perspective of the Porte in Istanbul, there was no such thing as a "vizier of Epirus": in terms of Ottoman administrative geography, the city of Ioannina was the capital of a district of the same name (Ott. Yanya), which was in turn part of the province of Rumeli. Ali Pasha's claim on the region of Epirus thus raises the question of what exactly is implied by the phrase "a benefactor to this country" (line 14): which, or, perhaps even more important, whose, country is being invoked here? The Greek word used for "country" (πατρίδα, *patrida*) in the poem could also be translated as "fatherland," a term that asserts the governor's deep bond with an imagined line of ancestors who held the area before him, all the way back to antiquity.

In the inscription, Ali Pasha and Pyrrhus are not only compared via their analogous legacies as strongman rulers of Epirus, united by a duty to serve their homeland; the text goes even further, asserting a genealogical kinship—Ali Pasha is designated the progeny, the "descendant" (απόγονος, *apogonos*, line 18), of Pyrrhus. This term is not typically used in Greek in a metaphorical sense; it implies an actual bond through a shared bloodline. Ali Pasha's connection with Pyrrhus is further reinforced with the description of the vizier as "another wondrous flame" (line 19). The word used for "flame" is not the common *fotia*, which also appears in this inscription in line 2, but the rarer term *pir*, creating an elegant pun on the name of Pyrrhus (*Piros*), which occurs at the end of the previous line. Thus Ali Pasha is another flame, another Pyrrhus, who through his cleansing abilities tears down the older city fabric only to construct it anew.

While the content of this inscription strives to link past and present, the style of the text does not follow an established epigraphic tradition. The inscription is written for the most part in what is commonly known as "demotic" or "political" verse, a fifteen-syllable iambic meter that had been one of the primary formats of popular Greek poetry from the later Byzantine period until the days of Ali Pasha.[28] In the Byzantine period, fifteen-syllable verse was commonly found in manuscripts and could also be performed orally, usually in an imperial court setting; its appearance in architectural epigraphy was exceedingly rare.[29] Attitudes changed under Ottoman rule, but throughout the early modern period comparable inscriptions seem to have been composed and executed exclusively within an ecclesiastical context, either appearing in church frescos or adorning icons.[30] From the perspective of the wider field of Byzantine and "post-Byzantine" epigrams, therefore, Ali Pasha's Greek inscriptions are highly unusual on two counts: they are secular texts, and they are carved in stone and appear on building exteriors, as opposed to being painted in a church interior. No one in Epirus would have seen anything quite like this before.

Yet there were plenty of people in Ioannina who would have been familiar with, and could appreciate, the Greek poetry used in this foundation inscription. The relative sophistication of the text, in terms of vocabulary and references to ancient history, points to an author who was highly educated and operated in elite intellectual circles, inevitably someone from among the city's Greek-speaking notables. Ioannina was a prominent center of the Greek Enlightenment movement at the turn of the century. Under Ali Pasha's tenure, there were two major academies for the local Christian population: the Kaplaneios and Balanos schools.[31] I submit that the leader of the former, Athanasios Psalidas (1767–1829), is one possible candidate for the authorship of the poem in question. The traveler William Haygarth described the curriculum Psalidas designed as steeped in the classics while promoting modern Greek literature:

> There are schools in Ioannina for instruction in the ancient Greek, and with the master of one of them, Athanas Psalidas, I was well acquainted. He was certainly the most learned man I met in Greece, well skilled in the ancient language of his country, and master of Latin, Italian, French, German and Russ. According to the information which he gave me, the cultivation of literature is making considerable advances amongst the modern Greeks. At his own school he taught Thucydides, Xenophon, Theophrastus, and Homer. Psalidas had published a metaphysical and theological work, entitled Ἀληθής Ευδαιμονία [*Alithis Evdaimonia, True Prosperity*]. He has also made a collection of songs and canzonets in the Romaic language entitled Ἔρωτος Ἀποτελέσματα [*Erotos Apotelesmata, The Consequences of Love*]. He is likewise a geographer, and is about to publish a map of Albania.[32]

The collection of songs mentioned in this passage, *Erotos Apotelesmata*, includes many poems in fifteen-syllable verse, the same style of the inscription's text.[33] As I will discuss in the next section, another possible author of the Ioannina inscription is Ioannis Vilaras (1771–1823), a well-known writer and physician in the service of Veli Pasha also living in the city at the time.[34] Vilaras was even more famous than Psalidas for his poetry, a good deal of which was written in demotic verse.[35]

One key point about the inscription is that it is written in a contemporary vernacular language, in contrast to an archaizing register looking to ancient Greek. Psalidas and Vilaras were actively engaged in what is commonly referred to as the "language question," a debate among scholars beginning in the late eighteenth century about whether a (then-hypothetical) Greek state should adopt as its official language the common dialect or a retrofitted version of ancient Greek.[36] Both men could be described as populist champions of the common tongue, maintaining that demotic Greek was a worthy steward of the preservation and advancement of what they understood to be their own cultural heritage all the way back to antiquity. With its references to Hellenistic and medieval rulers, all expressed in contemporary language, the Ioannina inscription uniquely reflects the specific intellectual milieu of Ali Pasha's court.[37] These figures, who have long been celebrated as catalysts of the Greek Enlightenment and incubators of revolution, were also clearly employed by the governor to formulate his own claims to legitimate rule.

Even though this text was written in a vernacular register, the question remains to what extent the inscription would have been accessible to people with only functional or limited literacy in Greek. It is possible that the general subject matter or even the precise language could have been conveyed to a wider audience via oral transmission. While the inscription itself is relatively long, the metrical beats and rhyming lines make it easier to commit the text to memory. The question also lingers whether the poem's extraordinary analogy between Ali Pasha and Pyrrhus is unique, a fleeting notion never to be repeated. A review of the accounts of travelers who met and conversed with Ali Pasha reveals that the governor was fully aware of Pyrrhus and his significance to the region and was in the habit of claiming descent from the ancient king on a regular basis. William Martin Leake writes:

> It must be admitted the success with which Alý has indulged his ambition in Greece and Albania, not only in defiance of the Porte, but hitherto with a constant increase of influence over the Supreme Government, is a proof of skill, foresight, and constancy of purpose, in which few statesmen or monarchs have ever excelled him. . . . He sometimes compares himself to Burros, because Pyrrhus was his predecessor in Epirus, and possibly because Pyrrhus is the only great man of antiquity he ever heard of except Alexander.[38]

Leaving aside Leake's snark, this passage reinforces the idea that Ali Pasha promoted an affinity with Pyrrhus owing to their common homeland of Epirus. When Thomas Hughes came to Ioannina, he was invited to a lively dinner party attended by the governor and some of his retinue: Psalidas, the archbishop of Ioannina; two leaders of the local Christian community; and a Muslim notable visiting from Istanbul. When it came time to offer toasts, "Ali gave the health of the Prince Regent, and the Royal

Family of Britain; in return for which we drank to the prosperity of his house and dynasty, and to the immortal memory of Pyrrhus, his heroic *ancestor*."[39] It is striking how closely this report mirrors the language of the architectural inscription, especially considering that this gathering took place in 1814, only a year before the creation of the epigraphic panel.

Furthermore, there is ample evidence that Ali Pasha's connections with antiquity pervaded popular culture, especially in the form of local Greek folk songs. Because of the fluid nature of oral tradition, it is often difficult to determine when a particular song was first composed and gained popularity. An important exception is the "Ballad of Ali Pasha" (*Fillada tou Alipasa*), published by the French Hellenist Émile Legrand, which chronicles Ali Pasha's dramatic last stand and mourns his execution at the hands of the sultan's men.[40] Although Legrand published this song in 1886, he relates in his preface to the text that he first transcribed the poem in Athens in 1875, as dictated by an old Epirote named Jean (Ioannis) Pagounis, who had been a baker in Ioannina and remembered the song from his youth, which could easily place this song shortly after Ali Pasha's death in 1822. This man was supposedly illiterate and could recite the some 650-line poem by heart "without hesitation."[41] The sympathetic tone of the poem itself and the opening invocation that Ali Pasha's soul find God's mercy (ραχμέτι, *rahmeti*)—a conventional Islamic prayer for the dead—indicates that the original composer was a Muslim from the Epirus region. This attribution serves as a stark reminder that the genre of Greek folk songs cannot be assumed to be the singular domain of Christians living in the Ottoman Balkans but rather reflects a local tradition shared by multiple confessions. The slain vizier is hailed in the opening lines of the ballad in evocative terms: "The renowned Ali Pasha, the hero of Epirus, / The awesome and terrible, the imitator of Pyrrhus."[42] Here, Ali Pasha is first and foremost designated as a formidable warrior from the region of Epirus, and the author does not invoke any of the governor's official Ottoman titles. The specific word used to describe Ali Pasha's relationship with Pyrrhus—μιμητής (*mimitis*), which can be translated as "imitator," or more poetically as "mirror"—again raises themes of regeneration and genealogy. As the "mirror" of Pyrrhus, Ali Pasha is presented as the contemporary embodiment of the foregone hero of Epirus. While the inscription commissioned for the walls of Ioannina was a unique product of Ali Pasha's court, it is equally important to note that in Ioannina these references to antiquity, and more specifically to Pyrrhus, extended beyond that rarefied circle and pervaded the popular imagination.

Finally, it is essential to note that the Greek inscription at the Ioannina citadel was also originally accompanied by another text, this one in Arabic (fig. 84). In 1970, the architectural historian Machiel Kiel was able to photograph the text in its original location, which was the left niche directly above the southern water entrance (see fig. 82).[43] The panel has gone missing in the intervening decades; it was no longer in place when I first visited Ioannina in 2012. It is somewhat unusual that the inscription in question is in Arabic and not Ottoman Turkish, though these languages are not mutually exclusive. That this inscription is relatively short means that anyone trained in reading the Qur'an, the standard curriculum in Muslim schools (of which there were several in Ioannina), should have been able to decipher the text.[44] As discussed in the previous chapter, Ali Pasha's court included both Christians and

FIGURE 84
Arabic inscription commemorating the renovation of Ioannina's city walls, 1815. Photo: Machiel Kiel.

Muslims who served as scribes, translators, and liaisons to their respective communities. To some extent, the pairing of the Greek and Arabic inscriptions above the southeastern citadel entrance, which provided immediate access to the governor's palace within the walls, reflected two parallel systems of education in the city.

This Arabic inscription itself was of very high quality, with three main lines of thuluth script cut in shallow relief, surrounded by a thin raised band forming a cartouche around the text:

(1) The patron of the charitable work and [ancient] remains
(2) And overlord of this praiseworthy fortress
(3) The victorious vizier Ali Pasha
(4) 1230[45]

The Hijri date of 1230 corresponds to the year 1815 given in the adjacent Greek inscription, an indication that both stone plaques were created at the same time for the gate. What's more, the Arabic text promotes similar themes of stewardship, in this case within the context of Islamic culture: the term "charitable work" (*hayr*) is a specific word typically used in the tradition of pious endowments (*vakıf*), which were used to fund the construction and maintenance of religious institutions like mosques. While the renovation of the city's walls was a secular project that probably could not have been technically covered by such an endowment, the use of this particular term would have conjured the associated connotations of philanthropy in the minds of Muslim viewers. At the same time, both inscriptions underscore Ali Pasha's dedication to the rebuilding of Ioannina's walls, which had gone without major restoration for centuries.[46] The Greek text goes even further to establish the governor's relationship with the ancient rulers of Epirus, a trope equally accessible to all members of the different confessions living under Ali Pasha's dominion, through public texts, popular poetry, and the vizier's own proclamations.

THE DEVELOPMENT OF HERALDIC INSIGNIA

Although the inscriptions above the southeastern citadel entrance are the only examples dating from Ali Pasha's time in Ioannina that have come down to us in some fashion, it seems that there was a much larger program designed for all five gates of the city's castle (labeled A–E in fig. 83). All of these portals feature rectangular-shaped niches similar in size and arrangement to those found at the southeastern gate (Gate B). It is possible that these niches held copies of the Greek and Arabic inscriptions or different texts on a similar theme.

FIGURE 85
Zoomorphic plaque above one of the gates to the walled district of Ioannina. Photo by author.

A number of the niches found above the gates of Ioannina were also flanked by zoomorphic figures, many of which do survive and remain in situ. These are significant because they are yet another example of how the governor went beyond the norms of self-presentation in Ottoman spatial contexts. A pair of zoomorphic plaques above Gate A feature lively animal scenes, the one on the left side depicting what appears to be a snake encountering a lion or panther, and the one on the right showing a similar feline creature with one of its front paws resting on an orb, while a stag appears in the background (fig. 85). Two other examples can be found above the arch of the northwest entrance to the Ioannina citadel (Gate E). These two plaques, which are almost mirror images of each other, can be described as more abstract depictions of lions, showing just the silhouette of the figures (fig. 86). Although the flattened rendering of these lions makes it appear as if a circular shape is protruding directly from their chests, we can assume that the animals are resting one of their front paws on an orb.

The practice of using zoomorphic figures as architectural decoration goes beyond the walls of Ioannina: plaques of similar size and iconography can be found in other fortifications that Ali Pasha constructed throughout the region. In the port city of Preveza, for example, on the southwestern bastion of the

POETIC JUSTICE 155

FIGURE 86
Zoomorphic plaque above one of the entrances to the southeastern citadel of Ioannina. Photo by author.

Agios Andreas Fortress, is a panel with a lion that closely resembles one of the examples from Ioannina (fig. 87; compare fig. 85). Instead of a stag, however, this plaque features on the right the figure of a person with his (?) hands raised, presumably in a gesture of intimidation or surprise. Even more interesting are a pair of panels above the entrance to Ali Pasha's triangular fortress on the Aktion peninsula facing Preveza, the one on the left showing a human figure reining in a chained lion, with a mosque distinguished by its minaret in the background (fig. 88). The plaque on the right, with a foundation date of 1812, features what seems to be a lion with something protruding from its mouth, either a ball of flame or the grislier option of a human hand (fig. 89).[47]

Many of the gateways of Ali Pasha's foundations are therefore adorned not only with striking inscriptions but also with a menagerie of fearsome beasts, especially lions. The lion has long functioned as a symbol for ruling authority in many cultures, especially those around the Mediterranean and in the Middle East. Examples from antiquity range from the facing pair above the main entrance of the Bronze Age citadel of Mycenae (ca. 1250 BCE) to Nebuchadnezzar's striding lions at the Ishtar Gate in Babylon (ca. 575 BCE). Fast-forward to the medieval period, when it was common for both Mamluk and Seljuk rulers to use felines, both lions and panthers, as heraldic blazons for particular rulers.[48] Despite this seemingly ubiquitous tradition of the lion as a signifier of power, Ali Pasha's extensive deployment of these feline figures on the gates of his fortifications is remarkable given the immediate context of Ottoman architectural practices.

Heghnar Watenpaugh has observed that the Ottoman ruling elite did not use personal emblems in the same way that their Mamluk predecessors did, perhaps owing to a stricter observance of the convention in Islamic societies to avoid figural representation in public settings, especially religious monuments.[49] As discussed earlier, the closest analogue to a blazon was the Ottoman sultan's *tuğra*, its use in architectural commissions implying the ruler's official support. In one remarkable example from Ali Pasha's tekke complex in the village of Hormova near Tepelena, two lions facing each other are carved in relief on the doorjamb of the main entrance to the mosque, something that was quite common in contemporary churches in the region but would have been unthinkable in, say, an Istanbul mosque. It therefore seems that these lions of Epirus are engaged in alternative visual traditions beyond the customs formulated by the Ottoman center.

As so often with iconographic programs, it is difficult to reach a definitive conclusion about the precise intention behind this imagery, or about how it was received. The location of most of these plaques above central points of entry to fortifications suggests an apotropaic or talismanic function, the figures designed to ward off enemies. Yet I maintain that many of these figural plaques respond to the wider Venetian practice of placing the official emblem of the republic—the lion of Saint Mark—on fortifications.[50] The legacy of the Serenissima was not a distant memory in this region: the Venetians once held several of the coastal territories that eventually came under Ali Pasha's rule, such as Preveza and Butrint, and the republic finally collapsed in the early years of the governor's rule. Examples of Saint Mark's lion abound throughout the eastern Mediterranean, but to best demonstrate a potential connection with Ali Pasha's constructions, we should look no further than the Venetian strongholds at the Ionian Islands of Corfu and Lefkada (known as Santa Maura to the Venetians) (see fig. 34). In Corfu Town, the so-called New Fortress, built in stages throughout the late sixteenth and early seventeenth centuries, prominently features a large rectangular plaque with the winged lion of Saint Mark above the main entrance to the citadel (fig. 90).[51] Meanwhile, the smaller fortress guarding the harbor at Lefkada has a similar, albeit smaller-scale, configuration, with the lion of Saint Mark carved in low relief and placed centrally over the main gate. There is another plaque on the exterior of the fortress with the striking image of the winged lion holding aloft a sword (fig. 91).

One factor that suggests a more direct connection between the zoomorphic plaques on Ali Pasha's foundations and the lion of Saint Mark is that several of the feline figures commissioned by the governor have a front paw resting on an orb. A globe is a generic symbol of

FIGURE 87
Zoomorphic plaque on the southwestern bastion of the Fortress of Agios Andreas in Preveza. Photo by author.

FIGURE 88
Zoomorphic plaque located on the left above the main entrance of the Aktion Fortress, Preveza. Photo by author.

FIGURE 89
Zoomorphic plaque located on the right above the main entrance of the Aktion Fortress, Preveza. Photo by author.

dominium, but this particular configuration is perhaps best interpreted as a modified translation of the Venetian lion holding under its paw an open codex, a reference to the Gospel of Saint Mark (see fig. 90). When Ali Pasha set out in the early nineteenth century to construct his own series of coastal fortifications and defensive city walls, the legacy of Venetian military might, symbolized in Venice's fortresses, still loomed large in the imaginations of those who lived in the former Venetian territories and among the Ottoman subjects just on the other side of this imperial border in mainland Epirus. It is especially tempting to compare the plaques at the Fortress of Aktion with the older Venetian relief embedded in the eastern face of the exterior curtain wall of the Santa Maura Fortress (see figs. 88 and 91). In the latter, the lion of Saint Mark wields a sword menacingly, either defending or storming a fortified castle; the former, which has a remarkably similar composition, features a chained male lion with a mosque in the background. The panel at Aktion may boast of the governor's ability to "tame" the lion of Venice, a republic that for many years had been his greatest foreign opponent, holding the Ionian Islands and their key footholds on the mainland. It is important to note the close proximity of these two images: one of the main strategic functions of the Aktion Fortress was to monitor the Santa Maura fortification across the bay, maintaining a direct sightline to the other structure and only a few kilometers away as the crow flies. Thus, at least in the case of Preveza, Ali Pasha's plaques deploying lion imagery may have been engaging in a site-specific visual competition across a vanishingly thin transimperial border.

That said, all of the figural plaques we find in Ioannina and Preveza would not necessarily have been understood as a literal appropriation of the lion of Saint Mark, but might have operated more loosely as references to the generic visual language of heraldry. As the symbol of Venice, the lion of Saint Mark is usually equipped with a fixed set of attributes: a halo, wings, codex, and sometimes a sword or cross. In Ali Pasha's foundations, however, the lions above gates are never distinguished by a halo or

FIGURE 90
Relief sculpture of the lion of Saint Mark above the main entrance to the Venetian "New Fortress" in Corfu Town. Photo by author.

wings. With these identifying markers eliminated, the lion is deactivated as the symbol of Venice and rendered available for use by Ali Pasha as a heraldic device.

In European travel accounts, Ali Pasha was frequently referred to as the "Lion of Ioannina." In an 1822 biography, Alphonse de Beauchamp claimed that "a coat of arms was *found* for [Ali Pasha] by one well skilled in heraldry; it consisted of a *Lion in a field Gules embracing three young Lions*, the emblem of his dynasty."[52] Additionally, in the local culture of Epirus, a brave warrior was often referred to as a lion, an animal that connotes bravery as well as ferocity.[53] This tradition is specifically found in Greek folk songs. For example, in the *Alipasiad*, the epic poem commissioned by Ali Pasha, the preamble explicitly describes its patron in such terms:

He is the crown of the Albanians, the lion [ασλάνι, *aslani*] of Rumelia,
....
Albania has not produced another warrior such as he.
The hero of the Albanians, the fearsome lion [λειοντάρι, *leiondari*].[54]

The *Alipasiad*'s narrator, Haji Sehreti, invokes not only the vocabulary in the Ottoman Turkish context of the lion (*aslan*) as a brave warrior, but also the Greek term denoting lion (*leiondari*), from which the English term is derived. In his account of visiting Ali Pasha in 1813, Thomas Hughes reported that when he met with the governor in the audience chamber of his palace at Litharitsa, the governor received his guests seated upon a lion's pelt.[55]

FIGURE 91
Plaque on the exterior of the Santa Maura Fortress in Lefkada. Photo by author.

It is thus no real surprise that another Greek inscription commissioned by Ali Pasha in 1814 makes explicit reference to the governor's personal emblem. This panel once appeared at the entrance to Ali Pasha's coastal fortress at Porto Palermo, last seen in place in the 1990s (fig. 92).[56] The main text consists of fourteen lines of Greek that form rhyming couplets:

1814 February
(1) O foreign seafarers turn your bows without fear
(2) [For] in the sea of Palermo, the anger of the wind disappears
(3) As for that which you now see on my [brow] like a star
(4) It is the trophy of victory, the glimmering castle
(5) With zeal the brides of Himara resurrected it
(6) Hostile to adversaries and amiable to friends
(7) Phaethon introduced me [and] Pyrrhus possessed me before
(8) Ali the foremost [and] the hero of Tepelena holds me [now]
(9) The master plenipotentiary in the parts of Epirus
(10) And an incomparable general with sword in hand
(11) He holds fifty thousand troops at his command
(12) Always fearless and courageous against his enemy
(13) In Ioannina the brave lion [λειοντάρι, leiondari] rests
(14) Born of Athena, raised by Ares[57]

160 ARCHITECTURAL REVOLUTION ON THE OTTOMAN FRONTIER

The photograph of this inscription in situ shows that this marble plaque was in virtually the same format and style of the metrical text found at Ioannina, evidence that they may have been created by the same masons. The inscription at Porto Palermo also appears as a poem in a 1935 edition of the collected works of Ioannis Vilaras, the famous writer from Ioannina, which strongly suggests that he is the author of this and possibly of all the metrical inscriptions commissioned by Ali Pasha.[58] Interestingly, there are a few small differences in vocabulary between the poem published in the Vilaras anthology and the architectural inscription itself—nothing that changes the overall meaning of the text, but perhaps evidence of a drafting process before the poem was committed to stone.[59] Another feature of the inscription that strengthens the connection to Vilaras is that it follows simplified spelling conventions introduced by the writer in his 1814 treatise *The Romaic Language* (*H Romeiki glosa*), published the same year the inscription was produced.[60] As mentioned above, Vilaras was a champion of demotic Greek in the ongoing "language debate," and this treatise proposes nothing less than an abandonment of ancient Greek orthography, which had been preserved in the modern written language over the centuries, in favor of a phonetic system of spelling.[61] That Vilaras was allowed the opportunity to pilot his radical new approach to the Greek language in such an open fashion—in an architectural inscription commissioned for one of Ali Pasha's fortifications—calls for a reassessment of the governor's role in the Greek Enlightenment and underscores the unorthodox nature of this epigraphic program, found in monuments across Epirus.

The inscription begins with the land itself—a small peninsula jutting into the bay

FIGURE 92
Greek inscription above the main entrance to the fortification at Porto Palermo, commemorating Ali Pasha's completion of the fortress in 1814. This photograph was taken in the 1990s, before the marble plaque disappeared. Photo: Auron Tare.

POETIC JUSTICE   161

of Porto Palermo—"speaking" in the first person, which prompts the viewer to consider the fortress's position within a deeper chronology of the landscape (see fig. 35). Compared to the inscription in Ioannina, the text here goes even further in its citations of antiquity by acknowledging again that Pyrrhus had once ruled the lands of Epirus and concluding with an astonishing description of Ali Pasha as "born of Athena" and "raised by Ares," the gods of wisdom and war in ancient Greece. Most notable for this discussion of Ali Pasha's use of figural plaques on public monuments, these references to classical mythology are combined with the contemporary concept in folklore of the brave hero as a lion (line 13). This inscription thus supports an interpretation of the feline figures above the gates of Ali Pasha's fortifications not as generic talismans but as heraldic insignia specific to the person of the governor, a reference that was simultaneously evoked in popular song. At Porto Palermo, the marble inscription was originally flanked by two smaller niches above the main doorway (see fig. 92). Although these spaces are now empty, given the decorative programs at Ali Pasha's fortresses in Ioannina and Preveza, it would not be surprising if they once contained some kind of lion imagery.

Especially considering that all the inscriptions and architectural imagery discussed so far appear on city gates or military outposts, the multiple descriptions of Ali Pasha as a fearless warrior seem somewhat conventional, standard fare for texts adorning fortifications. There are a few details in the inscription at Porto Palermo, however, that hint at a distinctive brand of leadership cultivated by Ali Pasha that could be exceedingly harsh. Line 5 claims that the "brides of Himara" rebuilt the fortress "with zeal." Himara, a settlement just north of Porto Palermo, was famous for its independence and resistance to the governor's rule.[62] Because the word for "brides" (νυφάδες, *nyfades*) in the poem is almost identical to, even interchangeable with, the term that describes the nymphs of Greek mythology (νύμφες, *nymfes*), it is possible that the author is generating a fantastical origin for the castle here. In this reading, the poet proposes that the fortress was built not by human hands but by spritely supernatural beings, which would support the concept of extending this landscape's timeline back to primeval days, as seen in the phrase "Phaethon introduced me" (line 7). Yet the specific choice of terminology suggests an alternative or even dual meaning in which the wives of Ali Pasha's known enemies were responsible for the construction of a fortification purposely designed to antagonize their homeland.[63] This claim of an all-female workforce should not be taken literally, but it would have been an exceptionally grave insult on the walls of a building a stone's throw from the town of Himara. This fantasy of violation and coercion is even more disturbing in its complex layers: the women of the region were not only drafted into the service of the vizier but went happily, "with zeal." While the meaning of the passage remains debatable, perhaps intentionally so, other poetic inscriptions unambiguously celebrate Ali Pasha's severe approach to justice.

MONUMENTS OF DESTRUCTION: THE MASSACRE AT GARDIKI

Like the public texts on the walls of Ioannina and the fortress at Porto Palermo, the third known case study of Ali Pasha's architectural epigraphy in Greek verse serves as a kind of foundation inscription, but for a far grislier monument. During his tenure as governor, Ali Pasha exercised his authority to wage war against several villages that he maintained were the source of frequent unrest and rebellion. Perhaps the most famous example is the governor's siege of Souli, a Christian enclave now in modern Greece located on the other side of the Pindus Mountains from Ioannina, which concluded in 1803 with an armistice agreement.[64] But there were other occasions when a particular village fell out of favor with Ali Pasha and suffered harsh consequences, among them the massacre of the people of Gardiki (Alb. Kardhiq), a now-abandoned village in present-day Albania located in a small valley off the main road between Tepelena and Gjirokaster (fig. 93). This massacre took place in the spring of 1812 and was immediately commemorated by the governor with an inscription fixed to the ruins of a roadside inn, the Han at Valiares, where the executions took place.

The massacre at Gardiki is a difficult story. Yet a sustained investigation of what happened there, using fieldwork and archival research, allows for a deeper understanding of Ali Pasha's role in shaping a narrative that has been so heavily mythologized by Western European interpreters and later historians. The sensational tales of ruthless despots and their petty blood feuds that frequently appear in travel accounts may be dismissed as another tired Orientalist trope, with the allegedly enlightened European observing—and, yes, being titillated by—such gruesome actions (fig. 94).[65] Gardiki is of particular significance not only because of the massacre itself but also given its aftermath, when Ali Pasha sought to mark the site with a memorial. This effort to immortalize acts of terror with physical reminders in the landscape forces us to reconsider our assumptions about architectural patronage. The epigraphy at Gardiki challenges the Kantian notion that any impulse to produce an aesthetic work, whether a building or a painting or a written

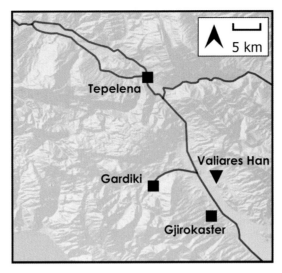

FIGURE 93
Map showing the location of the village of Gardiki and the Valiares Han. Courtesy of Matthew J. Jacobson.

text, is an inherently virtuous proposition.[66] Alongside more traditional forms of patronage, like Ali Pasha's commissioning of mosques and fortifications, the memorial at the Valiares Han participates in the manipulation of territory as a language of power.

Gardiki was a large village northwest of Gjirokaster. To reach the site today, one must follow the highway north of Gjirokaster along the Drino River Valley, on the road to Tepelena. Following a tributary of the Drino, the road opens to another, smaller river valley surrounded by mountains on all sides. After one passes a World War II monument to the Albanian soldier, the village of Gardiki comes into view on the left. The older settlement and fortress are situated on a conical hill overlooking the valley. After the massacre of 1812, the village was never fully repopulated, and to this day the remains of the nineteenth-century buildings remain crumbling next to the fortress, a veritable ghost town. A modern village named Prongji now sits at the foot

FIGURE 94
Drawn by W. Davenport and engraved by George Hunt, *The Vizier Ali Pacha, Giving the Fatal Signal, for the Slaughter of the Gardikiotes Shut up in the Khan of Valiare*. Lithograph, 25.4 × 36.5 cm. From W. Davenport, *Historical Portraiture of Leading Events in the Life of Ali Pacha* [...] (London: Thomas M'Lean, 1823). American School of Classical Studies at Athens, Gennadius Library.

of the hill, immediately visible from the ruins to the southeast (fig. 95). At the beginning of the nineteenth century, Gardiki was considered a prosperous fortified town inhabited by Muslims.[67] Its leading families owned much of the property in the surrounding area and cultivated the fields in the river valley below.[68]

The Gardiki massacre is described in the accounts of William Martin Leake, Henry Holland, Thomas Hughes, and François Pouqueville, all of whom visited the area in 1812–13, during the months directly following the event, and claimed to have heard the details from eyewitnesses.[69] The consensus of these accounts is that in March 1812, Ali Pasha's troops surrounded the village and took all the inhabitants into custody. Most of the women and children were sent away, to be resettled elsewhere. The adult males—the accounts claim anywhere from six to eight hundred men—were marched to the main road connecting Gjirokaster to Tepelena and were gathered in a roadside inn (*han*) in the village of Valiares (Alb. Valarë). There, Ali Pasha's soldiers locked the doors of the inn and executed the men inside. The governor ordered that the bodies be left in the inn and thus denied a proper burial, and that the site should be kept locked and deserted as a reminder to anyone passing along the road. As for Gardiki itself, it was not to be inhabited again, and a new village was constructed in the valley below to tend the deserted fields.

While the remains of the abandoned town are still visible today, there is no discernible trace of the inn at Valiares. This is not surprising, given that inns in this region were usually ad hoc structures that provided basic shelter, a kitchen, and an enclosure wall that could be locked at night. A watercolor sketch of a *han* on the other side of the Pindus Mountains provides an approximate idea of what the way station at Valiares may have looked like in Ali Pasha's day (fig. 96). This image reveals that such buildings usually resemble domestic architecture in that they feature a ground level of stone and an upper story of wattle-and-daub construction. Unlike religious foundations or fortifications, they were not meant to stand the test of time. Nevertheless, Ali Pasha sought to convert the inn at Valiares into what one of the European accounts described as a "monument of destruction" by placing a long poetic inscription carved in stone above its main gate after the massacre.[70]

The inscription itself also no longer survives, but it was described in detail by the several European travelers who saw it when they visited the *han*.[71] Leake gives the most information, reporting that the text had sixty-four verses, more than three times the length of the inscription in Ioannina. If that is correct, then it is likely that the inscription was carved on multiple panels fixed next to one another above the doorway. Leake also provides a sample of two lines from the original Greek text, which confirm that the inscription was in demotic verse and organized in rhyming couplets, the same format of the other two known Greek inscriptions commissioned by Ali Pasha. The full text of the poem is now lost, but Leake summarizes its content and quotes passages in translation. The inscription is supposed to begin with a dialogue between the personified *han* and the dead men inside, who explain why they can be found within its walls: "He that wishes to destroy the Moutzohousatic house / Will be sure to lose his life."[72] As noted earlier, the adjective "Moutzohousatic" refers to Ali Pasha's great-grandfather Mustafa, known locally in Albanian as Moutzo Housso, who had gained notoriety as a brigand leader in the area around Tepelena.[73] Again, the poet seeks to place the governor in a longer genealogy of local rulers. It is also fascinating to note how the building itself speaks, a rhetorical device also deployed in the inscription at Porto Palermo. Becoming animate, the *han* asks the dead men for an explanation of what has taken place there, thus anticipating the questions that a visitor may have when approaching the site. In the inscription, the massacred men continue:

> When Alý was a little boy, (μικρό παιδάκι) deprived of his father, with no brother, and only a mother, we [the Gardikiotes] ran with arms in our hands to cut him off. He escaped, skillful as he is, (ώς επιτήδιος), upon which we went to Garianí (Καργιανή) and burnt his houses. It is now fifty years since. It is for that deed that he slew us at the Khan; that he has sent our chief men to the island of the lake of Ioánnina, and there put them to death; that he has dispersed our families among all the kazás under his authority, has razed our unfortunate town to the ground, and ordered that it may remain a desert for ever. For he is a very just man, (Διότι είναι δίκαιος πολύ,) and in like manner slew the Khormovites, and ordered that not one should remain alive.[74]

At the end of the inscription, Ali Pasha himself concludes by speaking in the first person: "When I consider this terrible slaughter, I am much grieved, and I desire that so great an evil shall never occur again.... For which reason I give notice to all my neighbours that they must

FIGURE 95
The early nineteenth-century ruins of Gardiki, with the modern village of Prongji in the distance. Photo by author.

not molest my house (το οντζάκι μου να μη κακοποήσουν), but be obedient, in order that they may be happy (να υποτάσσωνται διά να ευτυχήσουν). This sad event took place the 15th of March, 1812, in the afternoon, το δειλινόν κοντά, i.e., near three o'clock."[75] When the traveler Henry Holland saw the inscription, he recognized the text as Greek verse, but he could not read it because the panels were too high above the ground. But Holland's local guard was familiar with the poem and was able to convey the gist: "such should be the fate of all who injured the family of Ali Pasha."[76] I would go one step further and argue that this was the unequivocal message of the entire site.

The inscription frames the massacre as an act of retaliation, the ultimate resolution of an injustice that had gone unaddressed for five decades. In the text, the men of Gardiki confess to their crimes, owning that they had tried to kill Ali when he was defenseless ("a little boy, deprived of his father") and, when they failed, "burnt his houses" in the village of Gariani (Alb. Karjan), located only a few kilometers north of the *han*. In the European accounts, this tale is further embellished to include the kidnapping and violation of Ali's mother and sister, a general theme of violence against women that may be echoed in the inscription at Porto Palermo, as discussed above.[77]

The text above the gate at Valiares offers a specific narrative that blends gruesome fact with convenient fiction. We can better understand this editorial process by examining several archival sources, which point to the more immediate political concerns that seem to have led to the decision to destroy Gardiki. Documents from Ali Pasha's chancery indicate that

FIGURE 96
William Haygarth, *Khan at the Foot of the Pindus at Malacasi* [Malakasi], 1810. Ink on paper, 27.5 × 40.5 cm. No. 28, Gennadius Collection. American School of Classical Studies at Athens, Gennadius Library.

the governor maintained a cordial correspondence with the headman of the town, Demir Ağa, primarily for the purpose of coordinating the gathering of troops in the service of the vizier.[78] In this archive, the first hint of what is to come appears in May 1811, when Ali Pasha's sons Veli and Muhtar wrote to their father from the front lines in Sophia (in what today is Bulgaria) that the notables of Gardiki among their ranks had asked them to intercede with their father. Veli and Muhtar requested that "he forgive the transgression" of the Gardikiotes.[79] While they offer no further information about this particular offense, probably because their father was already aware of it, the fact that Veli and Muhtar were addressing a sudden breakdown in relations makes it unlikely that they were referring to a decades-long vendetta. Diplomatic records from the British Library shed more light on the matter. George Foresti, the British consul in Ioannina at the time, reported in September 1811 that while occupying Corfu, the French had sent officers to Gardiki and Gjirokaster to distribute money and ammunition on the condition that the inhabitants take up arms against Ali Pasha. This information should be understood in the context of the deteriorating relationship between the vizier and his neighbors Beratlı İbrahim Pasha and Delvineli Mustafa Pasha, the local administrators nominally ruling the offending areas. "Ali Pasha has not yet decided upon the measures he will pursue against Gardiki and Argyrokastro [Gjirokaster]," Foresti continued. "I am endeavoring to impress upon him the necessity of making effectual exertions and subdue them, while he has desire, afforded him by the termination of his contest with Ibrahim Pasha.... I may venture to assure you that he will take instant and decisive measures."[80] Five months later, the men of Gardiki were dead. It is impossible to know how much impact the consul's advice had on Ali Pasha's decision. Yet it is worth noting that an event that Europeans routinely cited as evidence of the governor's bloodthirsty (read: Oriental) disposition seems to have been backed by an agent of the British Crown. At the same time, Ali Pasha's own scribes confirm in an official memorandum to Istanbul that the people of Gardiki had been accused of working with the French in a major conspiracy, and that the governor was mobilizing troops against them in an effort to maintain order.[81] The *Alipasiad* also recounts the story of Gardiki, and it implies that the village was destroyed because of its inhabitants' collusion with the rival governor Delvineli Mustafa Pasha.[82]

The question remains: if the massacre at Gardiki was a direct reaction to an alleged collaboration with the French, why does the public inscription at Valiares go to such lengths to suggest otherwise? The ghosts of the dead men divulge that they insulted the young Ali Pasha: "It is for that deed that he slew us at the Khan." The inscription shifts the context for this offense from the more abstract realm of international politics to something much more visceral and personal. At least twice the text evokes a threat to the "house" (οντζάκι, *otzaki*) of Ali Pasha, which, as explained in the introduction, is a term that comes from Ottoman Turkish (*ocak*), which literally translates as "hearth," thus conjuring notions of home and kin. This effort to reframe the nature of the offense perpetrated by the people of Gardiki anticipates a local audience that may have questioned such an extreme response to rumors of political intrigue, especially against a community that was generally known for being loyal to the governor. Even further contributing to this justification is the poet's decision to have the dead men speak for themselves, instead of giving a more impersonal description of the crime. This strategy shifts the responsibility for the massacre onto the men of Gardiki, while Ali Pasha, by contrast, acknowledges the grievous nature of the "terrible slaughter" and expresses his "desire that so great an evil shall never occur again." While the passage of the *Alipasiad* that recounts the destruction of Gardiki does not replicate the inscription precisely, it likewise confirms that the governor wanted that "dark day to be remembered throughout the world, / that, for as long as there is existence, / they will talk about this event, about what Ali Pasha of Tepelena has done."[83] Thus, no matter the rationale given for the massacre, the entire site functions as a clear warning to those who would contemplate any future actions against the governor, all of this during a time of internecine rivalry and foreign interference.

The destruction of Gardiki was remembered not only in song and written accounts but also in a physical monument preserved in the landscape itself. That Ali Pasha had the men moved from the village, which is tucked away in its own valley, to a way station on one of the most heavily trafficked routes in the region suggests that he had some kind of memorial in mind before the massacre took place. In the immediate aftermath, the posting of the inscription over the door of the *han* and Ali Pasha's express orders to burn Gardiki and block any future settlement there, so that "it may remain a desert for ever," both preserve these places as frozen in time. These actions effectively collapse chronological distance and elucidate a more affective response from visitors. And this was a place that Ali Pasha intended people to visit; Henry Holland says that he would not have gone to Gardiki had the governor not made a point of adding it to his itinerary.[84] Meanwhile, during his own stop at the site, Thomas Hughes reflected on the contrast between wandering around the remnants of an ancient city and visiting this haunting modern memorial:

> A chilling kind of sensation, like the fascination of some deadly spell, benumbs the senses, and almost stops the respiration of the traveller, who treads as it were, upon the prostrate corpse of a great city, just abandoned by the animating spirit. The feeling is far different from that which he experiences amidst the fine ruins of antiquity, whose aspect, mellowed down by time and unconnected with any terrible convulsion, inspires only pleasing melancholy, or animating reflections: but here the frightful contrast of a recent and terrible overflow appals him; his heart sickens at the sight; and whilst the deep silence is broken only by the breeze which sighs around the ruins or amidst the funereal cypresses which here and there wave over them, he almost expects to meet a spectre at every step he takes.[85]

It is the proximity in time to the event that Hughes seems to find most disturbing. While the other poetic inscriptions commissioned by Ali Pasha play with an expansive chronology, the text at Valiares transports the viewer to a very specific moment, down to the time of day: "This sad event took place the 15th of March, 1812, in the afternoon." The shifting voices in the text—from the personified *han* to the men of Gardiki lying within and, finally, to Ali Pasha himself—enliven the space and create an immersive environment.

Typically, modern war memorials (such as the World War II monument dedicated to Albanian soldiers, just a stone's throw from Gardiki) are constructed sometime after the fact and function as a tribute to those who have fallen. The site of the Gardiki massacre, by contrast, is a victory monument, designed above all to intimidate viewers, Ali Pasha's "neighbours" who pass along the road. It is not difficult to find parallels for this type of "monument of destruction." In an example that is also from World War II, during the invasion of Crete, soldiers fighting for the Reich set up inscriptions in both German and Greek recording the massacre of the village of Kandanos, which was supposed to be in retaliation for its inhabitants' participation in the Battle of Crete in 1941. In language that echoes the text at Gardiki, one sign reads, "On June 3, 1941, Kandanos was razed down to the foundations, never to be rebuilt again."[86]

Ultimately, the inscription at Valiares was not the sole memorial to Ali Pasha's fearsome reputation. In 1960, construction was completed on the *Monument of Zalongo*, a massive sculpture by the well-known artist George Zongolopoulos located near the modern village of Kamarina in Greece (fig. 97). Standing thirteen meters at its highest point, the massive abstract sculpture depicts six female figures linking hands. The downward arc created by the arms of the figures is continued into the natural curve of the rocky outcrop upon which they stand, tying the figures to the surrounding environment. The sculpture depicts the "Dance of Zalongo," a tale from Ali Pasha's war with the people of Souli in 1803, when it is said that a group of refugees trapped near the village of Zalongo jumped off the cliff edge rather than submit to the governor's men. The story was recounted by a local Greek author only about a decade later, and it quickly captured the imagination of Europeans and locals alike.[87] While the poetic inscription at Valiares deploys a rhetoric of justice, styling the massacre at Gardiki

FIGURE 97
George Zongolopoulos, *Monument of Zalongo*, 1960. Kamarina, Greece. Limestone blocks and concrete, 13 × 18 m. Photo by Andreas Papageorgiou.

as an unfortunate but necessary measure, the *Monument of Zalongo* demonstrates how easily such a narrative could spin beyond Ali Pasha's control. Once the governor was finally put to death by the sultan's troops, Ottoman administrators immediately set to work dismantling his carefully crafted public persona.

AFTERMATH

Ali Pasha finally met his end in February 1822, after a two-year siege of his capital in Ioannina. In order to prevent any of the governor's descendants from laying claim to the region, Ottoman soldiers also executed his sons, Veli, Muhtar, and Salih Pasha, decisively ending the Moutzohousatic house.[88] In the years following Ali Pasha's death, officials sent from Istanbul took a number of measures to undermine the vizier's spatial interventions. As mentioned in the introduction, his palace on the Litharitsa hill in Ioannina, which was burned in the chaos of the siege, was left standing and abandoned as a ruin (see fig. 6). A few years later, in 1838, this site was overshadowed by the construction of a massive army barracks (*kışlâ*), a relatively new type of structure that embodied the military reforms of Sultan Selim III and continued under Mahmud II (fig. 98).[89] Yet the most obvious act of excising the memory of Ali Pasha's rule can be found at the entrance gates in Ioannina's city walls, where Ottoman authorities seem to have systematically removed inscriptions commissioned by the vizier and replaced them with new panels that better adhered to the decorum of imperial epigraphy. There are at least three cases of this erasure (found at Gates A, C, and E in fig. 83) in which Ottoman Turkish inscriptions accompanied by the sultan's royal monogram (*tuğra*) have been fitted into niches originally designed to accommodate larger panels.[90] Again, these niches probably held inscriptions commemorating Ali Pasha's construction of the walls, similar to the surviving marble plaque of popular Greek verse

FIGURE 98
Edward Lear, *View of Ioannina from the South* (showing the ruins of Ali Pasha's palace on the Litharitsa hill in the foreground on the right and the Ottoman barracks building in the background), 1849. Ink, pencil, and watercolor on paper, 21.5 × 32.2 cm. MS Typ 55.26, Houghton Library, Harvard University.

now held in the city's Byzantine Museum (see figs. 81 and 82).

These new texts were a complete departure from the former vizier's epigraphic proclamations about being the hero of Epirus and descendant of great ancient kings, with nary a *tuğra* in sight. Above the main entrance portal to the walled city (Gate A), one can see today an Ottoman Turkish inscription dated 1259 H (1844–45), thus placed there about twenty years after Ali Pasha's death, paired with a nicely carved *tuğra* of Sultan Abdülmecid I bordered with a floral wreath (fig. 99).[91] The inscription begins with obeisance to the ruler, praising God "who gave [us] Abdülmecid Han." As a sign of humility, the name of the regional commander, Osman Nuri Pasha, appears only after three full lines of lavish praise for the sultan. Interestingly, this inscription does not seem to record any kind of major structural repairs or additions to the walls; rather, it commemorates the placing of the imperial monogram itself above the doorway: "it is with great pride that Osman Nuri Pasha affixes this awe-inspiring name to the gate of the fortress . . . the *tuğra* makes manifest the renown of victory." The repeated references to the sultan's triumphs and conquest (*muzaffer*, line 2; *zafer*, line 5) are somewhat formulaic. Yet the specific scenario of these panels—replacing inscriptions commissioned by Ali Pasha, considered a traitor to the empire—suggests that this later epigraphic intervention was designed as a conscious act of *damnatio memoriae* against the former vizier.[92] Ali Pasha's unorthodox approach to legitimizing his rule, which seems to have made no attempt to pay any respect whatsoever to the Ottoman sultan, was too risky an enterprise to let stand.

POETIC JUSTICE

FIGURE 99
The main entrance gate to the walled city of Ioannina. Photo by author.

The vizier's innovative program of public inscriptions and heraldic insignia, prominently presented in a variety of architectural settings, operates within the specific regional context of Epirus, while also intersecting with and improvising upon a range of visual, literary, and oral traditions. It is not entirely clear whether Ali Pasha intended such texts and engravings to be read as openly rebellious against imperial sovereignty—suffice it to say that he turned to alternative vocabularies of legitimacy that did not rely upon a glowing endorsement from the sultan. Unsurprisingly, after his execution, the new governing authorities in Ioannina felt compelled to neutralize these epigraphic experiments by putting up their own inscriptions and symbols, which look squarely to Istanbul in establishing hierarchies of power. Above the gates of Ioannina, the sultan's *tuğra* faces down Ali Pasha's lions, a frozen conversation between center and periphery.

Conclusion

In 2012, the Albanian prime minister, Sali Berisha, approached high-level officials in Turkey with an unusual request—to hand over the head of Ali Pasha. Almost two centuries earlier, after Ali Pasha was declared an enemy of the state, and the sultan's forces had laid siege for two years to his stronghold in Ioannina, the vizier was finally captured and killed. To demonstrate the Porte's ability to suppress rebellion, the wayward governor's head was taken back to Istanbul with great pomp and ceremony.[1] For a time, this prize was displayed in the first courtyard of the Topkapı Palace, accompanied by a written decree listing all of the ex-governor's crimes against the imperial order.[2] Thwarting a merchant's scheme to purchase the head and send it to London for popular exhibition, a former associate of Ali Pasha's managed to secure the head and saw to it that it was laid to rest alongside his sons and grandson in a cemetery beyond Istanbul's walls. The tombstone inscription, which is still there today, reads in Ottoman Turkish: "Here lies the head of the famous Ali Pasha of Tepelena, the former governor of the Yanya [Ioannina] *şancaḳ*, who distinguished himself in Albania with more than thirty years of transgression."[3] In this epitaph, even the Ottoman authorities grudgingly acknowledge the vizier's renown, describing Ali Pasha as "famous" (*meşhûr*), his fame, according to the text, primarily due to his persistence in pushing beyond the bounds of his rank. In Sharon Marcus's study of celebrity culture, the origins of which are traced to precisely the same period in which Ali Pasha came to power, she names defiance of the status quo as one of the most important elements of becoming a star in the modern sense.[4] At the time of his death, the vizier was thus already well on his way to becoming an international sensation.

Despite (or, more likely, because of) his ignominious end, Ali Pasha has recently enjoyed a revival as a figure of popular history, especially in Greece and Albania. Prime Minister Berisha himself praised the former Ottoman governor as "one of the most extraordinary personalities of the Albanian nation, the great politician, outstanding strategist, sterling diplomat, visionary statesman, and brave general who ... established a practically independent Albanian state."[5] In 2012, the centennial year of the foundation of modern Albania, Berisha had thought of one way that Turkey, a typically friendly ally, could join the people of Albania in celebrating their independence. During an official visit to Tirana by the Turkish defense minister, Berisha requested that Turkey exhume the head of Ali Pasha so that it might be laid to rest in the land of his birth.[6] The prime minister's proposal echoed the Ottoman sultan's demand for Ali

Pasha's head, a present-day attempt to reverse the sequence of actions that first brought the governor's remains to Istanbul almost two hundred years earlier. Ahmet Davutoğlu, at the time the foreign minister of Turkey, denied Berisha's request outright. Although Davutoğlu made no comment to reporters on the rationale behind his decision, Berisha later speculated that this was yet another attempt on behalf of Turkey's ruling AK Party to assert a neo-Ottomanist agenda: "the imperial wrath against [Ali Pasha] is not yet extinguished."[7] In an article covering this dispute, the Turkish journalist Murat Bardakçı countered the Albanian claim to the head, arguing that Ali Pasha's great-grandfather was a Mevlevi dervish from Kütahya, a large town in what is now northwest Turkey.[8] For this reason, the governor, whom the Porte allegedly referred to as "Anatolian Ali," should remain in the country of his ancestry. Bardakçı also observed that while the governor's head was now in Istanbul, the rest of his body had been buried in Ioannina, now part of modern Greece, thus exposing the fiction that surrendering Ali Pasha's head to Albania would make him physically whole again.

This diplomatic scuffle over the bones of a renegade pasha points to the obstinate fact that the history of the Ottoman Empire is alive and well in its former provinces. Ali Pasha continues to have cultural and political relevance today; he is a household name in Albania, Greece, and Turkey. Significantly, the debate about his head is couched in a wider discourse about communal identity and landscape, his earthly remains claimed and mapped onto multiple geographies.

In this book, I have demonstrated how Ali Pasha himself was likewise invested in staging his claims to territory through the patronage of a wide variety of architectural monuments and infrastructure projects. The traveler Richard Burgess, who visited Epirus in 1834, about a decade after the governor's death, observed, "At Yanina, every spot is connected with the name of Ali Pacha: his memory, like a haunting spirit, claims every thing for its own: if there is a house of a better appearance than the rest, he either began it, or planned it, or was the cause of its comparative splendour."[9] Ali Pasha was responsible for this "haunting spirit" by commissioning a multiplicity of structures that adhered to specific formal typologies and spatial configurations, establishing a distinctive brand throughout the region. The corpus of material under consideration here may thus be understood as specters within a haunted landscape, in the sense that these buildings are inextricably tied to a single individual who was deeply committed to the cultivation of his own personal mythology. In the aftermath of his execution, officials of the central government in Istanbul attempted to uncouple the name of the vizier from the monuments themselves, to deactivate this mythologizing process and render the structures and spaces usable again for the service of empire. In the citadel of Ioannina, Ali Pasha's unusual program of architectural epigraphy was superseded with *tuğra*s and inscriptions in Ottoman Turkish praising the name of the sultan as a glorious victor. Meanwhile, the palaces of the governor and his sons were demolished and replaced with army barracks and government offices. Yet despite these efforts to tamp down Ali Pasha's architectural experiments, the vizier's phantom still occupies these spaces, pointing to the stubborn endurance of local memory.

There is a recent movement in the humanities that some scholars have described as the "spectral turn." In this literature, ghostly traces and haunting memories are understood to be inherently destabilizing agents, imbued with the potential to challenge modern hegemonic narratives of linear time and the inevitable march of progress.[10] In other words, ghosts remind us of the past, but they can also make us question the present. Ali Pasha's engagements with the built environment in Ottoman Epirus were staged during a turbulent period, when the successful outcomes of the subsequent independence movements in Greece and Albania could by no means be considered a foregone conclusion.[11] In many cases, the buildings commissioned by the vizier were designed to provoke—from a monastic church dedicated to a preacher killed for sedition to coastal fortifications that stoked the anxiety of Ali Pasha's neighbors on the Ionian Islands before they were even completed.

The material under examination in this volume therefore raises a crucial question about the role of architecture during the age of revolution in the late eighteenth and early nineteenth centuries. In the Ottoman Empire, what could be considered subimperial conceptions of regional space were emerging throughout the provinces. Among a new *ayan* class of local rulers, Ali Pasha stands out as an ambitious patron of architecture, commissioning and appropriating a wide range of structures, in the process completely transforming the physical composition of the territory under his jurisdiction. Ali Pasha and the building specialists he employed developed distinctive architectural typologies that announced the governor's dominion, a spatial strategy that ushered in "the age of Ali Pasha." In addition to concentrating on urban centers, the governor invested in infrastructure networks of roads, way stations, and military installations both within his territory and along its borders. Drawing on imported building technology and local architectural traditions, he sought to consolidate a diverse population of different religious and ethnic communities, the Christian notables at his court becoming increasingly cosmopolitan in their connections to a wider zone of trade and intellectual culture.

The government in Istanbul at first tacitly accepted Ali Pasha's efforts to bring together a number of microregions under a unifying political order. This concession was part of a broader policy that delegated the administration of the empire to mediating "partners" who were savvy with respect to local political mores. Ali Pasha's increasing autonomy in matters of governance was intrinsically tied to a profound shift in architectural patronage. The erection of public buildings that had once been predominantly the prerogative of the royal family and administrators who had risen through the court hierarchy in Istanbul—especially Friday mosques, fortifications, and governor's palaces—now fell under the purview of local power holders. Ali Pasha's tendency in his architectural projects to ignore customary protocols for showing deference to the Porte, such as including a *tuğra* in a building's foundation inscription and his inclination to treat the population under his administration more like his own subjects than those of the sultan, sufficiently aroused the ire of the center to bring about his eventual downfall. The case of Epirus offers a view of Ottoman architecture from the edges of empire, where alternative futures were being imagined. What has been left behind from this period—both structural and archival—has been conjured here to tell the story of Ali Pasha. The result is a view of architectural patronage that can be defined not merely as a sum total of building commissions but as a reflection of a patron's worldview and aspirations—a material biography that can in turn go on to live a life of its own.

NOTES

Abbreviations

AAP   *Archeio Ali Pasa: Syllogis I. Chotzi, Gennadeiou Vivliothikis tis Amerikanikis Scholis Athinon* (Archive of Ali Pasha: Collection of I. Chotzi, Gennadius Library at the American School in Athens), edited by Vasilis Panagiotopoulos, Dimitris Dimitropoulos, and Panagiotis Michalaris. 5 vols. Athens: Institute for Neohellenic Research, 2007–18.

BOA   T. C. Cumhurbaşkanlığı Devlet Osmanlı Arşivleri (Republic of Turkey Presidential State Ottoman Archives), Istanbul

DİA   *Türkiye Diyanet Vakfı İslâm Ansiklopedisi* (Turkish Foundation of Religious Affairs Encyclopedia of Islam). 44 vols. Istanbul: Türkiye Diyanet Vakfı, 1988–2013

NA   National Archives of the United Kingdom, London

VGM   T. C. Vakıflar Genel Müdürlüğü (Republic of Turkey Directorate General of Pious Foundations), Ankara

Introduction

1. BOA, HAT. 401/21059 (1235 H/1820), HAT. 1263/48891 (1235 H/1819–20), C.DH. 69/3423 (1235 H/1819–20). See also Koçyiğit, *Kabudlu Mustafa Vasfi Efendi Tevârîh*, 105; Skiotis, "The Lion and the Phoenix," 169.

2. William Meyer to Thomas Maitland, Preveza, May 6, 1820, in Prevelakis and Merticopoulou, *Epirus*, 1:104.

3. BOA, HAT. 400/21018a (1237 H/1822).

4. Eric Hobsbawm popularized the concept of the late eighteenth and early nineteenth centuries as an age of revolution in his study of Western Europe, and there have been subsequent efforts to expand this geography and examine the age of revolution as a global phenomenon, including in the Ottoman Empire. See Hobsbawm, *Age of Revolution*; Philliou, *Biography of an Empire*; and Yaycıoğlu, *Partners of the Empire*.

5. Kenney, *Power and Patronage*, 3.

6. Galaty and Watkinson, "Practice of Archaeology," 8–12; Hamilakis, *Nation and Its Ruins*, 78–85; Moudopoulos-Athanasiou, *Early Modern Zagori*, 42.

7. For more on this tendency to use modern national boundaries to frame studies of the earlier Ottoman period in the Balkans, see Kiel, *Ottoman Architecture in Albania*; Kiel, *Art and Society of Bulgaria*; and Brouskari, *Ottoman Architecture in Greece*.

8. See Egro, *Historia dhe ideologjia*; Brouskari, *Ottoman Architecture in Greece*; Georgopoulou and Thanasakis, *Ottoman Athens*; and Moudopoulos-Athanasiou, *Early Modern Zagori*.

9. My approach to landscape as a social product shaped by ideology has been informed by the field of cultural geography. See Cosgrove, *Social Formation and Symbolic Landscape*, 13.

10. Turner, *From Ritual to Theatre*, 11; Hutcheon, *Theory of Parody*, 1–3; and Wheeler, "Negotiating Deviance and Normativity," 270.

11. Schechner, *Performance Studies*, 42.

12. Jackson, "Landscape as Theater," 5; Harding, "Presenting and Re-Presenting the Self," 119.

13. See, for example, Payne, *Ali Pacha*; Georgopoulou, "Land of the Great"; Muse, "Encountering Ali Pasha," 340–41.

14. This is the title under which the ballad was first published in its entirety in 1870, in Sathas, *Istorikai diatrivai*, 123–336.

15. There are at least three manuscript copies of this text: two in Greece, one at the Gennadius Library (MS Volides 12) and one at the National Library in Athens (EBE 2313), and one in the National Archives of Albania in Tirana (Collection F.143, MS D.1836).

16. Sathas, *Istorikai diatrivai*, 335.

17. Mert, "Âyan," 196.

18. McGowan, "Age of the Ayans," 658–63; Khoury, "Ottoman Centre," 140–43.

19. While Hourani focused on the administrative territory of greater Syria during the modernization reforms of the mid-nineteenth century (i.e., slightly later than the heyday of the *ayan*), his work was groundbreaking in that it proposed writing history through the view of "patrician" politics, rather than from the top-down perspective of the sultan and his advisors in Istanbul. Hourani, "Ottoman Reform and the Politics of Notables," 45. See also Gelvin, "'Politics of Notables' Forty Years After."

20. Sadat, "Urban Notables in the Ottoman Empire"; Nagata, *Some Documents on the Big Farms*; McGowan, *Economic Life in Ottoman Europe*, 171–72; İnalcık, "Emergence of Big Farms," 124; Veinstein, "On the *Çiftlik* Debate"; Özkaya, *Osmanlı İmparatorluğu'nda Ayanlık*, 125–40.

21. For more recent studies on the *ayan*, see Zens, "Ayanlık and Pasvanoğlu Osman Paşa"; Zens, "Ottoman Provincial Notables"; and Anastasopoulos, *Provincial Elites in the Ottoman Empire*.

22. Barkey, *Empire of Difference*, 17.

23. Yaycıoğlu, *Partners of the Empire*, 2, 13.

24. Hobsbawm, *Age of Revolution*, 53–55.

25. Acun, *Bozok Sancağı*, 14–22; Hamilton, "Observations on the Position of Tavium," 76; Duru, "Yozgat Çapanoğlu Camii ve Vakfiyeleri"; Yenişehirlioğlu, "Architectural Patronage," 329.

26. It has been theorized that the lighter-colored limestone used in the first phase of construction was taken from the nearby ancient site of Tavium. Goodwin, *History of Ottoman Architecture*, 400n52.

27. Weber, "Changing Cultural References," 200–201.

28. This scholarship includes catalogs that document the buildings of some of these *ayan* families. See especially Kuyulu, *Kara Osman-oğlu Ailesine ait Mimari Eserler*; and Acun, *Bozok Sancağı*.

29. Arel, "Gothic Towers and Baroque Mihrabs," 212.

30. Yenişehirlioğlu, "Architectural Patronage."

31. Bingöl, *İshak Paşa Sarayı*, 31; Yenişehirlioğlu, "Architectural Patronage," 330–31.

32. Weber, "Changing Cultural References," 200–203; Marino, "Investissements de Sulaymân Pacha al-'Azm."

33. Cantacuzino, *Architecture in Continuity*, 166.

34. Al-Asad, "Mosque of Muhammad 'Ali"; Fahmy, *All the Pasha's Men*, 73; Behrens-Abouseif, *Islamic Architecture in Cairo*, 168–70; and El-Ashmouni and Bartsch, "Egypt's Age of Transition."

35. Bodenstein, "Industrial Architecture in Egypt," 43–51; El-Ashmouni and Bartsch, "Egypt's Age of Transition," 56–65.

36. Kiel, "Vidin," 105; and Gradeva, "Osman Pazvantoğlu of Vidin," 131.

37. The foundation inscription on the mosque adjacent to the library gives a date of 1216 H (1801–2), suggesting that it was completed about one year earlier. Kiel, "Date of Construction," 118; Gradeva, "Osman Pazvantoğlu of Vidin," 122; and Zens, "Ayanlık and Pasvanoğlu Osman Paşa," 1–2.

38. Gradeva, "Osman Pazvantoğlu of Vidin," 121.

39. For the term "Ottomanization," see Bierman, "Ottomanization of Crete." See also Watenpaugh, *Image of an Ottoman City*, 9–10; Kafescioğlu, "'In the Image of Rūm,'" 70; Bierman, "Franchising Ottoman Istanbul"; Artan, "Questions of Ottoman Identity," 85; and Necipoğlu, *Age of Sinan*, 70–78.

40. Zandi-Sayek, *Ottoman Izmir*; Weber, *Damascus*; Dimitriadis, "Transforming a Late Ottoman Port-City"; Christensen, *Germany and the Ottoman Railways*; and Hanssen, Weber, and Philipp, *Empire in the City*.

41. This book also complements a growing body of literature on the built environment in the Ottoman Empire during the long eighteenth century, which explores an understudied period of Ottoman architectural history while tending to focus on developments in the capital. See Hamadeh, *City's Pleasures*; and Rüstem, *Ottoman Baroque*.

42. Artan, "Questions of Ottoman Identity," 96.

43. Durusu-Tanrıöver, "Ways of Being Hittite," 5–7; Anzaldúa, *Borderlands/La Frontera*, 79–80; and Lightfoot and Martinez, "Frontiers and Boundaries," 483.

44. Asher, "Sub-Imperial Palaces."

45. Hartmuth, "History of Centre-Periphery Relations," 27–28.

46. To understand how Ali Pasha compared with his peers in terms of his relationship with the center, one can look to 1808, when the new sultan, Mahmud II, convened a meeting of *ayan* notables in Istanbul, which resulted in the Sened-i İttifâk, a "deed of agreement" in which attendees asserted their loyalty to the sultan and committed themselves to the orderly administration of the empire. While the heads of the Çapanoğlu and Kara Osman-oğlu families signed the document, Ali Pasha declined the invitation to come to Istanbul altogether. Akyıldız and Hanioğlu, "Negotiating the Power of the Sultan," 30.

47. Necipoğlu, *Age of Sinan*, 115.

48. Necipoğlu, *Age of Sinan*, 115. See also Watenpaugh, *Image of an Ottoman City*, 9–10.

49. Rüstem, *Ottoman Baroque*, 211–12; Hamadeh, *City's Pleasures*, 12–13; Artan, "Architecture as a Theatre of Life," 75–76.

50. For the Tanzimat reforms, see Hanioğlu, *History of the Late Ottoman Empire*, 72–75; and Findley, "Tanzimat."

51. Tandan, *Architecture of Lucknow and Oudh*, 132–50.

52. Examples of such tomb complexes include those of Saadat Ali Khan in Lucknow and of Bahu Begam and Shuja-al-Dawla in Faizabad. Keshani, "Architecture and the Twelver Shi'i Tradition," 233.

53. Artan, "Questions of Ottoman Identity," 87.

54. Skiotis, "The Lion and the Phoenix," 41. There is some debate about when exactly Ali Pasha was born; most secondary sources estimate 1750. Ottoman Turkish sources usually distinguish the governor as "Tepedelenli," an epithet that refers to his hometown of Tepelena (Ott. Tepedelen).

55. For the purposes of administration, the premodern Ottoman Empire was divided into provinces (*eyâlet*), which were in turn divided into districts or subprovinces (*şancak* or *livâ*). This system changed quite a bit after the Tanzimat reforms of the mid-nineteenth century.

56. Skiotis, "The Lion and the Phoenix," 47.

57. Beydilli, "Tepedelenli Ali Paşa," 477; BOA, C.AS. 29/1345 (1205 H/1791). A few years later, around 1792–94, Ali Pasha arranged for his son Veli Pasha to be appointed to the position of *derbendler başbuğu*. BOA, C.AS. 853/36500 (1213 H/1799). It appears, however, that the position had been passed back to his father at some point, as Ali

Pasha was referred to as the *derbendler nezâreti* in 1812. BOA, C.DH. 22/1060 (1227 H/1812).

58. Halaçoğlu, "Derbend," 163.

59. Ali Pasha, for example, was sent to put down other rebellious governors, such as Kara Mahmud Buşatlı in Shkodra and Osman Pasvantoğlu. Skiotis, "The Lion and the Phoenix," 48.

60. BOA, C.AS. 853/36500 (1213 H/1799) and TS.MA. d. 9901 (1227 H/1812); J. P. Morier to Lord Howick, Zante, March 19, 1807, NA, FO 78/58; memorandum from Ali Pasha, Ioannina, May 21, 1811, in *AAP*, 2:209–11, no. 571.

61. Holland, *Travels in the Ionian Isles*, 98.

62. Hanley, "How Many Sancaks," 176.

63. Karamustafa, "Military, Administrative, and Scholarly Maps," 209. That said, there was a robust tradition of Ottoman portolan charts in the early modern period, exemplified by Piri Reis's maps. After the modernization reforms in the Ottoman Empire, administrative maps outlining provincial districts began to appear, and they can be found accompanying the *sâlnâme* (annual yearbooks) published in the late nineteenth and early twentieth centuries.

64. For the history of this region in the ancient and medieval periods, see Hammond, *Epirus*; and Veikou, *Byzantine Epirus*.

65. Ben-Ghiat, *Strongmen*, 7; Fischer, "Introduction," 17.

66. See Todorova, *Imagining the Balkans*.

67. Hughes, *Travels in Sicily, Greece, and Albania*, 1:474.

68. Sathas, *Istorikai diatrivai*, 129.

69. Hagen, "Legitimacy and World Order," 55–58.

70. Sathas, *Istorikai diatrivai*, 328.

71. In the 1970s, the historian Dennis Skiotis broke new ground by examining Ali Pasha according to documents from the Ottoman archives, but he never published his doctoral dissertation, and the full scope of his work has not received the attention it deserves. See "The Lion and the Phoenix" and "From Bandit to Pasha."

72. These documents have been published in their entirety by a team based at the Institute of Neohellenic Research, which is part of the National Hellenic Research Foundation, under the title *Archeio Ali Pasa (AAP)*.

73. Yaycıoğlu et al., "Mapping Ottoman Epirus," 146; see also the project's website at https://ottoman.sites.stanford.edu.

74. In this respect, I aim to emulate one of the most important biographies of Ali Pasha, *Istoria Ali Pasa tou Tepelenli*, the author of which, Panagiotis Aravantinos (d. 1870), lived in Epirus under Ottoman rule and made extensive use of local Greek chronicles and archival documents.

75. In the best-known recent volume on Ali Pasha, *Muslim Bonaparte*, Katherine Fleming takes up the cultural representation of Ali Pasha among Europeans and likewise examines diplomatic archival sources and published travel accounts. Reading these sources against the grain, Fleming highlights the tension between this external Orientalizing gaze and what she argues is Ali Pasha's own effort to use these mythologizing forces to his advantage. I am indebted to Fleming's critical approach, and in this book I shift the focus from the representation of Ali Pasha in Western Europe to how his own initiatives in self-display were perceived within the more immediate cultural and spatial context of the Ottoman Empire. Meanwhile, in an article reviewing several of Ali Pasha's palaces and fortifications, Christian Ottersbach also examines the most important travel accounts. See Ottersbach, "Bauen als Ausdruck von Souveränität."

76. Isa Blumi argues that Ali Pasha "was more likely to become the leader of an independent state than anyone in Peloponnese or Epirus at the time. . . . Who is to say that [he] would not be celebrated today as the founder of a quite plausible 'Tepelina,' 'Tepelenistan,' or the 'Kingdom of Yanya'?" Blumi, *Reinstating the Ottomans*, 52. Şükrü Ilıcak has observed that Ali Pasha's rise to power in many ways was reminiscent of the formative years of the Ottoman state under the house of Osman. Ilıcak, "Those Infidel Greeks," 14.

Chapter 1

1. Necipoğlu, *Architecture, Ceremonial, and Power*, 57. In Ottoman bureaucratic documents, the city of Istanbul is often referred to by the epithet Dersaâdet (Gate of Felicity), which is the monumental gateway in the second courtyard of the Topkapı Palace, where the sultan sat enthroned for state rituals.

2. Atasoy, *Otağ-ı Hümayun*, 56–63.

3. For an examination of provincial administration in the sixteenth and seventeenth centuries, see Kunt, *Sultan's Servants*. In the appendix, Kunt reproduces a register recording the income for all provincial administrators in 1527; in this list, none of these individuals holds more than one district.

4. See Bingöl, *İshak Paşa Sarayı*; and El-Ashmouni and Bartsch, "Egypt's Age of Transition," 56–65.

5. See *AAP*.

6. Byron traveled to what is present-day Greece and Albania with John Cam Hobhouse, a.k.a. Lord Broughton. The most thorough account of the trip is Hobhouse, *Journey Through Albania*.

7. Byron, *Childe Harold's Pilgrimage*, p. 88, canto 2, stanzas 54–55.

8. Hobhouse, *Journey Through Albania*, 1:99.

9. Tietze, *Mustafa Ali's Counsel for Sultans*, 2:104.

10. Tietze, *Mustafa Ali's Counsel for Sultans*, 2:105.

11. Ertuğ, "Saray," 117.

12. See Necipoğlu, *Architecture, Ceremonial, and Power*; Eldem, *Köşkler ve Kasırlar*; and Sözen, *Devletin Evi*.

13. Necipoğlu, *Sinan's Autobiographies*, 72.

14. Hamadeh, *City's Pleasures*, 29–31.

15. Peirce, *Imperial Harem*, 45–47; Ertuğ, "Saray," 120. For the prince's palace (*sarây-ı 'âmire*) in Manisa, see Tezcan, *Manisa nach Evliya Çelebi*, 110–13.

16. Burgess, *Greece and the Levant*, 1:65–68.

17. The new structure was built southeast of the ruined palace, approximately where the municipality's Byzantine Museum is located today (see no. 11 in fig. 14). BOA, FTG, photograph 3, from Yıldız Album YEE d. 404; Konstantios, *Kastro of Ioannina*, 31.

18. See Kiel, *Ottoman Architecture in Albania*, 4.

19. Kahraman and Dağlı, *Evliya Çelebi Seyahatnamesi*, 8:297; Dankoff and Elsie, *Evliya Çelebi in Albania*, 59.

20. Documents from the early nineteenth century describe how the central government in Istanbul sent architects and funds to construct or repair governors' residences in both Manastir and İzmit, for example. See BOA, HAT. 1273/49342 (1230 H/1814–15), and C.DH. 24/1186 (1223 H/1816), respectively.

21. BOA, C.DH. 18/894 (1232 H/1816).

22. BOA, HAT. 1273/49342 (1230 H/1814–15).

23. BOA, HAT. 50/2361a (1217 H/1802).

24. BOA, HAT. 629/31087a (1232 H/1816–17).

25. BOA, HAT. 1273/49342 (1230 H/1814–15).

26. In his recent article "Bauen als Ausdruck von Souveränität," Christian Ottersbach reviews some of Ali Pasha's palatial constructions in Ioannina and Preveza.

27. While Barbié du Bocage never traveled to Ioannina, he received detailed descriptions and drawings from correspondents such as François Pouqueville, the French consul assigned to Ali Pasha's court. Asvesta, "Barbié du Bocage," 49.

28. Leake, *Travels in Northern Greece*, 1:223. The Greek chronicler Aravantinos asserted that Ali Pasha bought up the houses in the citadel in 1789 in order to begin construction on his new palace. *Chronografia tis Ipeirou*, 1:148n2. A document in the Ali Pasha archive lists a number of workers employed in constructing the "kastro" of Ioannina in 1801. *AAP*, 1:184–87, no. 102. Meanwhile, many secondary sources claim that the date of foundation for this complex was 1795, a date that can be found in an unpublished history of Ioannina by Kosmas Balanos (d. 1808). Vranousis, *Istorika kai topografika*, 54.

29. Leake, *Travels in Northern Greece*, 1:253.

30. Papadopoulou, "Citadel of Ioannina," 168.

31. Papadopoulou, "Kastro Ioanninon," 89–95.

32. Necipoğlu, *Architecture, Ceremonial, and Power*, 32–33.

33. Osswald, "*Lieux de Pouvoir* to *Lieux de Mémoire*," 197n17.

34. Koçyiğit, *Kabudlu Mustafa Vasfi Efendi: Tevârîh*, 105.

35. Jean-Guillaume Barbié du Bocage provides the date of 1807 for this palace on his map. This must be the date of completion, as there is a report by French engineers listing artillery to be placed in the "chateau fort" of Litharitsa in 1806. Gennadius Library, Athens, MS 150.

36. Barbié du Bocage gives the construction date of Veli Pasha's palace as 1811. John Hobhouse's visit to Muhtar Pasha's palace in 1812 provides a *terminus ante quem* for this complex. Hobhouse, *Journey Through Albania*, 1:59.

37. VGM, Vakfiye 629/743/491.

38. Leake, *Travels in Northern Greece*, 1:223. See also Petronitis, "Architektones kai michanikoi," 371. The *terminus ante quem* for the palace is established by Leake's journey.

39. The walled city of Tepelena surrounds the ruins of an earlier Ottoman fortification, which Evliya Çelebi mentions. Bejko, "Kalaja e Tepelenës," 103. As discussed in chapter 4, while an inscription once located above the eastern gate to the citadel seems to bear the year 1819, this plaque must record the final date of completion or even subsequent repairs to the city walls, because Leake refers to the vizier's "fortress" as early as 1804. Leake, *Travels in Northern Greece*, 1:30. See also Smiris, *To diktio ton ochiroseon*, 136.

40. Leake, *Travels in Northern Greece*, 1:31.

41. Durham, *Burden of the Balkans*, 242.

42. Hobhouse, *Journey Through Albania*, 1:156.

43. Stoneman, *Luminous Land*, 166.

44. Fraser, "Books, Prints, and Travel," 343.

45. A French plan of the Agios Andreas Fortress produced in 1798 shows a large building overlooking the sea just south of the main gateway facing east, labeled "Commander's quarters" (*quartier du Commandant*). Ministère des armées de France, Service historique de la Défense, Vincennes, R-18-4-10-B-202 (see fig. 45).

46. Memorandum from Ali Pasha's silahdar, February 5, 1808, in *AAP*, 1:669–71, no. 361.

47. Holland, *Travels in the Ionian Isles*, 64.

48. Hughes, *Travels in Sicily, Greece, and Albania*, 1:423–24.

49. Hughes, *Travels in Sicily, Greece, and Albania*, 1:423–24; Goodison, *Historical and Topographical Essay*, 94.

50. Pouqueville, *Voyage dans la Grèce*, 2:207.

51. Leake, *Travels in Northern Greece*, 4:151–52.

52. Also, given that Leake was writing shortly after the Macartney Mission to Beijing in 1793, this reference to the Qing palace would have come easily to the mind of an educated British person.

53. Kahraman and Dağlı, *Evliya Çelebi Seyahatnamesi*, 8:287; Ergolavos, *Evliya Tselebi*, 56–57.

54. Van Bruinessen and Boeschoten, *Evliya Çelebi in Diyarbekir*, 133.

55. Kahraman and Dağlı, *Evliya Çelebi Seyahatnamesi*, 8:285; Ergolavos, *Evliya Tselebi*, 43–46.

56. Hughes, *Travels in Sicily, Greece, and Albania*, 2:239; Shtylla, "Ujësjellësi i vjetër i Kalasë së Gjirokastrës," 70; Hobhouse, *Journey Through Albania*, 1:46.

57. BOA, C.AS. 557/23363 (1263 H/1847); Dupré, *Voyage à Athenes et à Constantinople*, 22–23.

58. Holland, *Travels in the Ionian Isles*, 494.

59. William Meyer to Colonel Travers, Preveza, February 24, 1820, in Prevelakis and Merticopoulou, *Epirus*, 1:61. For the negotiations over

Parga, see Papers of Sir Robert Liston (1818), NA, FO 78/90.

60. BOA, MAD. d. 9767 (1241 H/1826).

61. Register of the labor of Mastouros Panos in Veliqot, Ioannina, October 11, 1808, in *AAP*, 1:796–97, no. 430.

62. Memorandum of Mifti Pagouris, Tepelena, August 2, 1809, in *AAP*, 2:92–93, no. 494.

63. Hughes, *Travels in Sicily, Greece, and Albania*, 1:501.

64. Hughes, *Travels in Sicily, Greece, and Albania*, 1:474. Katherine Fleming also stresses the importance of Ali Pasha's mobility. *Muslim Bonaparte*, 45.

65. Respectively, John Phillip Morier to Lord Harrowby, Ioannina, February 26, 1805, NA, FO 78/47; William Martin Leake to Lord Harrowby, Corfu, January 21, 1805, NA, FO 78/57; and Hobhouse, *Journey Through Albania*, 1:57.

66. Goodison, *Historical and Topographical Essay*, 93–94.

67. Makris and Papageorgiou, *To chersaio diktyo epikoinonias*, 127–31; Fleming, *Muslim Bonaparte*, 44–45; Hughes, *Travels in Sicily, Greece, and Albania*, 1:459. Keeping the bridge crossing the Vjosa River at the foot of Tepelena was an especially daunting and ongoing endeavor, and Ali Pasha requested help from several engineers, including the French colonel Vaudoncourt, on the project. Report by Guillaume de Vaudoncourt (1807), 105, Ministère des armées de France, Service historique de la Défense, Vincennes, MS 1663.

68. Shtylla, "Ndërtime inxhinierike të fillimit të shekullit XIXte," 82–83. A very similar construction style can be found in a number of bridges that were built during the time of Ali Pasha as part of an elaborate aqueduct system designed to bring water to the town of Gjirokaster. Shtylla, "Ujësjellësi i vjetër i Kalasë së Gjirokastrës."

69. For a discussion of the Arta-Ioannina road, which took about twelve hours to traverse, see Hobhouse, *Journey Through Albania*, 1:54; Leake, *Travels in Northern Greece*, 1:222. The Arta-Salaora causeway, which reportedly took anywhere from 2.5 to 5 hours to cross, is described in Hobhouse, *Journey Through Albania*, 1:45–46; Hughes, *Travels in Sicily, Greece, and Albania*, 1:436; Leake, *Travels in Northern Greece*, 1:201; and Cockerell, *Travels in Southern Europe*, 232–33.

70. Holland, *Travels in the Ionian Isles*, 78–79. Today, some remains of the station appear to be visible next to a modern dock.

71. Smiris, *To diktio ton ochiroseon*, 159–61; Hughes, *Travels in Sicily, Greece, and Albania*, 1:436.

72. Leake, *Travels in Northern Greece*, 1:220.

73. Chrisomallis to William Meyer, Preveza, April 7, 1821, in Prevelakis and Merticopoulou, *Epirus*, 1:334.

74. BOA, MAD. d. 9767 (1241 H/1826).

75. BOA, MAD. d. 9767 (1241 H/1826).

76. BOA, MAD. d. 9767 (1241 H/1826).

77. Knowles, "Introducing Historical GIS," xvii.

78. Brøndsted, *Interviews with Ali Pacha*, 65–68. The carriage drivers are mentioned in registers that list Ali Pasha's retinue in Ioannina. *AAP*, 1:121, no. 73, and 1:126, no. 74.

79. Haygarth, *Greece, a Poem*, 128.

80. Porter and Thevernart, *Palaces and Gardens of Persia*, 109.

81. For these railway projects, see Özyüksel, *Hejaz Railway*; and Christensen, *Germany and the Ottoman Railways*.

82. Hartmuth, "Visual Strategies," 384–85.

83. Hughes, *Travels in Sicily, Greece, and Albania*, 1:458. These paintings were also observed by Cockerell, in *Travels in Southern Europe*, 240–41.

84. Hughes, *Travels in Sicily, Greece, and Albania*, 1:423, 424.

85. For the dating of the Zekate House, see Riza, "Arkitektura dhe restaurimi i banesës së Zekateve," 107.

86. Hughes, *Travels in Sicily, Greece, and Albania*, 1:424.

87. For the importance of Vitruvius in eighteenth-century British architectural theory and practice, see Summerson, *Architecture in Britain*, 188–89.

88. Crook, *Greek Revival*, 82–83.

89. This inscription is recorded in part in Leake, *Travels in Northern Greece*, 1:498. It is discussed in more depth in chapter 4.

90. Hartmuth, "Visual Strategies," 384.

91. Riza, "Arkitektura dhe restaurimi i banesës së Zekateve," 116–17.

92. Holland, *Travels in the Ionian Isles*, 121. An example of the "ornamented staff" mentioned in the passage can be seen on display at the National History Museum in Athens (no. 3765). The label attributes the object to the court of Ali Pasha.

93. Hobhouse, *Journey Through Albania*, 1:61.

94. See, for example, Hughes, *Travels in Sicily, Greece, and Albania*, 1:498.

95. Comte Capo d'Istria (Ioannis Kapodistrias), "Notions sur Ali Vezir de Joannina," 1811, 7–8, Gennadius Library, Athens, MS 158.

96. This encounter is also described by the artist in Haygarth, *Greece, a Poem*, 125–26.

97. Register of bread distribution in Ali Pasha's court, Ioannina, March 26, 1801, in *AAP*, 1:120–29, no. 73.

98. Necipoğlu, *Architecture, Ceremonial, and Power*, 72.

99. Hughes, *Travels in Sicily, Greece, and Albania*, 1:471–75.

100. In the Ottoman Empire, an individual's military rank was signified by how many horse tails (*tuğ*) were attached to the standards that his troops would carry into battle. Generally, the sultan carried seven horse tails, the grand vizier five, and so on. Çoruhlu, "Tuğ," 331.

101. Dupré, *Voyage à Athenes et à Constantinople*, 14.

102. With the subsequent urban development of Ioannina, it is difficult to say where this palace once stood. But based on the location of the Church of Agia Ekaterini on the Barbié du Bocage map (see fig. 13, no. 9), the garden palace complex seems to have been located between the modern streets of Megalou Alexandrou, Voriou

Ipirou, Ioannou Vilara, and Evergeton. What is now the Suburban Wood of Ioannina (Periastiko Dasos Ioanninon) is probably the area that Barbié du Bocage labels the "deer park."

103. Hobhouse, *Journey Through Albania*, 1:70.

104. Hobhouse, *Journey Through Albania*, 1:70.

105. Cockerell, *Travels in Southern Europe*, 237.

106. Hobhouse, *Journey Through Albania*, 1:69.

107. Hobhouse, *Journey Through Albania*, 1:70.

108. Hamadeh, *City's Pleasures*, 48–49; Artan, "Architecture as a Theatre of Life."

109. Kinneir, *Journey Through Asia Minor*, 87.

110. Dupré, *Voyage à Athenes et à Constantinople*, 11.

111. BOA, HAT. 517/25252 (1238 H/1822–23). See also BOA, HAT. 518/25293 (1237 H/1822), and HAT. 518/25304 (1238 H/1822–23).

112. The search for Ali Pasha's treasure started immediately after his death, with documented episodes in the mid-nineteenth century and just after World War I. BOA, HR.SYS. 1721/64 (1859); and Mavrika, "Archaiologiki Ypiresia," 163. My thanks to Edhem Eldem for bringing the former documents to my attention.

113. William Meyer to Temple, Preveza, January 19, 1822, in Prevelakis and Merticopoulou, *Epirus*, 2:19.

114. Bohrer, *Orientalism and Visual Culture*, 55; Fraser, "Delacroix's *Sardanapalus*," 320–21.

115. Athanassoglou-Kallmyer, *French Images*, 29–34.

116. Dimakis, *Guerre de l'indépendance grecque*, 76; Decemberousse, *Ali-Pacha*, 31.

117. Johnson, "Delacroix's 'Oriental' Sources," 603; Athanassoglou, "More on Delacroix's Oriental Sources," 587; and Fraser, *Mediterranean Encounters*, 167.

118. Nochlin, "Imaginary Orient," 123.

119. These two registers are BOA, D.BŞM.MHF. d. 13344 (1237 H/1822); and D.BŞM.MHF. d. 13346 (1237 H/1822).

120. Özcan, "Muhallefât."

121. See Savaş, "Sivas Valisi Dağıstânî Ali Paşa'nın Muhallefâtı"; Karababa, "Investigating Early Modern Ottoman Consumer Culture"; and Çoşgel and Ergene, "Intergenerational Wealth Accumulation."

122. Another register itemizes Vasiliki's jewelry, also seized by the Ottoman soldiers. BOA, IE.DH. 35/3083 (1237 H/1821–22).

123. For example, see Leake, *Travels in Northern Greece*, 1:280, 2:611; Beauchamp, *Life of Ali Pacha*, 230; Hobhouse, *Journey Through Albania*, 1:101; Holland, *Travels in the Ionian Isles*, 574.

124. Payne, *Dalmatia and the Mediterranean*.

125. Elgood, *Arms of Greece*, 225.

126. El-Ashmouni and Bartsch, "Egypt's Age of Transition," 57.

127. Tandan, *Architecture of Lucknow and Oudh*, 137; Gude, "Hybrid Visions."

128. Hughes, *Travels in Sicily, Greece, and Albania*, 2:58.

129. Andreades, "Ali Pacha de Tébelin," 429. See also Skiotis, "From Bandit to Pasha," 221; and Sezer, "Tepedelenli Ali Pasha'nın Çiftlikleri," 75–76.

Chapter 2

1. Setton, *Papacy and the Levant*, 4:1052–59; Finkel, *Osman's Dream*, 160–61.

2. Strunck, "Barbarous and Noble Enemy," 219–20.

3. Blumi, *Reinstating the Ottomans*, 49.

4. Report by Guillaume de Vaudoncourt (1807), 120, Ministère des armées de France, Service historique de la Défense, Vincennes, MS 1663; Skiotis, "From Bandit to Pasha," 225.

5. Braudel, *La Méditerranée et le monde méditeranéen*, 99.

6. Darling, "Mediterranean as a Borderland," 55.

7. See Huntington, "Clash of Civilizations?"

8. Smiris, *To diktio ton ochiroseon*, 209–14.

9. Şakul, "Ottoman Attempts to Control the Adriatic," 255n2.

10. Petition of Ali Pasha to Lord Hamilton, Grevena, May 8, 1811, and "Response to Vizier Ali Pasha's Request," London, May 23, 1812, both in NA, FO 78/80.

11. Both Osman Pasvantoğlu and Mehmed Ali Pasha established themselves inside an existing fortified area—the Baba Vida Fortress in Vidin and the medieval Citadel of Cairo, respectively—yet neither seems to have made any significant additions or reconstructions to the defensive works in these structures (though Mehmed Ali Pasha did establish an arsenal and foundry in the citadel). Gradeva, "Osman Pazvantoğlu of Vidin," 119–20; Fahmy, *All the Pasha's Men*, 3–5; Bodenstein, "Industrial Architecture in Egypt," 46–50.

12. Philipp, *Acre*, 137–38; Pringle et al., "Qal'at Jiddin," 162.

13. Philipp, *Acre*, 137; Greene, "Keeping Out Napoleon."

14. Arel, "Gothic Towers and Baroque Mihrabs," 212–13.

15. See, for example, the tower house still standing in Paramythia, Greece. Charalambos, "Koulia Paramythias," 182. See also the Tower of Dervish Ali near Vlorë, Albania. Riza, "Arkitektura dhe restaurimi i kullave të Dervish Aliut."

16. BOA, C.HR. 26/1262 (1213 H/1798), and C.HR. 41/2024 (1213 H/1798).

17. Curlin, "'Remember the Moment'"; Neumeier, "Spoils for the New Pyrrhus," 327.

18. Şakul, "Ottoman Attempts to Control the Adriatic," 256; Loukatos, "I Preveza kata ta gegonota," 304.

19. The notable exception was Parga, which only submitted to Ottoman subjecthood in 1818. This deal with the British was brokered primarily by Ali Pasha. Papers of James Cocks (1817), NA, FO 78/89; and Papers of Robert Liston (1818), NA, FO 78/90.

20. Ali Pasha enumerated these positions in response to British "applications . . . made in order to understand what places on the sea coast of Albania belonged to him." Anthony Baker to Robert Adair, November 10, 1808, Hertfordshire Archives, Hertford, UK, DE/MI/85508.

21. Stuart, "Natural and Physical Resources of Epirus," 276.

22. The groundwork for the documentation and structural analysis of these fortresses has been laid in Karaiskaj, *Fortifications of Butrint*; Karaiskaj, *Pesë mijë vjet fortifikime*; and Smiris, *To diktio ton ochiroseon*.

23. Gilkes, *Albania*, 301–2; Veinstein, "Avlonya (Vlore)," 221–22.

24. BOA, C.HR. 151/7526 (1225 H/1810); George Foresti to Colonel Lowe, Ioannina, July 25, 1810, British Library, London, Add MS 20183; Skiotis, "The Lion and the Phoenix," 51–52.

25. Leake reports that one of the reasons Ali Pasha built the fortress at Porto Palermo was to deter the people of Himara from plundering vessels taking refuge in the harbor. William Martin Leake to Lord Mulgrave, Ioannina, August 22, 1805, NA, FO 78/57.

26. Gilkes, *Albania*, 241.

27. In a report dated August 1805, Leake wrote that "Ali Pasha has lately built a castle on the point of the peninsula" of Porto Palermo. Leake to Lord Mulgrave, Ioannina, August 22, 1805, NA, FO 78/57.

28. Himariotes to Commander Mocenigo, June 25, 1804, in Ars, *I Rosia kai ta pasalikia Alvanias*, 134–36, no. 39.

29. Leake noted the presence of a house, probably for the fortress commander, in addition to the church. *Travels in Northern Greece*, 1:88. The church is due east of the fortress. It has an inscription on the exterior that I read as the date [1]818, but this plaque is badly damaged. If the date is correct, then it is possible that Leake, who traveled to the site in 1805, saw an earlier iteration of the structure on the same spot or nearby.

30. Stuart, "Natural and Physical Resources of Epirus," 279.

31. Leake, *Travels in Northern Greece*, 1:11.

32. Burgess, *Greece and the Levant*, 1:48–49. The map is in the Bibliothèque nationale de France, Paris, Cartes et plans, GE D-421.

33. Memorandum from Bishop Ignatius to Ali Pasha, Corfu, September 13, 1804, in *AAP*, 1:441–46, no. 241; Commander Mocenigo to Italinsky, January 10, 1806, in Ars, *I Rosia kai ta pasalikia Alvanias*, 149–55, no. 46.

34. Leake, *Travels in Northern Greece*, 1:185. The tax-farming grant (*iltizam*) can be found in the BOA, C.ML. 554/22780 (1219 H/1804).

35. Leake, *Travels in Northern Greece*, 1:95; Davies, "Late Venetian Butrint," 281; Karaiskaj, "Fortifikimet mesjetare."

36. Carvajal and Palanco, "Castle of Ali Pasha at Butrint."

37. The Venetian fortress can also be seen on the late eighteenth-century map mentioned above—Bibliothèque nationale de France, Paris, Cartes et plans, GE D-421.

38. Carvajal and Palanco, "Castle of Ali Pasha at Butrint," 299. In 1801, Athanasios Psalidas told Ali Pasha that he had purchased military supplies in Corfu and was having them shipped immediately to "Vivari," probably a reference to the new fortress at the mouth of the channel. Athanasios Psalidas to Ali Pasha, Corfu, July 7, 1801, in *AAP*, 1:155–57, no. 89.

39. In 1811, Ali Pasha told the British consul George Foresti that he intended to have a fort constructed at Sagiada, but this structure seems never to have been built. George Foresti to Colonel Lowe, Ioannina, June 15, 1811, British Library, London, Add MS 20183.

40. Archival evidence indicates that Ali Pasha's agents did supply the fortress with artillery and built a new *saray* in the keep; see William Meyer to Mr. Kolovos, Preveza, February 11, 1820, in Prevelakis and Merticopoulou, *Epirus*, 1:52; and memorandum of Elmaz Metze to Ali Pasha, Istanbul, June 9, 1819, in *AAP*, 3:272–73, no. 1202.

41. Ibrahim Manzour, *Memoires sur la Gréce et l'Albanie*, 91.

42. The map, dated ca. 1806–12, is at the Bibliothèque nationale de France, Paris, Cartes et plans, GE D-17276. A document from 1807 mentions that Ali Pasha was also threatening Parga with men in Agia Kiriaki, a village due east of Parga, suggesting that the governor had surrounded the townspeople on multiple flanks. Ioannis Vlaspoulos to Hasan Aga Tsabari, Parga, August 7, 1807, in *AAP*, 1:603–4, no. 330. For Ali Pasha's disappointment about not receiving Parga from the French, see report by Guillaume de Vaudoncourt (1807), 113, Ministère des armées de France, Service historique de la Défense, Vincennes, MS 1663.

43. Özgüven, "*Palanka* Forts," 171; Finkel and Ostapchuk, "Outpost of Empire," 182n5.

44. Another inland example is the fortress at Kiafa, which Ali Pasha ordered built to monitor the Souli area in 1805 after the multiyear war with its inhabitants. Leake, *Travels in Northern Greece*, 1:227–29.

45. William Martin Leake to Lord Mulgrave, Ioannina, August 22, 1805, NA, FO 78/57.

46. Leake to Lord Hawkesbury, November 14, 1808, 15–16, NA, FO 78/57.

47. From 1797 to 1814, Lefkada was occupied by Venetian, French, Russian, and British forces.

48. Karabelas, "To kastro tis Boukas," 400–408.

49. Kahraman and Dağlı, *Evliya Çelebi Seyahatnamesi*, 8:282–83; Ergolavos, *Evliya Tselebi*, 32–34.

50. Karabelas, "To kastro tis Boukas," 411–12; Curlin, "'Remember the Moment,'" 278.

51. Karabelas, "Ottoman Fortifications in Preveza," 49, 56.

52. Şakul, "Ottoman Attempts to Control the Adriatic," 256; Sklavenitis and Nikolaou, "I deyteri katalipsi tis Prevezas," 3–6.

53. "Rapport concernant la mission de monsieur Ponceton pendant son séjour en Turquie," 1807, 2, Gennadius Library, Athens, MS 150.

54. Report of Charles Rowley, May 13, 1811, NA, FO 78/76.

55. Goodison wrote, "There is a second new fort, (in which also a seraglio is to be built,) nearly completed, at about one mile and a half from the town, towards the entrance to the gulph." *Historical and Topographical Essay*, 93.

56. An 1801 document from Ali Pasha's scriptorium mentions the "fortress at Punta," probably a reference to a fortification there, as Aktion was known as "Punta" to the Venetians.

Muhtar Pasha to Ali Pasha, Arta, June 27, 1801, in *AAP*, 1:142–45, no. 82. Leake noted the small fortress when he traveled in the area in June 1805. *Travels in Northern Greece*, 1:174. And work was under way for a moat there in 1807. Liaze Loulachos to Ali Pasha, Preveza, February 12, 1807, in *AAP*, 1:556–57, no. 300. For the inscription, see Karabelas, "O Anglos theologos Thomas S. Hughes," 138.

57. In 1801, Muhtar Pasha wrote to his father that the construction of bastions in Tekes and Plagia were under way, and that an old tower at Tekes was being repaired. Muhtar Pasha to Ali Pasha, Arta, June 27, 1801, in *AAP*, 1:142–45, no. 82. British diplomatic correspondence indicates that the construction was completed at Tekes in 1810. George Foresti to Colonel Lowe, Ioannina, July 4, 1810, British Library, London, Add MS 20183.

58. A French engineer named Captain Ponceton wrote that in April 1807 he oversaw at Plagia the construction of a new fortification 60 to 69 *toises* (a *toise* is approximately two meters) in length on top of what was referred to as the "old fort." "Rapport concernant la mission de monsieur Ponceton pendant son séjour en Turquie," 1807, 2–3, Gennadius Library, Athens, MS 150.

59. Kefallonitou, "Citadel of Antirrio," 113.

60. See, for example, the following registers: BOA, MAD. d. 3992 (1110 H/1699), MAD. d. 3367 (1127 H/1715), MAD. d. 3160 (1187 H/1773–74), and MAD. d. 3162 (1206 H/1791). For the map, see Bibliothèque nationale de France, Paris, Cartes et plans, GE DD-509.

61. Kefallonitou, "Citadel of Antirrio," 115.

62. Muhtar Pasha to Ali Pasha, Nafpaktos, January 24, 1807, in *AAP*, 1:549–51, no. 296.

63. BOA, D.BŞM. d. 41822 (1231 H/1816).

64. The moat of Preveza appears to have been particularly problematic, as indicated by a record of workers employed there in 1807. Liaze Loulachos to Ali Pasha, Preveza, February 12, 1807, in *AAP*, 1:556, no. 300.

65. Wolfe, "Walled Towns"; Duffy, *Fortress in the Age of Vauban*, 2–5.

66. This system can also be seen on the other side of the Adriatic in the fifteenth-century Venetian fortress at Ravenna, Italy.

67. Curlin, "'Remember the Moment,'" 278.

68. In some cases—for example, the bastions of Agios Andreas in Preveza—these upper battlements no longer survive.

69. Ibrahim Manzour, *Memoires sur la Gréce et l'Albanie*, 354.

70. Register of workers employed at the Ioannina citadel, Ioannina, September 19, 1801, in *AAP*, 1:184–87, no. 102.

71. Greek-speaking locals referred to this type of forced labor as *angareia*. Dimitropoulos, "Ochiromatikes kai oikodomikes ergasies," 43; Peacock, "Introduction," 19–20.

72. Hughes, *Travels in Sicily, Greece, and Albania*, 1:453.

73. The stone was sourced locally. The register says that the workers brought stone from "Ardomista," a village now named Loggades on the eastern side of the Ioannina lake. Additionally, in the Barbié du Bocage map of 1820, a quarry "for building stone" (*la pierre pour batir*) is indicated to the west of the city, just south of the road leading toward Paramythia (see fig. 13).

74. Darling, "Mediterranean as a Borderland," 59.

75. See, for example, Carvajal and Palanco, "Castle of Ali Pasha at Butrint," 300.

76. This document mentions that Petros was tasked with locating building specialists (μαστόρος) for Ali Pasha's new fortress in Souli. Letter to Master Petros, Ioannina, 1804, in *AAP*, 1:395–96, no. 205. See also Pouqueville, *Histoire de la régénération de la Grèce*, 1:95; Petronitis, "Architektones kai michanikoi," 367–72; Vaudoncourt, *Memoirs on the Ionian Islands*, 287; and Shuteriqi, *Petro Korçari*.

77. Leake, *Travels in Northern Greece*, 1:223, 253.

78. Philadelpheis, "Anaskafai Nikopoleos," 234–35; Petronitis, "Architektones kai michanikoi," 370; Karabelas, "H ochirosi tou exoterikou perivolou," 158. This plaque was paired with another inscription bearing the date 1223 AH (1807–8), the same year that appears on the Ottoman Turkish inscription on the southeastern bastion of the Fortress of Agios Andreas.

79. This tradition seems to have continued with Petros's son, who is recorded as working under a Master Thanos. Register of Ali Pasha's retinue, Ioannina, March 26, 1801, in *AAP*, 1:126, no. 74.

80. Gilkes, *Albania*, 303–4. See also Adhami, "Të dhëna rreth fizionomisë urbanistike dhe arkitektonike."

81. Anthony Baker to Robert Adair, November 10, 1808, Hertfordshire Archives, Hertford, UK, DE/MI/85508.

82. The full text of these reports, transcribed by Ileana Moroni, can be found in Neumeier, "Trans-Imperial Encounter," 31–44. The Gennadius collection has only half of Vaudoncourt's report; a complete version can be found in Ministère des armées de France, Service historique de la Défense, Vincennes, MS 1663.

83. Vaudoncourt, *Memoirs on the Ionian Islands*, 251, 82, 252, 287.

84. "Rapport du colonel Guillaume, commandant le Régiment d'artillerie à Cheval italienne, chevalier de la Couronne de fer, sur la mission qui lui a été confiée par S. A. I. [Son Altesse Impériale] le Prince Eugène Napoléon de France Vice Roi d'Italie; en Erzegovine, Albanie et Epire," 1807, 61, Gennadius Library, Athens, MS 150; Beauchamp, *Life of Ali Pacha*, 151.

85. "Rapport du colonel Guillaume," 1807, 59, Gennadius Library, Athens, MS 150.

86. "Rapport du colonel Guillaume," 1807, 61, Gennadius Library, Athens, MS 150.

87. "Rapport du colonel Guillaume," 1807, 62, Gennadius Library, Athens, MS 150.

88. "Rapport du colonel Guillaume," 1807, 65, Gennadius Library, Athens, MS 150. "Quarrés" is a now obsolete spelling of the word *carré*.

89. "Rapport du colonel Guillaume," 1807, 66 , Gennadius Library, Athens, MS 150.

90. Pouqueville, *Histoire de la régénération de la Grèce*, 1:95.

91. See, for example, Ostapchuk and Bilyayeva, "Ottoman Northern Black Sea Frontier," 163.

92. Greek historians remember this notorious event as the "destruction" (*chalasmos*) of Preveza.

93. Istanbul ended up sending a man named Abdullah Bey as *voyvoda* (mayor, governor), selected from among the ranks of the *kapıcıbaşı* (head of the palace doorkeepers) in the imperial court. BOA, C.BH. 40/1890 (1218 H/1803).

94. Fortification works were also thrown up at Ali Pasha's residence in Mitikas, directly facing the land border of Preveza to the north, as well as at Plagia and Tekes, facing Lefkada from the west. Muhtar Pasha assured his father that at Mitikas there were plenty of cannons facing the land border. Muhtar Pasha to Ali Pasha, Arta, June 27, 1801, in *AAP*, 1:142–45, no. 82.

95. Although unsigned, the letter seems to have been written by Yiankos Yiazitzi-zades, a Phanariot from Istanbul who had previously worked for Ali Pasha in Ioannina. Letter to Ali Pasha, November 17, 1801, in *AAP*, 1:202–5, no. 113.

96. "Treaty of Peace," 405. For the Ottoman-Russian treaty forming the Septinsular Republic, see BOA, C.HR. 85/4232 (1213 H/1799); Şakul, "Ottoman Attempts to Control the Adriatic," 256.

97. See, both in the Bibliothèque nationale de France, Paris, Cartes et plans, Vincenzo Coronelli, map of Preveza and Santa Maura, 1687, GE D-13092, and map of the region of Preveza, Vonitsa, and Lefkada, 1800, GE C-10202.

98. J. P. Morier to Charles James Fox, Ioannina, June 4, 1806, NA, FO 78/53.

99. William Meyer to Thomas Maitland, May 1820, in Prevelakis and Merticopoulou, *Epirus*, 1:115, no. 46. The British consul George Foresti also noted that "the fortifications of Preveza, of Port Palermo and those opposite Santa Maura, which command the town, the port and even the citadel of that island, as also the line of forts in the coast opposite Corfu were all erected by Aly Pacha in direct violation of treaties which were formerly concluded between Turkey and the Republic of Venice, and which have been since renewed in the favor of the Ionian Islands." Report by George Foresti, November 1820, NA, FO 78/96.

100. BOA, C.HR. 166/8278 (1219 H/1804).

101. Lowe added that the high commissioner should remind Ali Pasha that in the days of Venetian control, "the ancient treaties were respected and no works [were] ever erected in that spot." Colonel Lowe to George Foresti, Lefkada, May 26, 1810, British Library, London, Add MS 20168.

102. George Foresti to Colonel Lowe, July 4, 1810, British Library, London, Add MS 20183.

103. George Foresti to Colonel Lowe, July 4, 1810, British Library, London, Add MS 20183.

104. See, for example, supplies sent to Yanya, Arta, Preveza, and Parga in 1830. BOA, C.AS. 419/17395 (1246 H/1830). There were also repairs conducted at the fortresses in Preveza, Arta, and Parga in 1849. BOA, A.AMD. 14/36 (1265 H/1848–49).

105. Peacock, "Introduction," 19–20.

106. Süleyman Efendi to Ali Pasha, Istanbul, May 5, 1810, in *AAP*, 2:145, no. 541.

107. George Foresti to Colonel Lowe, July 4, 1810, British Library, London, Add MS 20183. See also petition of Ali Pasha to Lord Hamilton, Grevena, May 8, 1811, NA, FO 78/80.

108. Ostapchuk and Bilyayeva, "Ottoman Northern Black Sea Frontier," 163.

109. For this revisionist literature, see Agoston, "Disjointed Historiography"; and Şakul, "Evolution of Ottoman Military Logistical Systems."

110. "Rapport concernant la mission de monsieur Ponceton pendant son séjour en Turquie," 1807, 1, Gennadius Library, Athens, MS 150.

111. See, for example, BOA, C.DH. 87/4346 (1217 H/1802), and HAT 117/4748 (1217 H/1802).

112. In any case, the Porte evidently did not meet all his needs. Ali Pasha complained that, of the 147 long-range battering guns requested, only thirty-seven were actually sent for the fortresses in Preveza. BOA, C.AS. 385/15929 (1224 H/1809).

113. The foundry is mentioned in the register of immovable property belonging to Ali Pasha. BOA, MAD. d. 9767 (1241 H/1826). Leake reported that in this place Ali Pasha had settled a group of Bulgarians "whom he brought [there] in 1802 on his return from the Danube." Leake, *Travels in Northern Greece*, 1:222.

114. Athanasios Psalidas to Ali Pasha, Corfu, July 7, 1801, in *AAP*, 1:155–57, no. 89.

115. For an explanation of these registers and how they can be used, see Finkel and Ostapchuk, "Outpost of Empire," 154–55.

116. In Ali Pasha's time, the first indication of repair works at Nafpaktos (İnebahtı) comes in 1787, in the form of an order to cut down trees for repairs at the fortress. BOA, C.AS. 1164/51832 (1202 H/1787), and C.AS. 1174/52307 (1202 H/1788). In 1799, a *bina emini* was sent to Nafpaktos ordering the construction of carriages for the cannons and buildings belonging to the head of the local unit of Janissaries. BOA, D.BŞM.BNE. d. 16084 (1214 H/1799). It seems that this construction continued until at least until 1803; see BOA, C.AS. 1131/50236 (1216 H/1801), and HAT. 41/2065a (1218 H/1803); in this instance, the workers were not provided by Ali Pasha but rather by Ali Ağa, who was among those who held property in the area as a reward for his military service.

117. Muhtar Pasha to Ali Pasha, Nafpaktos, January 24, 1807, in *AAP*, 1:550, no. 296. There was a similar situation in 1818, when one Mimar Abdülkadir was brought in to take charge of further repairs at Nafpaktos. BOA, C.AS. 452/18832 (1233 H/1818). Yet perhaps the most important intervention came in 1816, and it is thoroughly documented in a *tamirat* register that records extensive repairs to both the Nafpaktos citadel and the fortress at

Antirrio, including the "structures of Muhtar Pasha's palace" and the curtain walls of the fortifications. BOA, D.BŞM. d. 41822 (1231 H/1816). Ali Pasha was notified by his agent in Istanbul that workers were being sent to Nafpaktos as early as October 1815 for this project. Hüseyin Bey to Ali Pasha, Istanbul, October 28, 1815, in *AAP*, 2:612, no. 814.

118. BOA, C.AS. 1103/48736 (1217 H/1801).

119. For this view, see Anscombe, "Continuities in Ottoman Centre-Periphery Relations," 243.

120. Goodison, *Historical and Topographical Essay*, 94; Leake, *Travels in Northern Greece*, 1:180–82.

121. Stuart, "Natural and Physical Resources of Epirus," 283; Leake, *Travels in Northern Greece*, 1:178; Goodison, *Historical and Topographical Essay*, 93–94. A map dated 1825 shows the depths of the strait. NA, MPI 1/42.

122. Hughes, *Travels in Sicily, Greece, and Albania*, 1:423.

123. For an example of such scholarship, see Necipoğlu, "Framing the Gaze."

124. See Langins, *Conserving the Enlightenment*.

Chapter 3

1. The 1878 map is based on demographic data compiled by the local chronicler Panagiotis Aravantinos, first published in 1857. Aravantinos, *Chronografia tis Ipeirou*, 2:320–93.

2. For the complexity of local identity in Epirus represented in European travel narratives, see Fraser, *Mediterranean Encounters*, 173–77.

3. For the term "religioscape," see Tanyeri-Erdemir, "Remains of the Day," 73.

4. Leake, *Travels in Northern Greece*, 4:285.

5. William Meyer to Hankey, Preveza, May 10, 1820, in Prevelakis and Merticopoulou, *Epirus*, 1:123.

6. William Meyer to Londonderry, Preveza, July 15, 1821, NA, FO 78/103.

7. Legrand, *Complainte d'Ali de Tébélen*, 23–25.

8. Skiotis, "The Lion and the Phoenix," 66.

9. Crane, "Ottoman Sultan's Mosques," 203–4.

10. Necipoğlu, *Age of Sinan*, 30.

11. Kinneir, *Journey Through Asia Minor*, 90; Acun, *Bozok Sancağı*, 14–56; Yenişehirlioğlu, "Architectural Patronage," 329; Duru, "Yozgat Çapanoğlu Camii ve Vakfiyeleri."

12. Acun, *Bozok Sancağı*, 57–115.

13. Al-Asad, "Mosque of Muhammad 'Ali," 41–42; Fahmy, *All the Pasha's Men*, 73; Behrens-Abouseif, *Islamic Architecture in Cairo*, 168–70; and El-Ashmouni and Bartsch, "Egypt's Age of Transition," 52–56.

14. Al-Asad, "Mosque of Muhammad 'Ali," 43.

15. Veli Pasha also commissioned a mosque in a village in the district of Arcadia (Ott. Arkadya), presumably when he was governor of the Peloponnese province. BOA, C.MF. 114/5668 (1224 H/1814). This may be the same mosque Pouqueville saw in Filiatra, which he attributes to Veli Pasha. Pouqueville, *Voyage dans la Grèce*, 6:23.

16. Sathas, *Istorikai diatrivai*, 262; Hughes, *Travels in Sicily, Greece, and Albania*, 2:327; Holland, *Travels in the Ionian Isles*, 453.

17. Machiel Kiel places a "thorough reconstruction [of the building] on the orders of Ali Pasha" around 1800. "Yanya," 319. Similar assertions can be found in Konstantios, *Kastro of Ioannina*, 37; and Papadopoulou, "Fethiye Mosque," 162.

18. Papadopoulou, "Fethiye Mosque," 162; Smiris, "Ta mousoulmanika temeni ton Ioanninon," 58; Leake, *Travels in Northern Greece*, 1:253–54.

19. Kiel, "Yanya," 319. See Delilbaşı, "1564 Tarihli Mufassal Yanya Livası Tahrir Defterlerine Göre Yanya Kenti ve Köleri," 4–5.

20. Osswald, "*Lieux de Pouvoir* to *Lieux de Mémoire*," 190.

21. During Evliya Çelebi's journey to Ioannina in 1670, he referred to the mosque in the inner citadel as the "Fethiye Mosque." Kahraman and Dağlı, *Evliya Çelebi Seyahatnamesi*, 8:288. The earliest known Ottoman archival document calling this mosque the "Fethiye" is an order from the late seventeenth century naming a new imam for the foundation. BOA, C.EV. 516/26086 (1107 H/1696).

22. Smiris, "Ta mousoulmanika temeni ton Ioanninon," 58; Osswald, "*Lieux de Pouvoir* to *Lieux de Mémoire*," 197n7; Vranousis, *Istorika kai topografika*, 35. It has been suggested that the name "Fethiye" is a direct reference to the Pammakaristos Church in Istanbul, the seat of the Orthodox Patriarchate, being converted to the Fethiye Mosque just a few years earlier, around 1590. Osswald, "*Lieux de Pouvoir* to *Lieux de Mémoire*," 190; Eyice, "Fethiye Camii." While the mosque in Istanbul was converted to celebrate Sultan Murad III's annexation of what are now Georgia and Azerbaijan, it is not clear which "conquest" the new mosque in the Ioannina citadel was referring to, or why the Ottoman authorities decided to revoke part of the original capitulation agreements at this particular moment.

23. Kiel, "Yanya," 319.

24. Eyice, "Arslan Paşa Camii," 401. The Ottoman Turkish inscription above the doorway of the mosque provides the year 1027 H (1617–18). The pious endowment document (*vakfiye*) was established two years earlier. VGM, Vakfiye 623/199/193 (1025 H/1616).

25. Smiris, "Ta mousoulmanika temeni ton Ioanninon," 59; Osswald, "*Lieux de Pouvoir* to *Lieux de Mémoire*," 190. It is tempting to imagine that a natural disaster, such as an earthquake or fire, compromised the structure to the point of requiring demolition, but there is no archival documentation to support this hypothesis.

26. See, for example, VGM, 183/24/181 (1215 H/1800).

27. The grille that can be found on the site today is a replica, produced in 1999 on the initiative of the Friends of Antiquity of Ioannina and the Philippou family. The original cover, which can be seen in several travelers' drawings contemporary with or shortly after Ali Pasha's time (see fig. 16), survived until World War II, when it was removed during the German occupation of the city. According

to the transcription of a now-lost tombstone located in this mausoleum, Ümmülgüsüm Hanım was the daughter of Kaplan Pasha of Delvina. Soulis, "Tourkikai epigrafai Ioanninon," 91; Skiotis, "From Bandit to Pasha," 228n2. Archival documents indicate that she established a cash endowment in her own name. VGM, Defter 877/38 and 406/43. These documents refer to Ümmülgüsüm Hanım as Ali Pasha's *halile*, or wife by Islamic law.

28. Smiris, "Ta mousoulmanika temeni ton Ioanninon," 53–58.

29. Hughes, *Travels in Sicily, Greece, and Albania*, 1:475.

30. Documents from the Ottoman archives refer not only to the mosque but also to a *medrese* and a *mekteb* (school) built by Ali Pasha in the city. BOA, C.EV. 374/18998 (1239 H/1824). A document from Ali Pasha's chancery reports that repairs were made to the mosque in 1809. Mifti Pagouri to Mastoros Themelis, Tepelena, August 16, 1809, in *AAP*, 2:96–97, no. 500.

31. Hobhouse, *Journey Through Albania*, 99.

32. Leake, *Travels in Northern Greece*, 1:52.

33. Lear, *Edward Lear in the Levant*, 115–16. An Ottoman plan of the Tepelena citadel that is undated but probably from the late nineteenth century also notes the mosque. BOA, PLK, p. 866.

34. BOA, HAT. 250/14174 (1227 H/1812); Holland, *Travels in the Ionian Isles*, 70.

35. Petsas, "Eidiseis ek tis 10is Archaiologikis Perifereias," 31–34. Unlike at Tepelena, however, the columns and capitals used in the outer arcade for the Preveza mosque seem to be reused, sourced from the nearby ancient city of Nikopolis. Several structures in Preveza, including Ali Pasha's "Bouka" palace and the Pantocrator Fortress, use spoliated material. Neumeier, "Spoils for the New Pyrhhus," 319–22.

36. A disturbance in the masonry on the façade of the Fethiye Mosque where the minaret joins the northern wall (see fig. 52) can be explained by the later demolition of an exterior porch that no longer survives, a portion of which can still be observed standing in an 1840s drawing by Dominique Papety. Louvre Museum, Paris, RF.1773.34.

37. According to an Ottoman source, the mosque was still standing at the end of the nineteenth century. *Sâlnâme-yi Vilâyet-i Yanya* (1306 H/1888–89), 96; Kiel, *Ottoman Architecture in Albania*, 92. For the pious endowment established by Ali Pasha for this mosque, see BOA, EV.MKT. 841/75 and 843/85 (1293 H/1876–77).

38. Mantzana, "Osman Şah (or Kurşunlu) Mosque"; Necipoğlu, *Sinan's Autobiographies*, 94.

39. Hartmuth, "History of Centre-Periphery Relations," 25.

40. This later renovation is evidenced by the neoclassical Ottoman interior decoration, with the *tuğra* (imperial monogram) of Sultan Abdülhamid II installed above the mihrab.

41. VGM, 629/743/491 (1219 H/1804).

42. Leake, *Travels in Northern Greece*, 1:482n1.

43. BOA, HAT. 250/14174 (1227 H/1812).

44. BOA, EV. d. 19962.

45. BOA, C.EV. 374/18998 (1239 H/1823).

46. Hasluck, *Christianity and Islam Under the Sultans*, 2:593–96. The only example that I have come across of another provincial power holder directly commissioning a tekke in this period is a Nakshibendi lodge located in Manisa, built by a member of the Kara Osman-oğlu family, which no longer survives. Kuyulu, *Kara Osmanoğlu Ailesine ait Mimari Eserler*, 157.

47. Nathalie Clayer mentions a few other tekkes associated with Ali Pasha that have not been included in the table because I could not locate any corroborating archival or material evidence for these foundations. Clayer, "Myth of Ali Pasha," 129.

48. In Ottoman documents and historical literature, the Arslan Pasha Mosque is alternatively paired with either a tekke/*zâvîye* or a *medrese*, suggesting that there was a degree of fluidity in the terms used to describe these accompanying institutions. BOA, C.EV. 37/1819 (1132 H/1720); Clayer, "Myth of Ali Pasha," 130; Papadopoulou, "Aslan Pasha Medrese."

49. Terzinoğlu, "Sufis in the Age of State-Building," 91–92; and Curry, *Transformation of Muslim Mystical Thought*, 65–72.

50. In the Ottoman documents that I have examined, the dervish lodges in question are alternatively referred to as a *tekke*, *zaviye*, or *dergâh*. Without exception, the archival documents from Ali Pasha's own chancery refer to these institutions exclusively by the term τεκές (*tekes*).

51. Mavrommatis, "Bektashis in 20th Century Greece," 220.

52. Androudis, "O Bektasikos tekes Dourbali Soultan," 241. The complex has tenuous links to Ali Pasha, though more archival research is needed to confirm the connection. Leake, *Travels in Northern Greece*, 4:413; Hasluck, *Geographical Distribution*, 111.

53. Several of these documents were first cited in Clayer, "Myth of Ali Pasha."

54. Hasluck, *Christianity and Islam Under the Sultans*, 2:586–93.

55. See Clayer, "Myth of Ali Pasha," 131–33.

56. The name of the preacher appointed to this mosque was Shaykh Yusuf Halife. BOA, HAT. 1571/13 (1242 H/1827).

57. Hughes, *Travels in Sicily, Greece, and Albania*, 2:23.

58. Pouqueville, *Voyage dans la Grèce*, 1:140.

59. Clayer, "Myth of Ali Pasha," 129.

60. BOA, DH.MKT. 473/2 (1319 H/1902). An earlier *vakıf* document, however, refers to this tekke as "constructed" (*binâ' ve inşâ'*) outright by Ali Pasha. VGM, Defter 865/36 (1265 H/1848–49).

61. Holland, *Travels in the Ionian Isles*, 130.

62. BOA, EV.MKT.CHT. 229/83 (1221 H/1806). The lodge is recorded in Ottoman documents as being in the "Zivadiye" neighborhood of the town, which was located at Ioannina's northern gate, thus connecting Muhtar Pasha's tekke with the lodge on the

Barbié du Bocage map. VGM, Defter 2411/37.

63. BOA, FTG, photograph 4, from Yıldız Album YEE d. 404.

64. Clayer, "Myth of Ali Pasha," 128; VGM, 580/379/207 (1220 H/1805).

65. A *vakıf* document dated about fifteen years after Ali Pasha's execution in 1822 confirms the death of the head of this tekke, Shaykh Ahmed Musir Efendi, who was presumably the leader of the complex when Ali Pasha was alive and may be the shaykh to whom Leake is referring. BOA, EV.KSD. 14/46 (1253 H/1837).

66. Leake, *Travels in Northern Greece*, 4:284.

67. Clayer, "Myth of Ali Pasha," 129.

68. The tekke at Preveza no longer survives. It is also uncertain where the site was located, though it may have been extra muros and north of the city, near the Muslim cemetery and the spring that fed the city. Karabelas, "O Italos politikos Francesco Guicciardini," 78; VGM, Defter 1771/30/35 and 902/63; Clayer, "Myth of Ali Pasha," 129.

69. BOA, C.EV. 462/23372 (1239 H/1824) and EV.MKT.CHT 281/92; Clayer, "Myth of Ali Pasha," 129.

70. Leake, *Travels in Northern Greece*, 1:31; Pouqueville, *Voyage dans la Grèce*, 1:291.

71. BOA, C.EV. 116/5772 (1219 H/1804).

72. Holland, *Travels in the Ionian Isles*, 504.

73. Kiel, *Ottoman Architecture in Albania*, 51. Before Ali Pasha, Kurt Ahmed Pasha held the all-important title "Commander of the Mountain Passes" (*derbendât başbuğu*). BOA, C.DH. 290/14493 (1201 H/1787).

74. Kiel, *Ottoman Architecture in Albania*, 51. There is a repair register for the citadel dated when Kurt Ahmed Pasha was still in power. Topkapı Palace, Istanbul, MA. d. 2729 (1197 H/1782–83).

75. Kiel, *Ottoman Architecture in Albania*, 62–65.

76. Skiotis, "From Bandit to Pasha," 230.

77. In his visit to the Durbali Sultan Tekke, François Pouqueville related that the shaykh there referred to the lodge as a "mad house." *Travels in Epirus*, 115. In Tepelena, Hughes recalled that they were accosted by a "mad dervish" who was wandering around Ali Pasha's newly built mosque. *Travels in Sicily, Greece, and Albania*, 2:252.

78. Kanetakis, *To kastro*, 126.

79. Tütüncü, "Corpus of Ottoman Inscriptions," 169.

80. See, for example, Hughes, *Travels in Sicily, Greece, and Albania*, 1:457.

81. Beydilli, "Yeniçeri," 453.

82. Register of bread distribution in Ali Pasha's court, Ioannina, March 26, 1801, in *AAP*, 1:120–24, no. 73.

83. See, for example, order of Ali Pasha to Master Koto regarding construction work at the Tekke of Shaykh Totzi, Ioannina (1808), in *AAP*, 2:792, no. 427; and declaration of the villagers from Dragoti, n.d., in *AAP*, 3:569–71, no. 1377.

84. This claim that Ali Pasha was a Bektashi was so important to the sculptor, Muntaz Dhrami, that he put his signature and the date of the work (2002) on the star itself.

85. Skiotis, "The Lion and the Phoenix," 6; Fleming, *Muslim Bonaparte*, 68–69; Yaycıoğlu, *Partners of the Empire*, 90–91.

86. John Phillip Morier to Lord Hawkesbury, Ioannina, June 30, 1804, NA, FO 78/44.

87. For a discussion of such restrictions in eighteenth-century Istanbul, see Hamadeh, *City's Pleasures*, 41–44.

88. Leake, *Travels in Northern Greece*, 1:49.

89. Gradeva, "From the Bottom Up," 137–38.

90. An early example is Khalid al-Qasri, governor under the Umayyad caliph ʿAbd al-Malik, who is said to have built a church for his mother next to the mosque in Kufa in the first half of the eighth century. Gharipour, "Preface," xxii.

91. See Christodoulidis, *Akolouthia kai vios tou en Agiois Patros Imon Kosma*. An abridged English translation can be found in Cavarnos, *St. Cosmas Aitolos*, 25–45.

92. Cavarnos, *St. Cosmas Aitolos*, 13–14, 41, 35.

93. Cavarnos, *St. Cosmas Aitolos*, 42–45.

94. The main gate and monastic quarters on the northwestern side of the complex appear to have been completely rebuilt very recently, sometime between 2007 and 2010.

95. As for the remains of the saint, they are said to have been transferred from the monastery to the archaeological museum in Fier in 1984. Other relics of the saint are kept in the Metropolitan Church in Athens. Elsie, *Historical Dictionary of Albania*, 95. There is still a simple funerary slab commemorating the saint in the tomb chamber of the monastery, which continues to be maintained and venerated with candles and wreaths.

96. Christopoulos, *Ta leipsana kai to monastiri Kosma tou Aitolou*, 570.

97. Cavarnos, *St. Cosmas Aitolos*, 47.

98. "ΆΝΗΓΕΡΘΗ ΕΚ ΒΑΘΡΩΝ / Ο ΘΕΙΟΣ ΚΑΙ ΙΕΡΟΣ ΟΥΤ/ΟΣ ΝΑΟΣ ΔΙΑ ΠΡΟΣΤΑ/ΓΗΣ ΚΑΙ ΠΡΟΤΡΟ-ΠΗΣ / ΤΟΥ ΥΨΗΛΟΤΑΤΟΥ ΒΕΖΥΡ / ΑΛΗ ΠΑΣΙΑ ΑΠΟ ΤΕΠΕΛΕ/ΝΗ." This inscription was first published in Christopoulos, *Ta leipsana kai to monastiri Kosma tou Aitolou*, 572.

99. Christopoulos, *Ta leipsana kai to monastiri Kosma tou Aitolou*, 572.

100. Fourka is a village near Konitsa in present-day Greece, the metropolitan of which presided in the nearby monastery of Agios Vellas.

101. My thanks to Sokol Çunga for bringing this volume to my attention. Alexoudis, *Syntomos istoriki perigrafi*, 82. Like the majority of Ali Pasha's communications with local notables and communities, these orders are written in Greek.

102. Alexoudis, *Syntomos istoriki perigrafi*, 82.

103. Alexoudis, *Syntomos istoriki perigrafi*, 82.

104. Koli Mitros is probably a nickname for the "Nikolaos Dimitriou" named in the inscription.

105. The village is in fact named Vasiliki, presumably after the patron of the church.

106. Inside the church is a splendid painting program, executed in two phases in 1839 and 1845. Panagiotopoulos, *Ieros Naos Agiou Nikolaou Vasilikis*, 27–28.

107. "ΑΝΕΚΑΙΝΙΣΘΗ ΕΚ ΘΕΜΕΛΙΩΝ Ο ΘΕΙΟΣ ΝΑΟΣ ΤΟΥ ΑΓΙΟΥ ΝΙΚΟΛΑΟΥ ΔΙ' ΕΞΟΔΩΝ ΤΩΝ ΕΓΧΩΡΙΩΝ / ΔΙΑ ΣΙΝΔΡΟΜΗΣ ΒΑΣΙΛΙΚΗΣ ΑΥΘΕΝΤΙΣΗΣ ΒΟΙΒΟΝΤΑΣ ΚΑΙ ΤΩΝ ΑΔΕΛΦΩΝ ΑΥΤΗΣ." The inscription is dated May 12, 1818.

108. According to Ottoman documents, Vasiliki also owned agricultural property (*çiftlik*) in the region, and even continued to receive a monthly salary from the revenues after the death of Ali Pasha. BOA, C.ML. 557/22866 (1239 H/1824).

109. Bozdoğan and Necipoğlu, "Entangled Discourses," 2.

110. One notable exception is the recent edited volume *Sacred Precincts*. See Gharipour, "Preface."

111. Kafescioğlu, *Constantinopolis/Istanbul*, 63–85; Necipoğlu, *Age of Sinan*, 103–4.

112. Necipoğlu, *Sinan's Autobiographies*, 92–99.

113. See especially Barkey, *Empire of Difference*; and Yaycıoğlu, *Partners of the Empire*.

114. Zimmi (Arb. *dhimmi*) is a legal term in Islamic law to designate the Christian or Jewish subject of a Muslim ruler, who would grant these non-Muslim communities the right to property, quality of life, and freedom to worship in exchange for paying a special tax (*cizye*). This institution or approach to the "People of the Book" in Islamic lands was upheld throughout the duration of the Ottoman Empire, until 1856, when the sultan issued an imperial edict that declared equality among all subjects of the empire. Masters, "Dhimmi"; and Kenanoğlu, "Zimmi Osmanlılar'da."

115. Neumann, "Hesitating but Challenging Closing Speech," 26.

116. Gradeva, "Ottoman Policy," 17–24.

117. These events resulted in an explosion of church-building activity that came to take on much more visibility and prominence, especially in the Ottoman capital. Girardelli, "Architecture, Identity, and Liminality," 233.

118. Kenanoğlu, *Osmanlı Millet Sistemi*, 292–97.

119. Masters, "Dhimmi," 186; and Kiel, *Art and Society of Bulgaria*, 192–202.

120. Giakoumis and Egro, "Ottoman Pragmatism," 90–93.

121. This seven-volume work was edited by Charalambos Bouras and Stavros Mamaloukos and appeared between 1979 and 2013. See also Bouras, *Byzantine and Post-Byzantine Architecture*.

122. Gilkes, *Albania*, 213–15.

123. Maximilian Hartmuth has identified several examples from the Ottoman Balkans in which Muslim and Christian craftsmen worked on religious monuments for a confessional group other than their own. Hartmuth, "In Search of the Provincial Artist," 78–88. For another example from Epirus, there is a document in the Ali Pasha archive in which a "Mastoro-Koto," the name suggesting an Albanian Christian, was called upon for construction work at the Tekke of Shaykh Totzi. *AAP*, 2:792, no. 427.

124. Barbié du Bocage seems to have been confused about the names of the different churches and monasteries on the island, though the locations appear to be correct. For example, the Filanthropinos Monastery, which is dedicated to Agios Nikolaos, is labeled "Agios Joanni" on the map (no. 18).

125. Delivorrias, "Some Thoughts," 133.

126. See Brouskari, *Ottoman Architecture in Greece*.

127. See Kiel, *Ottoman Architecture in Albania*. Like Greek historians, Albanian scholars also use the term "post-Byzantine" to describe Christian architecture erected under Ottoman rule. See, for example, Meksi and Thomo, "Arkitektura posbizantine."

Chapter 4

1. Archival records and published accounts suggest that it was still preserved in situ at least until the late 1980s. Institute of Cultural Monuments, Tirana, Burhan Dautaj, "Kalaja e Tepelenës," updated restoration report, October 25, 1985; and Bejko, "Kalaja e Tepelenës," 104. The curator at the Tepelena History Museum believes that the inscription was removed sometime after the fall of communism in Albania, during the 1990s. Auron Tare, email to author, June 3, 2021.

2. Although the mosque no longer stands, its proximity to the eastern gate of the Tepelena citadel can be determined from a sketch by Edward Lear in 1848 (see fig. 55) and a map at the BOA, PLK, 866.

3. I read "[ΙΜΠ]ΡΑΗΜ ΑΓΑΣ" in the upper left corner. There is a precedent for the names of Ali Pasha's agents appearing in public epigraphy. The governor's appointed administrators in Preveza, Bekir Ağa and Süleyman Bey, are named in a pair of Greek inscriptions dated 1808 that were once fixed above the main gate to the walled district immediately south of the Agios Andreas Fortress (see fig. 17). Philadelpheis, "Anaskafai Nikopoleos," 234–38; Petronitis, "Architektones kai michanikoi," 369–71; Karabelas, "To neo kastro 'sto Kyparissi,'" 12.

4. The date at the bottom of the plaque is noted in Bejko, "Kalaja e Tepelenës," 104; Kiel, "Tepedelen," 476; and Tütüncü, "Corpus of Ottoman Inscriptions," 174.

5. See Renda, *Batılılaşma Döneminde*; Gruber, "Like Hearts of Birds"; and Sezer, "Architecture of Bibliophilia," 184.

6. See Ameen, "Bilingual and Trilingual Inscriptions."

7. I use the term "linguistic landscape" as defined by Rodrigue Landry and Richard Y. Bourhis, to refer "to the visibility and salience of languages on public and commercial signs in a given territory or region." Landry and Bourhis, "Linguistic Landscape and Ethnolinguistic Vitality," 23.

8. For the phrase "epigraphic habits," see MacMullen, "Epigraphic Habit in the Roman Empire."

9. Revell, *Roman Imperialism and Local Identities*, 21. See also Sears, Keegan, and Laurence, *Written Space*

in the Latin West; and Eck, "Presence, Role, and Significance of Latin."

10. Cooley, *Res Gestae Divi Augusti*, 47–48.

11. What is considered one of the oldest surviving inscriptions from the Ottoman period, a text dated 1337 that lauds Orhan, the second Ottoman sultan, has generated a great deal of debate about the nature of early Ottoman statecraft. See Heywood, "1337 Bursa Inscription"; and Lowry, *Nature of the Early Ottoman State*, 33–44.

12. While there is still no major analytic study of Ottoman inscriptions, the following encyclopedias offer introductory overviews: Dijkema and Alparslan, "Kitâbât: 7. In Turkey"; and Alparslan, "Kitabe." There are several catalogs available, but they tend to target specific geographic regions or periods of time; see a summary of this literature in Dijkema, *Ottoman Historical Monumental Inscriptions*, 1–3. The Database for Ottoman Inscriptions is an effort currently under way to build a digital catalog of Ottoman inscriptions, beginning with Istanbul and with plans to expand beyond to the provinces; see http://info.ottomaninscriptions.com.

13. See Rhoby, *Postbyzantinische Epigramme*; and Laflı and Bozkuş, "Some Epigraphic and Archaeological Documents."

14. Dijkema and Alparslan, "Kitâbât: 7. In Turkey," 224.

15. For this specific inscription, see Konyalı, *Abideleri ve Kitabeleri ile Üsküdar Tarihi*, 1:260–61; Top, "İstanbul'daki Selatin Camilerin Kitabeleri," 140–46.

16. Kütükoğlu, *Osmanlı Belgelerinin Dili*, 71–75.

17. Keskiner, "Sultan Ahmed III (r. 1703–1730)," 292–93; Karateke, "Legitimizing the Ottoman Sultanate," 51.

18. Acun, *Bozok Sancağı*, 15.

19. Kana'an, "Waqf, Architecture, and Political Self-Fashioning," 125–28.

20. See Neumeier, "Rivaling Elgin" and "Spoils for the New Pyrrhus."

21. Hammond, *Epirus*, 568–69; Plutarch, *Lives, Volume IX*, 357–59.

22. Soulis, "Tourkikai epigrafai Ioanninon," 92; Philadelpheis, "Anaskafai Nikopoleos," 239–42; Petronitis, "Architektones kai michanikoi," 382; and Wace and Thompson, *Nomads of the Balkans*, 192.

23. The practice of indenting even-numbered lines in Greek inscriptions is referred to as *eisthesis*. Joseph W. Day, email to author, October 27, 2017; Hanink, "Epitaph for Atthis," 22.

24. A transcription of the original Greek text has been published in Soulis, "Tourkikai epigrafai Ioanninon," 92–93; and Steriadi, "Oi epigrafes tou kastrou," 114.

25. At Ioannina, the Byzantine masonry can be distinguished from that of the later Ottoman period, as it is typically characterized by courses of large, rough-cut fieldstones, the interstices filled with small pieces of brick and a thick mortar. An especially good example of this technique is the so-called Gate of Thomas on the western side of the outer walls, dated to the fourteenth century. Meanwhile, the Ottoman phasing has courses of small, rectangular-cut blocks, with a thinner application of mortar visible.

26. Papadopoulou, "Kastro Ioanninon," 39–43.

27. Kitromilides, *Enlightenment and Revolution*, 330; and Gallant, *Edinburgh History of the Greeks*, 90.

28. The term "political" does not necessarily imply political subject matter but rather comes from the Greek word *politikos* (civil, lay, municipal) and thus distinguishes the genre as a secular form of entertainment, as opposed to liturgical music. For more on political verse, see Bernard, *Writing and Reading Byzantine Secular Poetry*, 243–45; Jeffreys, "Nature and Origins of the Political Verse"; and Horrocks, *Greek*, 327–28. As Andreas Rhoby pointed out to me, some of the lines in this inscription (e.g., line 7, which is fourteen syllables) do not precisely adhere to the conventional scheme of the fifteen-syllable meter. Andreas Rhoby, email to author, June 17, 2021.

29. Drpić and Rhoby, "Byzantine Verses as Inscriptions," 433.

30. Rhoby, *Postbyzantinische Epigramme*, 4.

31. Kitromilides, *Enlightenment and Revolution*, 302–3. See also Floros, "*Paideia* in Ioannina."

32. Haygarth, *Greece, a Poem*, 128.

33. While this work was published anonymously, it is widely believed to be the work of Psalidas.

34. See Kechagioglou, "Ioannis Vilaras."

35. See Vilaras, *Apanta Ioannou Vilara*.

36. Kitromilides, *Enlightenment and Revolution*, 47–48, 270–72; and Horrocks, *Greek*, 442–45.

37. Meanwhile, Christine Philliou has observed a "classicizing tendency" among the Phanariot class in the Ottoman dependencies of Wallachia and Moldavia around precisely the same time. Philliou, *Biography of an Empire*, 12–13.

38. Leake, *Travels in Northern Greece*, 4:223.

39. Hughes, *Travels in Sicily, Greece, and Albania*, 2:53 (emphasis in the original).

40. See Legrand, *Complainte d'Ali de Tébélen*. The format of the "Ballad of Ali Pasha" draws an interesting parallel with the "Ballad of Alexander the Great" (*Fillada tou Megaleksandrou*), which was a modern Greek version of a Byzantine text that was repeatedly published from the seventeenth to nineteenth centuries. Galavaris, "Alexander the Great," 12. See also Minaoglou, *O Megalexandros stin Tourkokratia*.

41. Legrand, *Complainte d'Ali de Tébélen*, 8.

42. Legrand, *Complainte d'Ali de Tébélen*, 13.

43. Machiel Kiel, email to author, July 20, 2014. The inscription was still in situ until at least 1992. Petronitis, "Architektones kai michanikoi," 381–82. It is likely that this panel was one of a pair of inscriptions, because there is an empty niche of the same size on the other side of the central window located just above the doorway.

44. For the Islamic schools (*medrese*) that were in operation in Ioannina during the time of Ali Pasha, see Koulidas, *Ta Mousoulmanika vakoufia*, 244–55.

45. Machiel Kiel provided the following transcription: "(1) Sâḥib ul-hayr

46. In a similar vein, an Ottoman Turkish inscription once posted above one of the main gates to Preveza celebrates the governor's efforts in rebuilding the walls: "So worthy of praise abundant Preveza / Which Vizier Ali Pasha of Tepelena built anew / Almighty God will be merciful to his ancestors / The story of the *vali* of Yanya and Tırhala will be told from tongue to tongue." This inscription is now located in the Archaeological Museum at Nikopolis. Neumeier, "Spoils for the New Pyrrhus," 322.

47. The theory that the animal figure is gnawing on a human hand is supported by an older and much clearer photo of the plaque that shows the protruding mass to have five fingers, with one, the shorter thumb, pointing upward. Karabelas, "O Anglos theologos Thomas S. Hughes," 139.

48. Watenpaugh, *Image of an Ottoman City*, 198; Balog, "New Considerations on Mamluk Heraldry," 194–95; and Çağaptay, "Wings of the Double-Headed Eagle," 323–28.

49. Watenpaugh, *Image of an Ottoman City*, 205. And see Pancaroğlu, "Figural Ornament," 501–2.

50. In Christian art, the lion is the traditional symbol associated with Saint Mark the Evangelist. Saint Mark became closely associated with Venice after merchants spirited the relics of the saint from Alexandria to the city in the ninth century. Ferraro, *Venice*, 128.

51. Comescu, *Venetian Renaissance Fortifications*, 161.

52. A "field Gules" is a specific term used in heraldry to refer to a red background. Beauchamp, *Life of Ali Pacha*, 261 (emphasis in the original). According to François Pouqueville, the French consul of Ioannina, the designer of this coat of arms came from Bergamo, a city in the Lombardy region of northern Italy. *Histoire de la régénération de la Grèce*, 2:4n2.

53. For the use of the term "lion" to describe mercenary warriors, see Tair Papouli to Ali Pasha, Trikala, June 15, 1820, in *AAP*, 3:453, no. 1311. In this case, the writer uses the Ottoman Turkish word for lion (*aslan*).

54. Sathas, *Istorikai diatrivai*, 130.

55. Hughes, *Travels in Sicily, Greece, and Albania*, 1:443.

56. My thanks to Auron Tare, who brought this inscription to my attention and provided me with photographs from his fieldwork in the 1990s. Auron Tare, email to author, June 3, 2021. When I visited the site in 2014, the inscription was no longer in place.

57. Because the physical inscription is no longer available, I have based my translation on photographs provided to me by Auron Tare taken in the 1990s. The text of the Greek inscription was first transcribed and then translated into Albanian by the teacher Janko Pali in 1932. Auron Tare, email to author, June 3, 2021.

58. The editor of the anthology says that this text—which he describes as a "song"—is unpublished. The editor thus seems to have been unaware that the poem also appeared as an architectural inscription at the site of Porto Palermo. Vilaras, *Apanta Ioannou Vilara*, 113.

59. In line 8 of the poem in the collected volume, for example, Ali Pasha is described as "the great" (μέγας, *megas*), while the inscription uses the term "first" or "foremost" (πρώτος, *protos*).

60. For example, compare the first line of the poem as it was published in conventional modern Greek in the 1935 anthology with the inscription that once appeared above the doorway of the Porto Palermo fortress:

Στρίψτε τις πλώρες άφοβα θαλασσοπόροι ξένοι (*Apanta Ioannou Vilara*, 1935)
Στρίψτε τις πλόρες άφοβα θαλασοπόρη ξένη (Porto Palermo inscription, 1814)

The inscription replaces the letter omega with omicron and avoids double consonants and diphthongs, all spelling conventions that Vilaras proposed in *The Romaic Language*.

61. Kitromilides, *Enlightenment and Revolution*, 80.

62. There are numerous accounts of the ongoing conflict between the people of Himara and Ali Pasha. See Captain Spiro to Ali Pasha, Porto Palermo, April 15, 1800, in *AAP*, 1:100–102, no. 57; John Phillip Morier to Charles James Fox, Ioannina, June 10, 1806, NA, FO 78/53; Leake, *Travels in Northern Greece*, 1:80–90; and Stuart, "Natural and Physical Resources of Epirus," 279.

63. Leake claimed that one of Ali Pasha's motivations for constructing the Porto Palermo fortress was to keep the people of Himara in check. Leake, *Travels in Northern Greece*, 1:88–89.

64. The war with Souli ended in December 1803 with negotiations that allowed the besieged villagers to depart for the independent Parga. Veli Pasha to Ali Pasha, Souli, December 11, 1803, in *AAP*, 1:370–72, no. 201.

65. Fleming, *Muslim Bonaparte*, 172–75.

66. Guyer, "Feeling and Freedom," 141–42; and Damman, *Aesthetics and Morality*, 97–99.

67. The fortification dates back to the thirteenth and fourteenth centuries. Riza, "Arkitektura e vendbanimit-rrënojë," 97–98. See also Report of Guillaume de Vaudoncourt (1807), 107–8, Ministère des armées de France, Service historique de la Défense, Vincennes, MS 1663.

68. Holland, *Travels in the Ionian Isles*, 489.

69. See Holland, *Travels in the Ionian Isles*, 489–94; Leake, *Travels in Northern Greece*, 1:497–99; Hughes, *Travels in Sicily, Greece, and Albania*, 2:244–46; and Pouqueville, *Voyage dans la Grèce*, 3:383–401.

70. Hughes, *Travels in Sicily, Greece, and Albania*, 2:245.

71. Leake, *Travels in Northern Greece*, 1:497–99; Holland, *Travels in the Ionian Isles*, 492; and Hughes, *Travels in Sicily, Greece, and Albania*, 2:246. Pouqueville mentions the inscription but does not make clear whether he saw it himself. *Voyage dans la Grèce*, 3:400.

72. I have modified Leake's translation slightly (*Travels in Northern Greece*, 1:498), as he also provides the original verses in Greek:

Οντζάκι Μουτζοχουσάτικον ποίος
θέλει να χαλάση
Αύτος να είναι βέβαιος τον βίον
θέλει χάση.

73. Skiotis, "From Bandit to Pasha," 225.

74. Leake, *Travels in Northern Greece*, 1:498. In this and the following section of the inscription, Leake provides his own English translation along with the original Greek in parentheses for some key phrases.

75. Leake, *Travels in Northern Greece*, 1:498–99.

76. Holland, *Travels in the Ionian Isles*, 492.

77. Leake, *Travels in Northern Greece*, 1:499; Pouqueville, *Voyage dans la Grèce*, 3:269–70, 392.

78. For examples of these communications, see Demir Ağa Dosti to Ali Pasha, Gardiki, June 28, 1801, in *AAP*, 1:145–46, no. 83; and Demir Ağa to Ali Pasha, June 10, 1809, in *AAP*, 2:69–70, no. 477.

79. Veli Pasha and Muhtar Pasha to Ali Pasha, Sofia, May 5, 1811, in *AAP*, 2:201–3, no. 569.

80. George Foresti to Colonel Lowe, Ioannina, September 30, 1811, British Library, London, Add MS 20183.

81. BOA, C.AS. 255/10624 (1227 H/1812). See also BOA, HAT. 397/20927 (1227 H/1812).

82. Sathas, *Istorikai diatrivai*, 315–36.

83. Sathas, *Istorikai diatrivai*, 316.

84. Holland, *Travels in the Ionian Isles*, 489.

85. Hughes, *Travels in Sicily, Greece, and Albania*, 2:245.

86. Willingham, *Perilous Commitments*, 256; and McDonald, *Lost Battle*, 257.

87. Perraivos, *Istoria Souliou kai Pargas*, 2:39–40.

88. The graves of all three sons can be found alongside a tombstone marking the resting place of Ali Pasha's severed head in a cemetery in Istanbul's Zeytinburnu neighborhood. Berk, *Zaman Aşan Taşlar*, 303.

89. This building looked like a smaller version of the Selimiye Barracks in Istanbul, which were rebuilt a decade earlier, in 1828. For the construction of the barracks in Ioannina, see BOA, HAT. 591/29020 (1254 H/1838). This building no longer stands, but it can be seen clearly in an Ottoman panoramic view of Ioannina from 1899. BOA, FTG, photograph 3, from Yıldız Album YEE d. 404.

90. The inscription above Gate E (see fig. 83), one of the entrances to the southeastern citadel, commemorates the foundation of a new school located inside the enclosure. Soulis, "Tourkikai epigrafai Ioanninon," 95.

91. For a Greek translation of this inscription, see Soulis, "Tourkikai epigrafai Ioanninon," 96.

92. Ironically, the *tuğra* above one of the other gates to the Ioannina citadel (see fig. 83, Gate C) suffered the same fate: the sultan's monogram has been scratched away, probably after Ioannina became part of the nation-state of Greece in 1913.

Conclusion

1. BOA, C.DH. 135/6709 (1232 AH/1817).

2. Walsh, *Narrative of a Journey*, 63–66.

3. This transcription appears in Berk, *Zaman Aşan Taşlar*, 303.

4. Marcus, *Drama of Celebrity*, 21.

5. Berisha, "Biografia e Ali Pashë Tepelenës."

6. *Haberturk*, "Paşa'nın Kellesini Geri Verin!"

7. Berisha, "Biografia e Ali Pashë Tepelenës."

8. Bardakçı, "İşte, Arnavutlar'ın 'Bize Verin' Dedikleri."

9. Burgess, *Greece and the Levant*, 1:63.

10. Dziuban, "Introduction," 10; Davis, "Hauntology, Spectres, and Phantoms," 376–77.

11. Isa Blumi has discussed how the primordial foundation myths of modern nation-states in the Balkans can be limiting in that they "ignore counternarratives most scholars acknowledge exist." Blumi, *Reinstating the Ottomans*, 31.

BIBLIOGRAPHY

Primary Sources

Alexoudis, Anthimos. *Syntomos istoriki perigrafi tis Ieras Mitropoleos Velegradon*. Corfu: Ionia, 1868.

Aravantinos, Panagiotis. *Chronografia tis Ipeirou*. 2 vols. Athens: S. K. Vlastou, 1856–57.

———. *Istoria Ali Pasa tou Tepelenli*. Athens: S. K. Vlastos, 1895.

Ars, Grigoris L., ed. *I Rosia kai ta pasalikia Alvanias kai Ipeirou, 1759–1831: Engrafa rosikon archeion*. Athens: Institute of Neohellenic Research, 2007.

Beauchamp, Alphonse de. *The Life of Ali Pacha of Janina, Vizier of Epirus, Surnamed Aslan, or the Lion, from Various Authentic Documents*. London: Lupton Relfe, 1822.

Brockedon, William, Edward Francis Finden, and William Finden. *Finden's Illustrations of the Life and Works of Lord Byron*. 3 vols. London: John Murray, 1833–34.

Brøndsted, Peter Oluf. *Interviews with Ali Pacha of Joanina in the Autumn of 1812*. Edited by Jacob Isager. Athens: Danish Institute at Athens, 1999.

Bruinessen, Martin van, and Hendrik Boeschoten, eds. and trans. *Evliya Çelebi in Diyarbekir: The Relevant Section of the Seyahatname*. Leiden: Brill, 1988.

Burgess, Richard. *Greece and the Levant; Or, Diary of a Summer's Excursion in 1834*. 2 vols. London: Longman, Rees, Orme, Brown, and Green, 1835.

Byron, George Gordon, Lord. *Childe Harold's Pilgrimage: A Romaunt*. London: Thomas Davison, 1812.

———. *The Works of Lord Byron: With His Letters and Journals, and His Life, by Thomas Moore, Esq*. 17 vols. London: John Murray, 1832–33.

Christodoulidis, Sapfeiros. *Akolouthia kai vios tou en Agiois Patros Imon Kosma tou Ieromartyros kai Isapostolou*. Venice: Nikolaos Glikis, 1814.

Cockerell, Charles R. *Travels in Southern Europe and the Levant, 1810–1817*. London: Longmans, Green, 1903.

Coronelli, Vincenzo. *Description geographique et historique de la Morée, reconquise par les Venitiens, du royaume de Negrepont, des lieux circonvoisins et de ceux qu'ils ont soûmis dans la Dalmatie, et dans l'Epire*. Paris: Chez Nicolas Langlois, 1687.

Dankoff, Robert, and Robert Elsie, eds. and trans. *Evliya Çelebi in Albania and Adjacent Region (Kosovo, Montenegro, Ohrid)*. Leiden: Brill, 2000.

Davenport, W. *Historical Portraiture of Leading Events in the Life of Ali Pacha, Vizier of Epirus, Surnamed the Lion, in a Series of Designs*. London: Thomas M'Lean, 1823.

Decomberousse, François-Isaac-Hyacinthe. *Ali-Pacha: Melodrame en trois actes et a grand spectacle*. Paris: Chez J. Esneaux and Chez Barba, 1822.

Dupré, Louis. *Voyage à Athenes et à Constantinople*. Paris: Dondey-Dupré, 1825.

Durham, Mary Edith. *The Burden of the Balkans*. London: Edward Arnold, 1905.

Ergolavos, Spiros. *Evliya Tselebi: Taxidi stin Ipeiro*. Ioannina: Ekdoseis Ipeiros, 1995.

Goodison, William. *A Historical and Topographical Essay upon the Islands of Corfu, Leucadia, Cephalonia, Ithaca, and Zante*. London: Thomas and George Underwood, 1822.

Haygarth, William. *Greece, a Poem, in Three Parts*. London: Bulmer and Co., 1814.

Hobhouse, John Cam. *A Journey Through Albania and Other Provinces of Turkey in Europe and Asia to Constantinople During the Years 1809 and 1810*. 2 vols. Philadelphia: M. Carey and Son, 1817.

Holland, Henry. *Travels in the Ionian Isles, Albania, Thessaly, Macedonia, &c. During the Years 1812–1813*. London: Longman, Hurst, Rees, Orme, and Brown, 1815.

Hughes, Thomas Smart. *Travels in Sicily, Greece, and Albania*. 2 vols. London: J. Mawman, 1820.

Ibrahim Manzour Efendi. *Memoires sur la Gréce et l'Albanie pendant le gouvernment d'Ali-Pacha*. Paris: P. Ledoux, 1827.

Kahraman, Seyit Ali, and Yücel Dağlı, eds. *Günümüz Türkçesiyle Evliya Çelebi Seyahatnamesi*. 10 vols. Istanbul: Yapı Kredi Yayınları, 2003–11.

Kinneir, John Macdonald. *Journey Through Asia Minor, Armenia, and Koordistan, in the Years 1813 and 1814*. London: John Murray, 1818.

Koçyiğit, Ömer, ed. *Kabudlu Mustafa Vasfi Efendi: Tevârîh*. Sources of Oriental Languages and Literatures 124. Cambridge: Harvard University Press, 2016.

Leake, William Martin. *Travels in Northern Greece*. 4 vols. London: J. Rodwell, 1835.

Lear, Edward. *Edward Lear in the Levant: Travels in Albania, Greece, and Turkey in Europe, 1848–1849*. Edited by Susan Hyman. London: J. Murray, 1988.

Legrand, Émile. *Complainte d'Ali de Tébélen, Pacha de Janina: Poème historique en dialecte épirote*. Paris: Imprimerie Nationale, 1886.

Necipoğlu, Gülru, ed. *Sinan's Autobiographies: Five Sixteenth-Century Texts*. Critical edition and translation by Howard Crane and Esra Akın. Leiden: Brill, 2006.

Panagiotopoulos, Vasilis, Dimitris Dimitropoulos, and Panagiotis Michalaris, eds. *Archeio Ali Pasa: Syllogis I. Chotzi, Gennadeiou Vivliothikis tis Amerikanikis Scholis*

Athinon. 5 vols. Athens: Institute for Neohellenic Research, 2007–18.

Payne, John Howard. *Ali Pacha; Or, The Signet-Ring: A Melodrama, in Two Acts, as Performed at Covent-Garden Theatre, London*. New York: E. M. Murden, 1823.

Perraivos, Cristoforos. *Istoria Souliou kai Pargas*. 2 vols. Venice: Nikolaos Glikis, 1815.

Plomer, William. *Ali the Lion*. London: J. Cape, 1936.

Plutarch. *Lives, Volume IX: Demetrius and Antony, Pyrrhus and Gaius Marius*. Translated by Bernadotte Perrin. Loeb Classical Library 101. Cambridge: Harvard University Press, 1920.

Pouqueville, François. *Histoire de la régénération de la Grèce*. 4 vols. Paris: Firmin Didot, 1824.

———. *Travels in Epirus, Albania, Macedonia, and Thessaly*. London: Richard Phillips, 1820.

———. *Voyage dans la Grèce*. 6 vols. Paris: Firmin Didot, 1821.

Prevelakis, Eleutherios, and K. Kalliataki Merticopoulou, eds. *Epirus, Ali Pasha, and the Greek Revolution: Consular Reports of William Meyer from Preveza*. 2 vols. Athens: Akademia Athenon, 1996.

Remérand, Gabriel. *Ali de Tébélen: Pacha de Janina (1744–1822)*. Paris: Paul Geuthrer, 1928.

Sâlnâme-yi Vilâyet-i Yanya [Yearbook of the province of Yanya]. Vol. 5. Ioannina: Maṭba'a-yi Vilâyet, 1306 H (1888–89).

Sathas, K. N., ed. *Istorikai diatrivai*. Athens: A. Koromilas, 1870.

Stuart, R. "On the Natural and Physical Resources of Epirus." *Journal of the Royal Geographical Society of London* 39 (1869): 276–96.

Tietze, Andreas, ed. and trans. *Mustafa Ali's Counsel for Sultans of 1581: Edition, Translation, Notes*. 2 vols. Vienna: Österreichische Akademie der Wissenschaften, 1979–82.

"Treaty of Peace Between Charles VI [...] and Achmet Han Sultan of the Turks: Done in the Congress at Passarowitz in Servia, the 21st day of July 1718." In *A General Collection of Treatys of Peace and Commerce, Manifestos, Declarations of War, and Other Publick Papers [...]*, 4 vols., 4:401–13. London: J. J. and P. Knapton et al., 1732.

Vaudoncourt, Guillaume de. *Memoirs on the Ionian Islands [...]*. London: Baldwin, Cradock, and Joy, 1816.

Vilaras, Ioannis. *Apanta Ioannou Vilara*. Edited by Georgios A. Vavaretos. Athens: Petros Dimitrakos, 1935.

———. *H Romeiki glosa*. Corfu: n.p., 1814.

Walsh, Robert. *Narrative of a Journey from Constantinople to England*. Philadelphia: Carey, Lea & Cary, 1828.

Secondary Sources

Acun, Hakkı. *Bozok Sancağı (Yozgat İli)'nda Türk Mimarisi*. Ankara: Türk Tarih Kurumu, 2005.

Adhami, Stilian. "Të dhëna rreth fizionomisë urbanistike dhe arkitektonike të qytetit Mesjetar të Voskopojës." *Monumentet* 3 (1972): 95–118.

Agoston, Gabor. "Disjointed Historiography and Islamic Military Technology: The European Military Revolution Debate and the Ottomans." In *Essays in Honour of Ekmeleddin İhsanoğlu*, vol. 1, edited by Mustafa Kaçar and Zeynep Durukal, 567–82. Istanbul: IRCICA, 2006.

Akyıldız, Ali, and Şükrü Hanioğlu. "Negotiating the Power of the Sultan: The Ottoman Sened-I İttifak (Deed of Agreement), 1808." In *The Modern Middle East: A Sourcebook for History*, edited by Camron Michael Amin, Benjamin Fortna, and Elizabeth Frierson, 22–30. Oxford: Oxford University Press, 2016.

Al-Asad, Mohammad. "The Mosque of Muhammad 'Ali in Cairo." *Muqarnas* 9 (1992): 39–55.

Alparslan, Ali. "Kitabe." *DİA* 26 (2002), 76–81.

Ameen, Ahmed. "Bilingual and Trilingual Inscriptions of the Ottoman Buildings in Greece." *International Journal of Turkology* 11 (2021): 4–38.

Anastasopoulos, Antonis, ed. *Provincial Elites in the Ottoman Empire: Halcyon Days in Crete V*. Rethymno: Crete University Press, 2005.

Andreades, Andreas. "Ali Pacha de Tébelin, économist et financier." *Revue des études grecques* 25 (1912): 427–60.

Androudis, Paschalis. "O Bektasikos tekes Dourbali Soultan sto Ireni (Asprogeia) Farsalon." In *Ta Farsala kai i eyryteri periochi tous: Praktika diethnous epistimonikou synedriou*, 239–56. Farsala: Municipality of Farsala, 2016.

Anscombe, Frederick. "Continuities in Ottoman Centre-Periphery Relations, 1787–1915." In *The Frontiers of the Ottoman World*, edited by A. C. S. Peacock, 235–53. Oxford: Oxford University Press, 2009.

Anzaldúa, Gloria. *Borderlands/La Frontera: The New Mestiza*. San Francisco: Aunt Lute, 1987.

Arel, Ayda. "Gothic Towers and Baroque Mihrabs: The Post-Classical Architecture of Aegean Anatolia in the Eighteenth and Nineteenth Centuries." *Muqarnas* 10 (1993): 212–18.

Artan, Tülay. "Architecture as a Theatre of Life: Profile of the Eighteenth Century Bosphorus." PhD diss., Harvard University, 1989.

———. "Questions of Ottoman Identity and Architectural History." In *Rethinking Architectural Historiography*, edited by Dana Arnold, Elvan Altan Ergut, and Belgin Turan Özkaya, 85–109. New York: Routledge, 2003.

Asher, Catherine. "Sub-Imperial Palaces: Power and Authority in Mughal India." *Ars Orientalis* 23 (1993): 281–302.

Asvesta, Aliki. "Barbié du Bocage in the Gennadius Library: A Preliminary Investigation." In *New Griffon 12: Hidden Treasures at the Gennadius Library*, edited by Maria Georgopoulou, 45–56. Athens: American School of Classical Studies, 2011.

Atasoy, Nurhan. *Otağ-ı Hümayun: Ottoman Imperial Tent Complex*. Istanbul: Aygaz, 2000.

Athanassoglou, Nina. "More on Delacroix's Oriental Sources." *Burlington Magazine* 121, no. 918 (1979): 587–91.

Athanassoglou-Kallmyer, Nina. *French Images from the Greek War of Independence, 1821–1830: Art and Politics Under the Restoration*. New Haven: Yale University Press, 1989.

Balog, Paul. "New Considerations on Mamluk Heraldry." *Museum Notes* 22 (1977): 183–211.

Bardakçı, Murat. "İşte, Arnavutlar'ın 'Bize Verin' Dedikleri Tepedelenli'nin Bal Torbasındaki Kellesi." *Haberturk*, February 17, 2013. http://www.haberturk.com/yazarlar/murat-bardakci/820857-iste-arnavutlarin-bize-verin-dedikleri-tepedelenlinin-bal-torbasindaki-kellesi.

Barkey, Karen. *Empire of Difference: The Ottomans in Comparative Perspective*. Cambridge: Cambridge University Press, 2008.

Behrens-Abouseif, Doris. *Islamic Architecture in Cairo: An Introduction*. Leiden: Brill, 1989.

Bejko, Skënder. "Kalaja e Tepelenës." *Monumentet* 2 (1971): 103–10.

Ben-Ghiat, Ruth. *Strongmen: Mussolini to the Present*. New York: W. W. Norton, 2020.

Berisha, Sali. "Biografia e Ali Pashë Tepelenës, Berisha: Strateg i shquar dhe pararendës I Rilindjes." *NOA*, October 4, 2015. https://noa.al/lajmi/2015/10/520224.html.

Berk, Süleyman. *Zaman Aşan Taşlar: Zeytinburnu'nun Tarihi Mezar Taşlar*. Istanbul: Zeytinburnu Belediyesi Kültür Yayınları, 2016.

Bernard, Florid. *Writing and Reading Byzantine Secular Poetry, 1025–1081*. Oxford: Oxford University Press, 2014.

Beydilli, Kemal. "Tepedelenli Ali Paşa." *DİA* 40 (2011), 477–79.

———. "Yeniçeri." *DİA* 43 (2013), 450–62.

Bierman, Irene. "Franchising Ottoman Istanbul: The Case of Ottoman Crete." In *Seven Centuries of Ottoman Architecture: "A Supra-National Heritage,"* edited by Nur Akin, Afife Batur, and Selçuk Batur, 199–204. Istanbul: YEM, 2001.

———. "The Ottomanization of Crete." In *The Ottoman City and Its Parts: Urban Structure and Social Order*, edited by Irene Bierman, Rifa'at Abou-El-Haj, and Donald Preziosi, 53–76. New Rochelle: Aristide Caratzas, 1991.

Bingöl, Yüksel. *İshak Paşa Sarayı*. Istanbul: Türkiye İş Bankası Kültür Yayınları, 1998.

Blumi, Isa. *Reinstating the Ottomans: Alternative Balkan Modernities, 1800–1912*. New York: Palgrave Macmillan, 2011.

Bodenstein, Ralph. "Industrial Architecture in Egypt from Muhammad 'Ali to Sadat: A Field Survey." In *Workplaces: The Transformation of Places of Production, Industrialization, and the Built Environment in the Islamic World*, edited by Mohammad al-Asad, 41–80. Istanbul: Bilgi University Press, 2010.

Bohrer, Frederick. *Orientalism and Visual Culture: Imagining Mesopotamia in Nineteenth-Century Europe*. Cambridge: Cambridge University Press, 2003.

Bouras, Charalambos. *Byzantine and Post-Byzantine Architecture in Greece*. Athens: Melissa Publishing, 2006.

Bouras, Charalambos, and Stavros Mamaloukos, eds. *Ekklisies stin Ellada meta tin Alosi: Churches in Greece, 1453–1850*. 7 vols. Athens: Ethniko Metsovio Politechnio, 1979–2013.

Bozdoğan, Sibel, and Gülru Necipoğlu. "Entangled Discourses: Scrutinizing Orientalist and Nationalist Legacies in the Architectural Historiography of the 'Lands of Rum.'" *Muqarnas* 24 (2007): 1–6.

Braudel, Fernand. *La Méditerranée et le monde méditerranéen à l'époque de Philippe II*. Paris: A. Colin, 1966.

Brouskari, Ersi, ed. *Ottoman Architecture in Greece*. Athens: Hellenic Ministry of Culture, 2009.

Çağaptay, Suna. "On the Wings of the Double-Headed Eagle: *Spolia in Re* and Appropriation in Medieval Anatolia and Beyond." In *Spolia Reincarnated: Afterlives of Objects, Materials, and Spaces in Anatolia from Antiquity to the Ottoman Era*, edited by Ivana Jevtić and Suzan Yalman, 309–40. Istanbul: ANAMED, 2018.

Cantacuzino, Sherban, ed. *Architecture in Continuity: Building in the Islamic World Today; The Aga Khan Award for Architecture*. New York: Aperture, 1985.

Carvajal, José C., and Ana Palanco. "The Castle of Ali Pasha at Butrint." In *Butrint 4: The Archaeology and Histories of an Ionian Town*, edited by Inge Lyse Hansen, Richard Hodges, and Sarah Leppard, 289–308. Oxford: Oxbow Books, 2012.

Cavarnos, Constantine. *St. Cosmas Aitolos: Great Missionary, Awakener, Illuminator, and Holy Martyr of Greece*. 3rd ed. Belmont, MA: Institute for Byzantine and Modern Greek Studies, 1985.

Charalambos, Sotirios. "Koulia Paramythias." In *Ottoman Architecture in Greece*, edited by Ersi Brouskari, 182. Athens: Hellenic Ministry of Culture, 2009.

Christensen, Peter H. *Germany and the Ottoman Railways: Art, Empire, and Infrastructure*. New Haven: Yale University Press, 2017.

Christopoulos, Panagiotis. *Ta leipsana kai to monastiri Kosma tou Aitolou*. Athens: Idiotiki, 1987.

Clayer, Nathalie. "The Myth of Ali Pasha and the Bektashis: The Construction of an 'Albanian Bektashi National History.'" In *Albanian Identities: Myth and History*, edited by Stephanie Schwandner-Sievers and Bernd J. Fischer, 127–33. Bloomington: Indiana University Press, 2002.

Comescu, Dragoş. *Venetian Renaissance Fortifications in the Mediterranean*. Jefferson, NC: McFarland, 2016.

Cooley, Alison E., ed. and trans. *Res Gestae Divi Augusti: Text, Translation, and Commentary*. Cambridge: Cambridge University Press, 2009.

Çoruhlu, Tülin. "Tuğ." *DİA* 41 (2012), 330–32.

Çoşgel, Metin, and Boğaç Ergene. "Intergenerational Wealth Accumulation and Dispersion in the Ottoman Empire: Observations from

Eighteenth-Century Kastamonu." *European Review of Economic History* 15, no. 2 (2011): 255–76.

Cosgrove, Denis. *Social Formation and Symbolic Landscape*. 2nd ed. Madison: University of Wisconsin Press, 1998.

Crane, Howard. "The Ottoman Sultan's Mosques: Icons of Imperial Legitimacy." In *The Ottoman City and Its Parts: Urban Structure and Social Order*, edited by Irene Bierman, Rifa'at Abou-El-Haj, and Donald Preziosi, 173–243. New Rochelle: Aristide Caratzas, 1991.

Crook, J. Mordaunt. *The Greek Revival: Neo-Classical Attitudes in British Architecture, 1760–1870*. London: John Murray, 1972.

Curlin, James. "'Remember the Moment When Previsa Fell': The 1798 Battle of Nicopolis and Preveza." In *Preveza B: Proceedings of the Second International Symposium for the History and Culture of Preveza (16–20 September 2009)*, edited by Nikos D. Karabelas and Michael Stork, 2 vols., 1:265–96. Preveza: University of Ioannina, Municipality of Preveza, Actia Nicopolis Foundation, 2010.

Curry, John. *The Transformation of Muslim Mystical Thought in the Ottoman Empire: The Rise of the Halveti Order, 1350–1650*. Edinburgh: Edinburgh University Press, 2010.

Damman, Elisabeth Schellekens. *Aesthetics and Morality*. London: Bloomsbury, 2008.

Darling, Linda. "The Mediterranean as a Borderland." *Review of Middle East Studies* 46, no. 1 (2012): 54–63.

Davies, Siriol. "Late Venetian Butrint: 16th–18th Centuries." In *Butrint 4: The Archaeology and Histories of an Ionian Town*, edited by Inge Lyse Hansen, Richard Hodges, and Sarah Leppard, 280–88. Oxford: Oxbow Books, 2012.

Davis, Colin. "Hauntology, Spectres, and Phantoms." *French Studies* 59, no. 3 (2005): 373–79.

Delilbaşı, Melek. "1564 Tarihli Mufassal Yanya Livası Tahrir Defterlerine Göre Yanya Kenti ve Köleri." *Belgeler: Türk Tarih Belgeleri Dergisi* 17, no. 21 (1996): 1–40.

Delivorrias, Angelos. "Some Thoughts on the Secular Art of Hellenism Under Foreign Rule." In *From Byzantium to Modern Greece: Hellenic Art in Adversity, 1453–1830*, edited by Angelos Delivorrias, 133–45. Athens: Benaki Museum, 2005.

Dijkema, F. *The Ottoman Historical Monumental Inscriptions in Edirne*. Leiden: Brill, 1977.

Dijkema, F., and Ali Alparslan. "Kitâbât: 7. in Turkey." In *Encylopaedia of Islam*, 5:223–25. Leiden: Brill, 1986.

Dimakis, Jean. *La guerre de l'indépendance grecque: Vue par la presse française (période de 1821 à 1824); Contribution à l'étude de l'opinion publique et du movement philhellénique en France*. Thessaloniki: Institute for Balkan Studies, 1968.

Dimitriadis, Sotirios. "Transforming a Late Ottoman Port-City: Salonica, 1876–1912." In *Well-Connected Domains: Towards an Entangled Ottoman History*, edited by Pascal Firges, Tobias Graf, Christian Roth, and Gülay Tulasoğlu, 207–21. Leiden: Brill, 2014.

Dimitropoulos, Dimitrios. "Ochiromatikes kai oikodomikes ergasies tou Ali pasa stin Preveza." In *Preveza B: Proceedings of the Second International Symposium for the History and Culture of Preveza (16–20 September 2009)*, edited by Nikos D. Karabelas and Michael Stork, 2 vols., 2:41–51. Preveza: University of Ioannina, Municipality of Preveza, Actia Nicopolis Foundation, 2010.

Drpić, Ivan, and Andreas Rhoby. "Byzantine Verses as Inscriptions: The Interaction of Text, Object, and Beholder." In *A Companion to Byzantine Poetry*, edited by Wolfram Hörandner, Andreas Rhoby, and Nikos Zagklas, 430–58. Leiden: Brill, 2019.

Duffy, Christopher. *The Fortress in the Age of Vauban and Frederick the Great, 1660–1789*. London: Routledge, 1985.

Duru, Mehmet. "Yozgat Çapanoğlu Camii ve Vakfiyeleri." *Vakıflar Dergisi* 13 (1981): 71–89.

Durusu-Tanrıöver, Müge. "Ways of Being Hittite: Empire and Borderlands in Late Bronze Age Anatolia and Northern Syria." *Studia Orientalia Electronica* 9, no. 2 (2021): 3–27.

Dziuban, Zuzanna. "Introduction: Haunting in the Land of the Untraumatized." In *The Spectral Turn: Jewish Ghosts in the Polish Post-Holocaust Imaginaire*, edited by Zuzanna Dziuban, 7–47. Bielefeld: transcript, 2019.

Eck, Werner. "The Presence, Role, and Significance of Latin in the Epigraphy and Culture of the Roman Near East." In *From Hellenism to Islam: Cultural and Linguistic Change in the Roman Near East*, edited by Hannah Cotton, Robert Hoyland, Jonathan Price, and David Wasserstein, 15–42. Cambridge: Cambridge University Press, 2006.

Egro, Dritan. *Historia dhe ideologjia: Një qasje kritike studimeve osmane në historiografinë moderne shqiptare*. Tirana: Instituti i Historisë, 2007.

El-Ashmouni, Marwa, and Katharine Bartsch. "Egypt's Age of Transition: Unintentional Cosmopolitanism During the Reign of Muhammad 'Alî (1805–1848)." *Arab Studies Quarterly* 36, no. 1 (2014): 43–74.

Eldem, Sedad. *Köşkler ve Kasırlar*. 2 vols. Istanbul: Yüksek Mimarlık Bölümü Rölöve Kürsüsü, 1973.

Elgood, Robert. *The Arms of Greece and Her Balkan Neighbors in the Ottoman Period*. London Thames & Hudson, 2009.

Elsie, Robert. *Historical Dictionary of Albania*. 2nd ed. Lanham, MD: Scarecrow Press, 2010.

Ertuğ, Zeynep Tarım. "Saray." *DİA* 36 (1999), 117–21.

Eyice, Semavi. "Arslan Paşa Camii." *DİA* 3 (1991), 401–2.

———. "Fethiye Camii." *DİA* 12 (1995), 460–62.

Fahmy, Khaled. *All the Pasha's Men: Mehmed Ali, His Army, and the Making of Modern Egypt*. Cairo: American University in Cairo Press, 1997.

Ferraro, Joanne M. *Venice: History of the Floating City*. Cambridge: Cambridge University Press, 2012.

Findley, Carter Vaughn. "The Tanzimat." In *The Cambridge History of Turkey*, vol. 4, *Turkey in the Modern World*, edited by Reşat Kasaba, 11–37. Cambridge: Cambridge University Press, 2008.

Finkel, Caroline. *Osman's Dream: The History of the Ottoman Empire*. New York: Basic Books, 2006.

Finkel, Caroline, and Victor Ostapchuk. "Outpost of Empire: An Appraisal of Ottoman Building Registers as Sources for the Archeology and Construction History of the Black Sea Fortress of Özi." *Muqarnas* 22 (2005): 150–88.

Fischer, Bernd. "Introduction." In *Balkan Strongmen: Dictators and Authoritarian Rulers of Southeast Europe*, edited by Bernd Fischer, 1–18. London: Hurst, 2007.

Fleming, Katherine. *The Muslim Bonaparte: Diplomacy and Orientalism in Ali Pasha's Greece*. Princeton: Princeton University Press, 1999.

Floros, Ioannis N. "*Paideia* in Ioannina During the So-Called *Tourkokratia* (18th Century–Beginning 20th Century)." Master's thesis, University of Johannesburg, 2005.

Fraser, Elisabeth. "Books, Prints, and Travel: Reading in the Gaps of the Orientalist Archive." *Art History* 31, no. 3 (2008): 342–67.

———. "Delacroix's Sardanapalus: The Life and Death of the Royal Body." *French Historical Studies* 26, no. 2 (2003): 315–49.

———. *Mediterranean Encounters: Artists Between Europe and the Ottoman Empire, 1774–1839*. University Park: Penn State University Press, 2017.

Galaty, Michael L., and Charles Watkinson. "The Practice of Archaeology Under Dictatorship." In *Archaeology Under Dictatorship*, edited by Michael L. Galaty and Charles Watkinson, 1–18. Boston: Springer, 2006.

Galavaris, George. "Alexander the Great Conqueror and Captive of Death: His Various Images in Byzantine Art." *Canadian Art Review* 16, no. 1 (1989): 12–18, 74–77.

Gallant, Thomas W. *The Edinburgh History of the Greeks, 1768 to 1913*. Edinburgh: Edinburgh University Press, 2015.

Gelvin, James. "The 'Politics of Notables' Forty Years After." *Middle East Studies Association Bulletin* 40, no. 1 (2006): 19–29.

Georgopoulou, Maria. "'The Land of the Great, the Home of the Brave': Echoes of the Greek War of Independence on Stage." 1821 Commemorative Lecture Series: The Greek War of Independence Revisited. Hellenic Centre, June 11, 2021. https://www.youtube.com/watch?v=IDk1ugoGSXc&t=15s.

Georgopoulou, Maria, and Konstantinos Thanasakis, eds. *Ottoman Athens: Archaeology, Topography, History*. Athens: Gennadius Library and Aikaterini Laskaridis Foundation, 2019.

Gharipour, Mohammad. "Preface: Non-Muslim Sacred Sites in the Muslim World." In *Sacred Precincts: The Religious Architecture of Non-Muslim Communities Across the Islamic World*, edited by Mohammad Gharipour, xi–xxv. Leiden: Brill, 2015.

Giakoumis, Konstantinos, and Dritan Egro. "Ottoman Pragmatism in Domestic Inter-Religious Affairs: The Legal Framework of Church Conversion and Construction in the Ottoman Empire and the 1741 Firman of Ardenicë Monastery." *Ipeirotika Chronika* 44 (2010): 73–127.

Gilkes, Oliver. *Albania: An Archaeological Guide*. New York: I. B. Tauris, 2013.

Girardelli, Paolo. "Architecture, Identity, and Liminality: On the Use and Meaning of Catholic Spaces in Late Ottoman Istanbul." *Muqarnas* 22 (2005): 233–64.

Goodwin, Godfrey. *A History of Ottoman Architecture*. London: Thames & Hudson, 1971.

Gradeva, Rossitsa. "From the Bottom Up and Back Again Until Who Knows When: Church Restoration Procedures in the Ottoman Empire, Seventeenth–Eighteenth Centuries (Preliminary Notes)." In *Political Initiatives "From the Bottom Up" in the Ottoman Empire*, edited by Antonis Anastasopoulos, 135–63. Rethymno: Crete University Press, 2012.

———. "Osman Pazvantoğlu of Vidin: Between Old and New." In *The Ottoman Balkans, 1750–1830*, edited by Frederick Anscombe, 115–61. Princeton: Markus Wiener, 2006.

———. "Ottoman Policy Towards Christian Church Buildings." *Études balkaniques* 4 (1994): 14–36.

Greene, Annie. "Keeping Out Napoleon: The Fortress-City of Acre." Stambouline, October 7, 2015. http://www.stambouline.info/2015/10/keeping-out-napoleon.html.

Gruber, Christiane. "Like Hearts of Birds: Ottoman Avian Microarchitecture in the Eighteenth Century." *Journal18: A Journal of Eighteenth-Century Art and Culture* 11 (Spring 2021). https://www.journal18.org/5689.

Gude, Tushara Bindu. "Hybrid Visions: The Cultural Landscape of Awadh." In *India's Fabled City: The Art of Courtly Lucknow*, edited by Stephen Markel, 69–102. Los Angeles: Los Angeles County Museum of Art, 2010.

Guyer, Paul. "Feeling and Freedom: Kant on Aesthetics and Morality." *Journal of Aesthetics and Art Criticism* 48, no. 2 (1990): 137–46.

Haberturk. "Paşa'nın Kellesini Geri Verin!" February 1, 2013. *HaberTurk*. http://www.haberturk.com/dunya/haber/818790-pasanin-kellesini-geri-verin.

Hagen, Gottfried. "Legitimacy and World Order." In *Legitimizing the Order: The Ottoman Rhetoric of State Power*, edited by Hakan T. Karateke and Maurus Reinkowski, 55–83. Leiden: Brill, 2005.

Halaçoğlu, Yusuf. "Derbend." *DİA* 9 (1994), 162–64.

Hamadeh, Shirine. *The City's Pleasures: Istanbul in the Eighteenth Century*. Seattle: University of Washington Press, 2008.

Hamilakis, Yannis. *The Nation and Its Ruins: Antiquity, Archaeology, and National Imagination in Greece*. Oxford: Oxford University Press, 2007.

Hamilton, W. J. "Observations on the Position of Tavium." *Journal of the Royal Geographical Society of London* 17 (1837): 74–81.

Hammond, N. G. L. *Epirus: The Geography, the Ancient Remains, the History, and the Topography of Epirus and Adjacent Areas*. Oxford: Clarendon Press, 1967.

Hanink, Johanna. "The Epitaph for Atthis: A Late Hellenistic Poem on Stone." *Journal of Hellenic Studies* 130 (2010): 15–34.

Hanioğlu, Şükrü. *A Brief History of the Late Ottoman Empire*. Princeton: Princeton University Press, 2008.

Hanley, Will. "How Many Sancaks?" *Journal of the Ottoman and Turkish Studies Association* 9, no. 2 (2022): 173–77.

Hanssen, Jens, Stefan Weber, and Thomas Philipp, eds. *The Empire in the City: Arab Provincial Capitals in the Late Ottoman Empire*. Würzburg: Ergon-Verlag, 2002

Harding, Frances. "Presenting and Re-Presenting the Self: From Not-Acting to Acting in African Performance." *TDR: The Drama Review* 43, no. 2 (1999): 118–35.

Hartmuth, Maximilian. "The History of Centre-Periphery Relations as a History of Style in Ottoman Provincial Architecture." In *Centres and Peripheries in Ottoman Architecture: Rediscovering a Balkan Heritage*, edited by Maximilian Hartmuth, 18–29. Stockholm: Cultural Heritage Without Borders, 2010.

———. "In Search of the Provincial Artist: Networks, Services, and Ideas in the Ottoman Balkans and the Question of Structural Change." PhD diss., Sabancı University, 2011.

———. "The Visual Strategies of Late Ottoman Provincial Strongmen and the Problem of the Didactic Use of Images in Islam." In *14th International Congress of Turkish Art Proceedings*, edited by Frédéric Hitzel, 381–88. Paris: Collège de France, 2013.

Hasluck, Frederick. *Christianity and Islam Under the Sultans*. Edited by Margaret Hasluck. 2 vols. Oxford: Clarendon Press, 1929.

———. "Geographical Distribution of the Bektashli." *Annual of the British School at Athens* 21 (1914–16): 84–124.

Heywood, Colin. "The 1337 Bursa Inscription and Its Interpreters." *Turcica* 36 (2004): 215–32.

Hobsbawm, Eric. *The Age of Revolution: 1789–1848*. New York: Vintage Books, 1996.

Horrocks, Geoffrey. *Greek: A History of the Language and Its Speakers*. 2nd ed. New York: John Wiley & Sons, 2010.

Hourani, Albert. "Ottoman Reform and the Politics of Notables." In *Beginnings of Modernization in the Middle East: The Nineteenth Century*, edited by William Polk and Richard Chambers, 41–68. Chicago: University of Chicago Press, 1968.

Huntington, Samuel P. "The Clash of Civilizations?" *Foreign Affairs* 72, no. 3 (1993): 22–49.

Hutcheon, Linda. *A Theory of Parody: The Teachings of Twentieth-Century Art Forms*. 2nd ed. Urbana: University of Illinois Press, 2000.

Ilıcak, Şükrü, ed. *"Those Infidel Greeks": The Greek War of Independence Through Greek Archival Documents*. Leiden: Brill, 2021.

İnalcık, Halil. "The Emergence of Big Farms, Çiftliks: State, Landlords, and Tenants." In *Contributions à l'histoire économique et sociale de l'Empire Ottoman*, edited by J. L. Bacqué-Grammont and P. Dumont, 105–26. Louvain: Peeters, 1983.

Jackson, J. B. "Landscape as Theater." *Landscape* 23, no. 1 (1979): 3–7.

Jeffreys, Michael J. "The Nature and Origins of the Political Verse." *Dumbarton Oaks Papers* 28 (1974): 141–95.

Johnson, Lee. "Delacroix's Oriental Sources." *Burlington Magazine* 120, no. 906 (1978): 603–15.

Kafescioğlu, Çiğdem. *Constantinopolis/Istanbul: Cultural Encounter, Imperial Vision, and the Construction of the Ottoman Capital*. University Park: Penn State University Press, 2009.

———. "'In the Image of Rūm': Ottoman Architectural Patronage in Sixteenth-Century Aleppo and Damascus." *Muqarnas* 16 (1999): 70–96.

Kana'an, Ruba. "Waqf, Architecture, and Political Self-Fashioning: The Construction of the Great Mosque of Jaffa by Muhammad Aga Abu Nabbut." *Muqarnas* 18 (2001): 120–40.

Kanetakis, Giannis. *To kastro: Simvoli stin poleodomiki istoria ton Ioanninon*. Athens: Techniko Epimelitirio Elladas, 1994.

Karababa, Eminegül. "Investigating Early Modern Ottoman Consumer Culture in the Light of Bursa Probate Inventories." *Economic History Review* 65, no. 1 (2012): 194–219.

Karabelas, Nikos D. "O anglos lochagos William Leake stin Preveza, ti Nikopoli kai to Aktio." *Prevezanika Chronika* 43–44 (2007): 164–263.

———. "O anglos theologos Thomas S. Hughes stin Preveza kai ti Nikopoli." *Prevezanika Chronika* 41–42 (2005): 53–144.

———. "O italos politikos Francesco Guicciardini stin Preveza kai ti giro periochi." *Ipeiroton Koinon* 1 (2005): 59–92.

———. "To kastro tis Boukas (1478–1701): I ochiromeni Preveza mesa apo tis piges." In *Preveza B: Proceedings of the Second International Symposium for the History and Culture of Preveza (16–20 September 2009)*, edited by Nikos D. Karabelas and Michael Stork, 2 vols., 1:400–412. Preveza: University of Ioannina, Municipality of Preveza, Actia Nicopolis Foundation, 2010.

———. "To neo kastro 'sto Kyparissi': To simerino kastro tou Agiou Andrea." Paper presented at the Municipal Cultural Center in Preveza, Greece, May 12, 2012. https://oxford.academia.edu/NikosDKarabelas.

———. "H ochirosi tou exoterikou perivolou tou kastrou tou Agiou Andrea tis Prevezas kai ta enteichismena se auti lithina anaglyfa." *Prevezanika Chronika* 51–52 (2015): 134–78.

———. "Ottoman Fortifications in Preveza in 1702: The First Phase of the Castle of Iç Kale." *Osmanlı Tarihi Araştırma ve Uygulama Merkezi Dergisi* 32, no. 2 (2012): 47–66.

Karaiskaj, Gjerak. *The Fortifications of Butrint*. Translated and edited by Andrew Crowson. London: Butrint Foundation, 2009.

———. "Fortifikimet mesjetare pranë kanalit të Vivarit në Butrint dhe restaurimi I tyre." *Monumentet* 11 (1976): 148–53.

———. *Pesë mijë vjet fortifikime në Shqipëri*. Tirana: Shtëpia Botuese "8 Nëntori," 1981.

Karamustafa, Ahmet. "Military, Administrative, and Scholarly Maps and Plans." In *The History of Cartography*, vol. 2, bk. 1, *Cartography in the Traditional Islamic and South Asian Societies*, edited by J. B. Harley and David Woodward, 209–27. Chicago: University of Chicago Press, 1992.

Karateke, Hakan T. "Legitimizing the Ottoman Sultanate: A Framework for Historical Analysis." In *Legitimizing the Order: The Ottoman Rhetoric of State Power*, edited by Hakan T. Karateke and Maurus Reinkowski, 13–52. Leiden: Brill, 2005.

Kechagioglou, Dimitris. "Ioannis Vilaras." In *I palaioteri pezografia mas: Apo tis arches tis os ton proto pagkosmio polemo*, vol. 2, edited by Nasos Vagenas, Giannis Dallas, Kostas Stergiopoulos, and Panagiotis Moullas, 104–13. Athens: Sokolis, 1999.

Kefallonitou, Frankiska. "Citadel of Antirrio (or Castle of Roumeli)." In *Ottoman Architecture in Greece*, edited by Ersi Brouskari, 113–15. Athens: Hellenic Ministry of Culture, 2009.

Kenanoğlu, M. Macit. *Osmanlı Millet Sistemi: Mit ve Gerçek*. Istanbul: Klasik, 2004.

———. "Zimmi Osmanlılar'da." *DİA* 44 (2013), 438–40.

Kenney, Ellen. *Power and Patronage in Medieval Syria: The Architecture and Urban Works of Tankiz al-Nasiri*. Chicago: Middle East Documentation Center, 2009.

Keshani, Hussein. "Architecture and the Twelver Shi'I Tradition: The Great Imambara Complex of Lucknow." *Muqarnas* 23 (2006): 219–50.

Keskiner, Bora. "Sultan Ahmed III (r. 1703–1730) as a Calligrapher and Patron of Calligraphy." PhD diss., SOAS University of London, 2012.

Khoury, Dina Rizk. "The Ottoman Centre Versus Provincial Power-Holders: An Analysis of the Historiography." In *The Cambridge History of Turkey: The Late Ottoman Empire, 1603–1839*, edited by Suraiya Faroqhi, 135–56. New York: Cambridge University Press, 2006.

Kiel, Machiel. *The Art and Society of Bulgaria in the Turkish Period*. Assen, Netherlands: Van Gorcum, 1985.

———. "The Date of Construction of the Library of Osman Pazvantoğlu in Vidin: A Note on the Chronogram of the Ottoman Inscription of the Library and Identity of Its Poet." *Études balkaniques* 16, no. 3 (1980): 116–19.

———. *Ottoman Architecture in Albania, 1385–1912*. Istanbul: IRCICA, 1990.

———. "Tepedelen." *DİA* 40 (2011), 475–76.

———. "Vidin." *DİA* 43 (2013), 103–6.

———. "Yanya." *DİA* 43 (2013), 317–21.

Kitromilides, Paschalis. *Enlightenment and Revolution: The Making of Modern Greece*. Cambridge: Harvard University Press, 2013.

Knowles, Anne Kelly. "Introducing Historical GIS." In *Past Time, Past Place: GIS for History*, edited by Anne Kelly Knowles, xi–xx. Redlands: ESRI Press, 2002.

Konstantios, Dimitris. *The Kastro of Ioannina*. Athens: Archaeological Receipts Fund, 2000.

Konyalı, İbrahim Hakkı. *Abideleri ve Kitabeleri ile Üsküdar Tarihi*. 2 vols. Istanbul: Türkiye Yeşilay Cemiyeti Yayınları, 1976.

Koulidas, Konstantinos I. *Ta Mousoulmanika vakoufia tis poleos ton Ioanninon*. Ioannina: Ipeirotiko Imerologio, 2004.

Koupari, Neonilli. "I techni stin avli tou Ali-Pasa oi martyries ton periigiton." *Ipeirotika Chronika* 44 (2010): 413–41.

Kunt, Metin. *The Sultan's Servants: The Transformation of Ottoman Provincial Government, 1550–1650*. New York: Columbia University Press, 1983.

Kütükoğlu, Mübahat. *Osmanlı Belgelerinin Dili*. Istanbul: Kubbealtı Akademisi Kültür ve Sanat Vakfı, 1994.

Kuyulu, İnci. *Kara Osman-oğlu Ailesine ait Mimari Eserler*. Erzurum: Atatürk Üniversitesi, 1996.

Laflı, Ergün, and Yıldız Deveci Bozkuş. "Some Epigraphic and Archaeological Documents from Western Anatolia During the Late Ottoman Period." *Post-Medieval Archaeology* 48, no. 2 (2014): 285–310.

Landry, Rodrigue, and Richard Y. Bourhis. "Linguistic Landscape and Ethnolinguistic Vitality: An Empirical Study." *Journal of Language and Social Psychology* 16, no. 1 (1997): 23–49.

Langins, Janis. *Conserving the Enlightenment: French Military Engineering from Vauban to the Revolution*. Cambridge: MIT Press, 2004.

Lightfoot, Kent, and Antoinette Martinez. "Frontiers and Boundaries in Archaeological Perspective." *Annual Review of Anthropology* 24 (1995): 471–92.

Loukatos, Spiros D. "I Preveza kata ta gegonota kai tis diethneis sinthikes teli 17ou aiona eos kai tis arches tou 19ou aiona." In *Preveza B: Proceedings of the Second International Symposium for the History* and *Culture of Preveza (16–20 September 2009)*, edited by Nikos D. Karabelas and Michael Stork, 2 vols., 1:297–305. Preveza: University of Ioannina, Municipality of Preveza, Actia Nicopolis Foundation, 2010.

Lowry, Heath. *The Nature of the Early Ottoman State*. Albany: State University of New York Press, 2003.

MacMullen, Ramsay. "The Epigraphic Habit in the Roman Empire." *American Journal of Philology* 103, no. 3 (1982): 233–46.

Makris, Giorgos, and Stefanos Papageorgiou. *To chersaio diktyo epikoinonias sto kratos tou Ali Pasa Tepelenli: Enischysi tis kentrikis exousias kai apopeira dimiourgias eniaias agoras*. Athens: Papazisis, 1990.

Mantzana, Kristallo. "Osman Şah (or Kurşunlu) Mosque." In *Ottoman Architecture in Greece*, edited by Ersi Brouskari, 208–10. Athens: Hellenic Ministry of Culture, 2009.

Marcus, Sharon. *The Drama of Celebrity*. Princeton: Princeton University Press, 2019.

Marino, Brigitte. "Les investissements de Sulaymân Pacha al-'Azm à Damas." *Annales islamologiques* 34 (2001): 209–26.

Masters, Bruce. "Dhimmi." In *Encyclopedia of the Ottoman Empire*, edited by Gábor Ágoston and Bruce Masters, 185–86. New York: Facts on File, 2009.

Mavrika, Virginia. "I Archaiologiki Ypiresia apenanti se 'thisavrothires' kai 'oneiropoles': Anazitontas ton thisavro tou Ali Pasa sto Kastro ton Ioanninon." In *Ipeiros, 1881–1945: Archeia kai archaiotites*, edited by K. I. Soueref, 161–90. Ioannina: Etaireia Ipeirotikon Meleton, 2017.

Mavrommatis, Giorgos. "Bektashis in 20th Century Greece." *Turcica* 40 (2008): 219–51.

McDonald, Callum. *The Lost Battle: Crete, 1941*. New York: Free Press, 1993.

McGowan, Bruce. "The Age of the Ayans." In *An Economic and Social History of the Ottoman Empire, 1300–1914*, edited by Halil İnalcık and Donald Quataert, 639–758. Cambridge: Cambridge University Press, 1994.

———. *Economic Life in Ottoman Europe: Taxation, Trade, and the Struggle for Land*. Cambridge: Cambridge University Press, 1981.

Meksi, Aleksandër, and Pirro Thomo. "Arkitektura posbizantine në Shqipëri (bazilikat)." *Monumentet* 21 (1981): 99–138.

Mert, Özcan. "Âyan." *DİA* 4 (1991), 195–98.

Michell, George. *The Royal Palaces of India*. London: Thames & Hudson, 1994.

Minaoglou, Charalambos. *O Megalexandros stin Tourkokratia*. Thessaloniki: Kyriakidis, 2012.

Moudopoulos-Athanasiou, Faidon. *The Early Modern Zagori of Northwest Greece: An Interdisciplinary Archaeological Inquiry into a Montane Cultural Landscape*. Leiden: Sidestone Press, 2022.

Muse, Amy. "Encountering Ali Pasha on the London Stage: No Friend to Freedom?" *Romanticism* 17, no. 3 (2011): 340–50.

Nagata, Yuzo. *Some Documents on the Big Farms (çiftliks) of the Notables in Western Anatolia*. Tokyo: Institute for the Study of Languages and Cultures of Asia and Africa, 1976.

Necipoğlu, Gülru. *The Age of Sinan: Architectural Culture in the Ottoman Empire*. Princeton: Princeton University Press, 2005.

———. *Architecture, Ceremonial, and Power: The Topkapi Palace in the Fifteenth and Sixteenth Centuries*. Cambridge: MIT Press, 1991.

———. "Framing the Gaze in Ottoman, Safavid, and Mughal Palaces." *Ars Orientalis* 23 (1993): 303–42.

Neumann, Christoph K. "A Hesitating but Challenging Closing Speech." In *Seven Centuries of Ottoman Architecture: "A Supra-National Heritage,"* edited by Nur Akin, Afife Batur, and Selçuk Batur, 24–29. Istanbul: YEM, 2001.

Neumeier, Emily. "Rivaling Elgin: Ottoman Governors and Archaeological Agency in the Morea." In *Antiquarianisms: Contact, Conflict, and Comparison*, edited by Benjamin Anderson and Felipe Rojas, 134–60. Oxford: Oxbow Books, 2017.

———. "Spoils for the New Pyrrhus: Alternative Claims to Antiquity in Ottoman Greece." *International Journal of Islamic Architecture* 6, no. 2 (2017): 311–37.

———. "Trans-Imperial Encounter on the Ionian Sea." In *Tesserae of Preveza's History*, edited by Nikos D. Karabelas, 11–54. Preveza: Actia Nicopolis Foundation, 2018.

Nochlin, Linda. "The Imaginary Orient." *Art in America* 71, no. 5 (1983): 119–31, 187–91.

Osswald, Brendan. "From *Lieux de Pouvoir* to *Lieux de Mémoire*: The Monuments of the Medieval Castle of Ioannina Through the Centuries." In *Discrimination and Tolerance in Historical Perspective*, edited by Gudmundur Halfdanarson, 187–99. Pisa: Pisa University Press, 2008.

Ostapchuk, Victor, and Svitlana Bilyayeva. "The Ottoman Northern Black Sea Frontier at Akkerman Fortress: The View from a Historical and Archaeological Project." In *The Frontiers of the Ottoman World*, edited by A. C. S. Peacock, 137–70. Oxford: Oxford University Press, 2009.

Ottersbach, Christian. "Bauen als Ausdruck von Souveränität: Die Festungen und Paläste des Ali Pasa von Tepelene." In *Herrschaft–Architektur–Raum: Festschrift für Ulrich Schütte zum 60. Geburtstag*, edited by Stephanie Hahn and Michael H. Sprenger, 165–81. Berlin: Lukas Verlag, 2008.

Özcan, Tahsin. "Muhallefât." *DİA* 30 (2020), 405–6.

Özgüven, Burcu. "*Palanka* Forts and Construction Activity in the Late Ottoman Balkans." In *The Frontiers of the*

Ottoman World, edited by A. C. S. Peacock, 171–87. Oxford: Oxford University Press, 2009.

Özkaya, Yücel. *Osmanlı İmparatorluğu'nda Ayanlık*. Ankara: Türk Tarih Kurumu, 1994.

Özyüksel, Murat. *The Hejaz Railway and the Ottoman Empire: Modernity, Industrialisation, and Ottoman Decline*. London: I. B. Tauris, 2014.

Panagiotopoulos, Petros. *Ieros Naos Agiou Nikolaou Vasilikis*. Kalabaka: Iera Mitropolis Stagon kai Meteoron, 2018.

Pancaroğlu, Oya. "Figural Ornament in Medieval Islamic Art." In *A Companion to Islamic Art and Architecture*, edited by Finbarr Barry Flood and Gülru Necipoğlu, 501–20. Hoboken, NJ: Wiley, 2017.

Pantoulas, Michalis. *Kosmas Aitolos: Ta eikonografika (1779–1961)*. Ioannina: Michalis Pantoulas, 2015.

Papadopoulou, Varvara. "Aslan Pasha Medrese." In *Ottoman Architecture in Greece*, edited by Ersi Brouskari, 163. Athens: Hellenic Ministry of Culture, 2009.

———. "Citadel of Ioannina." In *Ottoman Architecture in Greece*, edited by Ersi Brouskari, 168–69. Athens: Hellenic Ministry of Culture, 2009.

———. "Fethiye Mosque." In *Ottoman Architecture in Greece*, edited by Ersi Brouskari, 162. Athens: Hellenic Ministry of Culture, 2009.

———. "Kastro Ioanninon: H istoria ton ochiroseon kai tou oikismou." In *To kastro ton Ioanninon*, edited by Varvara Papadopoulou, 37–104. Ioannina: Ministry of Culture, 8th Ephorate of Byzantine Antiquities, 2009.

Papastratou, Dori. *Chartines eikones: Orthodoksa thriskevtika charaktika, 1665–1899*. Athens: Papastratos, 1986.

Payne, Alina, ed. *Dalmatia and the Mediterranean: Portable Archeology and the Poetics of Influence*. Leiden: Brill, 2013.

Peacock, A. C. S. "Introduction: The Ottoman Empire and Its Frontiers." In *The Frontiers of the Ottoman World*, edited by A. C. S. Peacock, 1–27. Oxford: Oxford University Press, 2009.

Peirce, Leslie. *The Imperial Harem: Women and Sovereignty in the Ottoman Empire*. Oxford: Oxford University Press, 1993.

Petronitis, Argiris. "Architektones kai michanikoi stin ipiresia tou Ali Pasa." In *Figos: Timitikos tomos gia ton Kathigiti Sotiri Dakari*, 367–89. Ioannina: University of Ioannina Press, 1994.

Petsas, Fotios. "Eidiseis ek tis 10is Archaiologikis Perifereias (Ipeirou)." *Archaiologiki Efimeris* 89–90 (1950–51): 31–49.

Philadelpheis, Alexandros. "Anaskafai Nikopoleos: Christianika mnimeia Prevezis." *Praktika Archaiologikis Etaireias* (1914): 219–41.

Philipp, Thomas. *Acre: The Rise and Fall of a Palestinian City, 1730–1831*. New York: Columbia University Press, 2001.

Philliou, Christine. *Biography of an Empire: Governing Ottomans in an Age of Revolution*. Berkeley: University of California Press, 2011.

Porter, Yves, and Arthur Thevernart. *Palaces and Gardens of Persia*. Paris: Flammarion, 2003.

Pringle, Denys, Andrew Petersen, Martin Dow, and Caroline Singer. "Qal'at Jiddin: A Castle of the Crusader and Ottoman Periods in Galilee." *Levant* 26 (1994): 135–66.

Renda, Günsel. *Batılılaşma Döneminde: Türk Resim Sanatı, 1700–1850*. Ankara: Türk Tarih Kurumu Basımevi, 1977.

Revell, Louise. *Roman Imperialism and Local Identities*. Cambridge: Cambridge University Press, 2009.

Rhoby, Andreas. *Postbyzantinische Epigramme in inschriftlicher Überlieferung (PBEiÜ)*. Vienna: Austrian Academy of Sciences Press, 2020.

Riza, Emin. "Arkitektura dhe restaurimi i banesës së Zekateve, Gjirokastër." *Monumentet* 13 (1977): 107–32.

———. "Arkitektura dhe restaurimi i kullave të Dervish Aliut në fshatin Dukat (Vlorë)." *Monumentet* 18 (1979): 105–20.

———. "Arkitektura e vendbanimit-rrënojë të Kardhiqit." *Monumentet* 17 (1979): 97–120.

Rüstem, Ünver. *Ottoman Baroque: The Architectural Refashioning of Eighteenth-Century Istanbul*. Princeton: Princeton University Press, 2019.

Sadat, Deena. "Urban Notables in the Ottoman Empire: The Ayan." PhD diss., Rutgers University, 1969.

Şakul, Kahraman. "The Evolution of Ottoman Military Logistical Systems in the Later Eighteenth Century: The Rise of a New Class of Military Entrepreneur." In *War, Entrepreneurs, and the State in Europe and the Mediterranean, 1300–1800*, edited by Jeff Fynn-Paul, 307–27. Leiden: Brill, 2014.

———. "Ottoman Attempts to Control the Adriatic Frontier in the Napoleonic Wars." In *The Frontiers of the Ottoman World*, edited by A. C. S. Peacock, 253–70. Oxford: Oxford University Press, 2009.

Savaş, Saim. "Sivas Valisi Dağıstânî Ali Paşa'nın Muhallefâtı XVIII: Asrın Sonunda Osmanlı Sosyal Hayatına Dâir Önemli Bir Belge." *TTK Belgeler* 15, no. 19 (1993): 249–92.

Schechner, Richard. *Performance Studies: An Introduction*. 3rd ed. New York: Routledge, 2013.

Sears, Gareth, Peter Keegan, and Ray Laurence, eds. *Written Space in the Latin West, 200 BC to AD 300*. London: Bloomsbury, 2013.

Setton, Kenneth M. *The Papacy and the Levant (1204–1571)*. Vol. 4, *The Sixteenth Century from Julius III to Pius V*. Philadelphia: American Philosophical Society, 1984.

Sezer, Hamiyet. "Tepedelenli Ali Pasha'nın Çiftlikleri Üzerine Bir Araştırma." *Belleten-Türk Tarih Kurumu* 62, no. 233 (1998): 75–106.

Sezer, Yavuz. "The Architecture of Bibliophilia: Eighteenth-Century Ottoman Libraries." PhD diss., Massachusetts Institute of Technology, 2016.

Shtylla, Valter. "Ndërtime inxhinierike të fillimit të shekullit XIXte në disa krahina të Shqipërisë së Jugut." *Monumentet* 21 (1981): 69–97.

———. "Ujësjellësi i vjetër i Kalasë së Gjirokastrës." *Monumentet* 20 (1980): 69–82.

Shuteriqi, Dhimitër. *Petro Korçari: Kryearkitekt Ali Pashë Tepelenës*. Tirana: Shtëpia Botuese "8 Nëntori," 1987.

Skiotis, Dennis N. "From Bandit to Pasha." *International Journal of Middle East Studies* 2, no. 3 (1971): 219–44.

——— [Dionysios Skiotis]. "The Lion and the Phoenix: Ali Pasha and the Greek Revolution." PhD diss., Harvard University, 1971.

Sklavenitis, Spiros, and Chrisa Nikolaou. "I deyteri katalipsi tis Prevezas (1806) mesa apo tis anafores tou proxenou tis Eptanisou Politeias Nikolaou Zampeli." In *Preveza B: Proceedings of the Second International Symposium for the History and Culture of Preveza (16–20 September 2009)*, edited by Nikos D. Karabelas and Michael Stork, 2 vols., 2:3–27. Preveza: University of Ioannina, Municipality of Preveza, Actia Nicopolis Foundation, 2010.

Smiris, Giorgos. *To diktio ton ochiroseon sto pasaliki ton Ioanninon (1788–1822)*. Ioannina: Etaireia Ipeirotikon Meleton, 2004.

———. "Ta mousoulmanika temeni ton Ioanninon kai i poleodomia tis Othomanikis Polis." *Ipeirotika Chronika* 34 (2000): 9–90.

Soulis, Christos. "Tourkikai epigrafai Ioanninon." *Ipeirotika Chronika* 8 (1933): 84–98.

Sözen, Metin. *Devletin Evi: Saray*. Istanbul: Sandoz Kültür Yayınları, 1990.

Steriadi, Tatiana. "Oi epigrafes tou kastrou." In *To kastro ton Ioanninon*, edited by Varvara Papadopoulou, 111–17. Ioannina: 8th Ephorate of Byzantine Antiquities, 2009.

Stoneman, Richard. *A Luminous Land: Artists Discover Greece*. Los Angeles: J. Paul Getty Museum, 1998.

Strunck, Christina. "The Barbarous and Noble Enemy: Pictorial Representations of the Battle of Lepanto." In *The Turk and Islam in the Western Eye, 1450–1750: Visual Imagery Before Orientalism*, edited by James G. Harper, 217–40. Farnham: Ashgate, 2011.

Summerson, John. *Architecture in Britain, 1530 to 1830*. 3rd ed. Harmondsworth: Penguin, 1958.

Tandan, Banmali. *The Architecture of Lucknow and Oudh, 1722–1856: Its Evolution in an Aesthetic and Social Context*. Cambridge: Zophorus, 2008.

Tanyeri-Erdemir, Tuğba. "Remains of the Day: Converted Anatolian Churches." In *Spolia Reincarnated: Afterlives of Objects, Materials, and Spaces in Anatolia from Antiquity to the Ottoman Era*, edited by Ivana Jevtić and Suzan Yalman, 71–96. Istanbul: ANAMED, 2018.

Terndrup, Alison. "Cross-Cultural Spaces in an Anonymously Painted Portrait of the Ottoman Sultan Mahmud II." Master's thesis, University of South Florida, 2015.

Terzinoğlu, Derin. "Sufis in the Age of State-Building and Confessionalization." In *The Ottoman World*, edited by Christine Woodhead, 86–102. London: Routledge, 2012.

Themeli-Katifori, Despina. "O Spiridon Ventouras ki i antidikia tou me ton Ali-Pasa." *Eptanisiaki Protochronia* 1 (1960): 203–15.

Todorova, Maria. *Imagining the Balkans*. Oxford: Oxford University Press, 2009.

Top, F. Gülsüm Ersoy. "İstanbul'daki Selatin Camilerin Kitabeleri." Master's thesis, Dokuz Eylül Üniversitesi, 2002.

Turner, Victor. *From Ritual to Theatre*. New York: PAJ Publications, 1982.

Tütüncü, Mehmet. "Corpus of Ottoman Inscriptions in Southern Albania." In *Ca' Foscari, Venezia e i Balcani*, edited by Giampiero Bellingeri and Giuseppina Turano, 155–88. Venice: Edizioni Ca' Foscari, 2015.

Veikou, Myrto. *Byzantine Epirus: A Topography of Transformation, Settlements of the Seventh–Twelfth Centuries in Southern Epirus and Aetoloacarnanina, Greece*. Leiden: Brill, 2012.

Veinstein, Gilles. "Avlonya (Vlore), une étape de la Voie Egnatia dans la seconde moitié du XVIE siècle?" In *Halcyon Days in Crete II: The Via Egnatia Under Ottoman Rule (1380–1699)*, edited by Elizabeth Zachariadou, 217–26. Rethymno: Crete University Press, 1996.

———. "On the Çiftlik Debate." In *Landholding and Commercial Agriculture in the Middle East*, edited by Çağlar Keyder and Faruk Tabak, 35–57. Albany: State University of New York Press, 1991.

Vranousis, Leandros. *Istorika kai topografika tou mesaionikou kastrou ton Ioanninon*. Athens: Etaireia Ipeirotikon Meleton, 1968.

Wace, Alan John Bayard, and M. S. Thompson. *The Nomads of the Balkans: An Account of Life and Customs Among the Vlachs of Northern Pindus*. London: Methuen & Co., 1914.

Watenpaugh, Heghnar. *The Image of an Ottoman City: Imperial Architecture and Urban Experience in Aleppo in the 16th and 17th Centuries*. Leiden: Brill, 2004.

Weber, Stefan. "Changing Cultural References: Architecture of Damascus in the Ottoman Period (1516–1918)." In *Multicultural Urban Fabric and Types in the South and Eastern Mediterranean*, edited by Maurice Cerasi, A. Petruccioli, A. Sarro, and Stefan Weber, 189–223. Würzburg: Ergon Verlag in Kommission, 2007.

———. *Damascus: Ottoman Modernity and Urban Transformation (1808–1918)*. Aarhus: Aarhus University Press, 2009.

Wheeler, Britta. "Negotiating Deviance and Normativity: Performance Art, Boundary Transgressions, and Social Change." In *Performance: Critical Concepts in Literary and Cultural Studies*, edited by Philip Auslander, 4 vols., 4:269–88. London: Routledge, 2003.

Willingham, Matthew. *Perilous Commitments: Britain's Involvement in Greece and Crete, 1940–41*. Staplehurst: Spellmount, 2005.

Wolfe, Michael. "Walled Towns During the French Wars of Religion (1560–1630)." In *City Walls: The Urban Enceinte in Global Perspective*, edited by James D. Tracy, 327–31. Cambridge: Cambridge University Press, 2000.

Yaycıoğlu, Ali. *Partners of the Empire: The Crisis of the Ottoman Order in the Age of Revolutions*. Stanford: Stanford University Press, 2016.

Yaycıoğlu, Ali, Antonis Hadjikyriacou, Fatma Öncel, Erik Steiner, and Petros Kastrinakis. "Mapping Ottoman Epirus (MapOE, http://mapoe.stanford.edu/)." *Journal of the Ottoman and Turkish Studies Association* 9, no. 2 (2022): 145–52.

Yenişehirlioğlu, Filiz. "Architectural Patronage of *Ayan* Families in Anatolia." In *Provincial Elites in the Ottoman Empire: Halcyon Days in Crete V*, edited by Antonis Anastasopoulos, 321–42. Rethymno: Crete University Press, 2005.

Zachariadou, Elizabeth. "Glances at the Greek Orthodox Priests in the Seventeenth Century." In *Living in the Ottoman Ecumenical Community: Essays in Honor of Suraiya Faroqhi*, edited by Vera Constantini and Markus Koller, 307–16. Leiden: Brill, 2008.

Zandi-Sayek, Sibel. *Ottoman Izmir: The Rise of a Cosmopolitan Port, 1840–1880*. Minneapolis: University of Minnesota Press, 2007.

Zens, Robert. "The *Ayanlık* and Pasvanoğlu Osman Paşa of Vidin in the Age of Ottoman Social Change, 1791–1815." PhD diss., University of Wisconsin–Madison, 2004.

———. "Ottoman Provincial Notables in the Eighteenth Century: A Comparative Study." In *Perspectives on Ottoman Studies: Papers from the 18th Symposium of the International Committee of Pre-Ottoman and Ottoman Studies (CIEPO) at the University of Zagreb*, edited by Ekrem Causevic, Nenad Moacanin, and Vjeran Kursar, 245–52. Berlin: LIT Verlag, 2010.

INDEX

Italicized page references indicate illustrations. Endnotes are referenced with "n" followed by the endnote number.

Abdülhamid I, 113, 145
Adam, Frederick, 65
Ahmed III, 145
age of revolutions, 179n4
    in the Ottoman sphere, 10, 16, 63
Agia-Anthousa, fortress at, 76, *76*, 85
Agios Andreas Fortress, Preveza, 77–78, 82, *82*–83, 85, 88, 91, 157, 182n45
    Ali Pasha's residence in, 39, 77
    inscription on the southwestern bastion, 155–56
Agios Georgios, Preveza, 78, 79, 85, 86, 88–91, 98
    Ali Pasha's residence in, 77
Agios Nikolaos, church of (endowed by Vasiliki), 133–34
    foundation inscription, *134*
Ahmad Pasha (al-Jazzar), 71
Ahmed Hurşid Pasha, 57–58
Aktion, triangular fortress at, 41, 78, 92–94
    inscription above the entrance, 156, 158, *158*
Ali Pasha (Tepedelenli)
    in Albanian historiography, 118, 123
    carriage of, 49
    chancery of, 22, 26, 28, 85
    court of, 25, 45–46, 51, 52–53
    death of, 1, 153, 170, 175
    depictions in art and literature, 8, 58–59
    early life of, 18, 165–66, 180n54
    erasure of the legacy of, 6–7, 170–71, 173, 176
    landed estates of, 47–49, *48*, 66
    as the "Lion of Ioannina," 155–59
    military campaigns of, 20, 72, 91–92, 115–16, 181n59
    as Moutzo Housso's descendant, 52, 165, 170
    movable property of, 56, 60–63, *61*, *64*, *65*
    offices and titles of, 18, 46–47, 180n54; as commander of the passes (*derbendler başbuğu*), 46–47,
    pious endowments (*vakıf*) founded by, 22, 106, 154
    portraits of, 4, 54, *55*, 65, 123–24, *124*
    religious views of, 103–104, 123–24, 190n84
    territory governed by, 2, *5*, 18–19, 74–77
    treasure of, 57–58, 60, 63, 184n102
Alipasiad, 8–9, 18, 19–20, 168
Anthimos (Metropolitan of Berat), 131
Antirrio, fortress at, 79, *80*
Apollonia, 125, 130
Ardenica Monastery, 125
Arslan Pasha Mosque, Ioannina, 106, 108, 110, *110*, 112, 113, 117
Arta, 43–44, 46, 77, 82
    Ali Pasha's residence in, 44
As'ad Pasha (al-'Azm), 13
â'yân (local notables), 9–10, 179n19
    as patrons of architecture, 11–12, 15–16

Baker, Anthony, 88
Balanos, Kostas, 108
Bardakçı, Murat, 176
Battle of Lepanto, the (painting by Giorgio Vasari), 67–68, *68*
Battle of Nikopolis. *See under* Nikopolis
Bayezid II, 79, 108, 122
de Beauchamp, Alphonse, 159
Beçisht, dervish lodge commissioned by Ali Pasha at, 122
Behram Pasha, 31
Bekir Ağa, 88, 191n3
Berisha, Sali, 175–76
Beylerbeyi Mosque, Istanbul, 113, *114*
du Bocage, Jean-Denis Barbié, 33, 120, 182n27
Bouka, castle at, Preveza, 41, 77–78, 82
    Ali Pasha's palace at, 39–41, 50, 90
    Venetian plans of, *40* (*see also* Coronelli, Vincenzo)
Bunila, Ali Pasha's foundry in, 96, 187n113

Burgess, Richard, 30, 176
Buşatlı Kara Mahmud (governor of Shkodra), 181n59
Buşatlı Mehmed Pasha (governor of Shkodra), 122
Butrint, 54, 72, 74, 75, *75*, 76, 83, 157
    Ali Pasha's network of fortresses in, 21, 74–75, 96
    See also Confederation of Continental Cities
Byron, George Gordon, Lord, 26–27, 58, 181n6

Çapanoğlu family (notables of Yozgat), 11–12, 56
Çapanoğlu Mosque, Yozgat, 11, *11*, 105, 145–46, *146*
Christodoulidis, Sapfeiros, 126
Christos (master architect), 87, 91
churches, 74, 125
    conversion into mosques, 106, 108–10, 188n22
    in Ottoman architecture, 135–36
    See also Agios Nikolaos; Shen Mary; Theotokos
çiftlik (farming villages), 10, 47, 49
Cihanoğlu family (notables of Aydın), 12, 71
Confederation of Continental Cities, 72, 74, 78, 91–92
Corfu, 69, 73, 74, 75, 92, 96
    New Fortress of, 157, *159*
    See also Ionian Islands
Coronelli, Vincenzo, 79, 82
Counsel for Sultans (*Nushatü's-Selâtin*) (book by Mustafa Ali), 28

Davutoğlu, Ahmet, 176
Death of Sardanapalus, the (painting by Eugène Delacroix), 58–60, *59*
Delvina, 30–31, 44, 74
    mosque commissioned by Ali Pasha in, 113
Demir Ağa (of Gardiki), 167
dervish lodges, 103, 116–19, 123–24
    See also individual buildings
Despotate of Epirus, 106–8
dizdâr ağası (castle warden), 43

Doğubayazıt, *13*, 26
Durbalı Sultan dervish lodge, Farsala, 118

Elbasan, dervish lodge endowed by Ali Pasha in, 119
epigraphy, 144, 192nn11–12
  in the Ottoman provinces, 145–46
  tuğra (sultanic monogram), 144–46, 157, 170–71
Epirus, 19–20, 150, 152–53, 177
  coastline of, 72
  demographics of, 101, *102*
  local architectural style of, 46, 113
  main roads in, 49, 119, 121, 138, 163–64, 183n79 (*see also* Pente Pigadia)
  mountain passes of, 48
  trade and manufacture in, 62–3
  as travel destination in the nineteenth century, 23

Fethiye Mosque (formerly the Orthodox Cathedral of Archangel Michael), Ioannina, 37, 106–10, *107*, *109*, *112*, *113*, 136, *137*, *139*, 187nn21–22
Fillada tou Alipasa (Ballad of Ali Pasha), 152
Foresti, George, 167
fortifications, 43–44, 69, 81–87, 91, 97–98
  See also individual fortresses

gardens, 38–39, 55–57
  See also under Ioannina; Veli Pasha
Gardiki, 44, *163*, 166
  massacre of, 163–64, *164*, 167
Giannena. *See* Ioannina
Gjirokaster, 74, 83, 123, 167
  Ali Pasha's residence in, 44–45
  citadel of, *71*, 83
  See also Zekate House
Great Imambara, Lucknow, 16, *17*
Greek Enlightenment, 151–52
Greek Revival movement, 51
Greek War of Independence, 1–2, 103, 150
Gulf of Corinth, 79
Gulf of Arta, 46, 91

Haji Sehreti, 8, 159
  See also Alipasiad
haṣṣa mi'mârları (corps of royal architects), 15
Haygarth, William, 53, 151
Himara, 73, 74, 160–61, 185n25, 193n62

Hobhouse, John, Lord Broughton, 28, 111, 181n6
Holland, Henry, 120, 122, 164, 166, 168
Hormova, dervish lodge and mosque endowed by Ali and Muhtar Pasha in, 117–19, 123, 157
Hughes, Thomas, 50, 97, 110, 119, 159, 164, 168–69

İbrahim Pasha (governor of Berat), 20, 44, 73, 95, 167
Igoumenitsa, 75
Ioannina, 1, 37, 108, 120, 150, 171, 176
  Byzantine Museum of, 146, 170–71, 182n17
  churches; of Agia Ekaterini, 138; the Agia Marina church complex, 138; of Agios Nikolaos Kopanon, 138
  dervish lodges endowed by Ali and Muhtar Pasha, 117, 119–21, 183n102, 189n60
  demographics during Ali Pasha's reign, 136–38
  Ali Pasha's garden palace complexes, 32, 54–55, *56*, 183–84n102
  inner citadel (*iç kale*), 1, 3, 33–37, 156; Ali Pasha's palace in the, 32, 33, 34, *35*, *36*, 36–37, 51, 54, 182n28
  northern citadel, 117
  outer walls, 150, 83, 85–88, 192n25; inscriptions at, 147–54, *147*, *148*, *149*, *154*, *155*, 172
  See also Arslan Pasha Mosque; Fethiye Mosque
Ionian Islands, 69
  Ali Pasha's designs against, 97
  See also Septinsular Republic
Iosaf (Metropolitan of Berat), 130–31, 133
İshak Pasha (Çıldıroğlu), 13, 26
  See also Doğubayazıt
Ishtar Gate, Babylon, 156
İzzet Mehmet Pasha Mosque, Safranbolu, 113, *114*

Kapodistrias, Ioannis, 53
Kara Osman-oğlu family (notables of Western Anatolia), 180n46, 189n46
Karbunara, dervish lodge endowed by Ali and Muhtar Pasha, in 122
Karlowitz, Treaty of, 79
Kastoria, 85
Kiafa, fortress at, 185n44
Kolovos, Spiros, 53

Korçë (Koritsa), 87–88
Kosmas Aitolos, Saint, 125–29, *128*, 133
Kurt Ahmed Pasha (governor of Berat), 18, 126
  dervish lodge and tomb of, Berat, 122–23, *122*
Kütahya, 176

Lampros (master architect), 87, 91
Lausanne, Treaty of, 118
Leake, William Martin, 33, 103, 115, 121, 152, 164–65
Lear, Edward, 111
Lefkada, 69, 71, 73, 77, 78, 79, 88–89, 91–94, 157
  Santa Maura Fortress in, *82*, 158, 160
Legrand, Émile, 153
Likurs, fortress at, 74, *75*
Litharitsa hill, Ioannina
  Ali Pasha's palace on, 7, 32, 33, 37–38, 41–43, 89, 171
  palaces of Muhtar and Veli Pasha, 32, 33, 38, 50, 182n36
Lowe, Colonel, 94

Mahmud II, 1, 170
  Sened-i İttifâk (Deed of Agreement), 180n46
Mahmud Pasha (son of Veli and grandson of Ali Pasha), 52
malikâne (tax-farming grants), 10
Mamluks, 156–57
Manastır (Bitola), 31
Manzour, Ibrahim, 85
Mehmed Ali Pasha, 13–14, 26, 71, 184n11
  Shubra palace, Cairo, 63
  Mehmed Ali Pasha Mosque, Cairo, 105, *105*
  sabil-kuttab of, Cairo, 13, *14*
Mehmed II, 77
Metsovo, 85
Meyer, William, 1, 58, 92, 103
military architecture. *See* fortifications
Mimar Sinan, 15–16, 113
  as author of *Tuhfetü'l-Mimârin* (Choice Gift for the Architects), 29
  See also Trikala: Osman Shah Mosque
Missolonghi, 79
Mitikas, Ali Pasha's residence in, 187n94
Molista, 85
monastic church dedicated to Saint Kosmas Aitolos, 125–26, *127*, 129–33, *130*, *132*

Montéléone, Don Santo, 85
Monument of Zalongo (sculpture by George Zongolopoulos), Kamarina, 169–70, *170*
Morier, John, 45
Moschopolis (Voskopojë), 88
mosques, 21, 104–106, 135–36
　See also individual mosques
Muhammad Ağa Abu Nabbut (of Jaffa), 145–6
Muhtar Pasha, 17, 73, 79–81, 87, 96, 110, 167
　affinity to dervish orders, 123
　death of, 170
Mustafa Pasha (governor of Delvina), 94, 96, 167–68
Mycenae, 146, 156

Nafpaktos (Lepanto), 72, 79
　Ottoman fortress in, 96, 187n116, 187n117
Napoleonic Wars, 20, 23, 72,
Nawabs of Awadh, 16, 64
Nikopolis
　Ali Pasha using spolia from, 189n35
　Battle of, 72, 146
non-Muslim communities, 101–3
　religious building restrictions imposed on, 124–25, 135–36
　tolerance enjoyed under Ali Pasha, 124–25

Ohrid, Ali Pasha's dervish lodge in, 119
Osman Pasha (Pasvantoğlu), 14, 71, 181n59, 184n11
Oswald, General, 94
Ottoman architecture
　Baroque style in, 26, 37, 50–51, 63, 122, 136
　preservation and study of Ottoman monuments in Greece and Albania, 7–8, 140
　in the sixteenth century, 15–16
Ottoman government
　imperial government, 8–10, 31, 71–72, 91–92, 94–97, 150, 170, 182n20
　provincial administration, 9–10, 18, 31, 180n55 (see also *â'yân*)
palaces, 25–26, 28, 34, 52–53
　See also individual palaces and residences
Pantocrator, fortress of, Preveza, 78, 98–99
Parga, 71, 72, 75, 83, 184n19
　Ali Pasha's mansion in, 44–5
　See also Confederation of Continental Cities
Passarowitz, Treaty of, 92
Patras, 79
patronage of architecture, 8, 11–12, 14–17, 23–24, 104–5, 112–13, 177
　See also â'yân; Ottoman architecture
Panos (master architect), 45
Pente Pigadia, inn at, 46–7, *47*, 69
Petros of Korçë (master architect), 23, 33, 38, 87–88, 91, 186n76, 186n79
Plagia, fortress at, 79, 85, 89, 186n57, 186n58
Ponceton, Captain, 89–90, 94
Porte, the. *See under* Ottoman government
Porto Palermo, 72, 75, 92, 160
　fortress at, 73–4
　inscription at the entrance to, 160–62, *161*, 193n57
Pouqueville, François, 88–89, 94, 119, 164, 182n27
Preveza, 40, 72, 75, 77–78, 88–89, 157
　Ali Pasha's mosque in, 112, 115–16
　Ali Pasha's dervish lodge in, 119, 190n68
　city walls of, 33, *36*; inscription at the main gates of, 193n46
　conquest by Ali Pasha, 91–92
　See also Agios Andreas; Agios Georgios; Bouka; Confederation of Continental Cities; Pantocrator
Psalidas, Athanasios, 96, 151–52
Pyrrhus, 147, 160, 162
　as "ancestor" of Ali Pasha, 150–53

Res Gestae Divi Augusti (*The Deeds of the Divine Augustus*), 143
roads, 6–7, 20, 25, 48, *49*
　See also under Epirus
Russo-Ottoman War of 1806, 77

Sagiada, 75, 185n39
Salaora, Ali Pasha's palace in, 46
Salih Pasha (son of Ali Pasha), 18
　death of, 170
Saranda, 73, 74, 76
Selim III, New Order (*Nizam-i Cedid*) reforms of, 19–20, 170
Selimiye Mosque, Konya, 113
　Selimiye Mosque, Üsküdar, 144, *145*
Septinsular Republic, 72, 92, 94, 115
Seyahatnâme (Evliya Çelebi's *Book of Travels*), 30, 43, 77, 122
Shen Meri Church, Labova e Kryqit, 136, *138*

Silistra, 31
Sinan. *See* Mimar Sinan
Sofia, 31
Souli, 104, 186n76
　Ali Pasha's war with, 20, 94, 106, 163, 193n64
　"Dance of Zalongo," 169
Stathis (master architect), 87
Sufi dervish orders, 117, 123–24
Süleyman Bey, 88, 191n3

Tavium, 180n26
Tekes, fortress at, 79, 84, 85, 94, 98
tekkes. *See* dervish lodges
Tepelena (Tepedelen), 6, 83, 87, 89, 141, 182n39
　Ali Pasha's dervish lodge at, 119, 121–22
　Ali Pasha's palace at, 27, 38–39, 87, 111
　Ali Pasha's mosque at 110–11, 116, 191n2
　bridge over the river Vjosa, 183n67
　citadel of, 38, *38*–39, 111, 182n39; inscriptions at, 141–43, *142*
　view of the city in Byron's *Childe Harold*, 26–28
Theotokos Church, Roupsia, 130
Tilsit, Treaty of, 76
Tirnavos. *See under* Veli Pasha
Topkapı Palace, Istanbul, 23, 28, 34, 41, 54, 175
Trikala, 103
　dervish lodges endowed by Ali Pasha in, 119–21
　Osman Shah Mosque, 113, *114*
tuğra. *See under* epigraphy

Ümmülgüsüm Hanım (wife of Ali Pasha), 110, 188–189n27

Valiares, inn at, 163–65, *163*
　inscription at, 165–66, 168–70
Vasiliki (wife of Ali Pasha), 21, 62, 125, 184n122, 191n108
　See also Agios Nikolaos
Vasilis (master architect), 45
de Vauban, Sébastien Le Prestre, 98
de Vaudoncourt, Frédéric-François Guillaume, 23, 88–91, 97–98
Veli Pasha, 18, 110, 123, 146, 152, 167
　death of, 170
　as *derbendler başbuğu*, 180n57
　Gülbahçe residence of, Tirnavos, 44
　mosque and *medrese* complex of, Ioannina, 38, 106, 115–16, *115*
　mosque of, Arcadia, 188n15

INDEX 209

Veliqot, Ali Pasha's palace in, 45
Venice, Republic of,
    effects of collapse in the Ionian Islands, 67–69, 91
    the lion of Saint Mark, 157–59
Ventouras, Spiridon, 65, 69
Vilaras, Ioannis, 152, 161
    I romeiki glosa (The Romaic Language), 161
Vlora, 72, 73, 76
Vonitsa, 72, 77, 83

Yiankos (agent of Ali Pasha), 92
Yozgat, 145–46
    See also Çapanoğlu; Çapanoğlu Mosque

Zahir al-'Umar, 71
Zekate House, Gjirokaster, 50, 51

BLS BUILDINGS, LANDSCAPES, AND SOCIETIES SERIES

SERIES EDITOR
Jesús Escobar, Northwestern University

ADVISORY BOARD
Cammy Brothers
Chanchal Dadlani
D. Fairchild Ruggles
Volker Welter
Carolyn Yerkes

OTHER BOOKS IN THE SERIES
The Nature of Authority: Villa Culture, Landscape, and Representation in Eighteenth-Century Lombardy by Dianne Harris

The Romanesque Revival: Religion, Politics, and Transnational Exchange by Kathleen Curran

Cities and Saints: Sufism and the Transformation of Urban Space in Medieval Anatolia by Ethel Sara Wolper

The Renaissance Perfected: Architecture, Spectacle, and Tourism in Fascist Italy by D. Medina Lasansky

Constantinopolis/Istanbul: Cultural Encounter, Imperial Vision, and the Construction of the Ottoman Capital by Çiğdem Kafescioğlu

The Culture of Architecture in Enlightenment Rome by Heather Hyde Minor

Making Modern Paris: Victor Baltard's Central Markets and the Urban Practice of Architecture by Christopher Mead

Architecture and Statecraft: Charles of Bourbon's Naples, 1734–1759 by Robin L. Thomas

Gunnar Asplund's Gothenburg: The Transformation of Public Architecture in Interwar Europe by Nicholas Adams

Freedom and the Cage: Modern Architecture and Psychiatry in Central Europe, 1890–1914 by Leslie Topp

Air Conditioning in Modern American Architecture, 1890–1970 by Joseph M. Siry

The Accidental Palace: The Making of Yıldız in Nineteenth-Century Istanbul by Deniz Türker

Isfahan: Architecture and Urban Experience in Early Modern Iran by Farshid Emami

Marrakesh and the Mountains: Landscape, Urban Planning, and Identity in the Medieval Maghrib by Abbey Stockstill